Christian Understandings of the Future

Christian Understandings of the Future

The Historical Trajectory

Amy Frykholm

Fortress Press
Minneapolis

CHRISTIAN UNDERSTANDINGS OF THE FUTURE

The Historical Trajectory

Cover image: Teal and Yellow Abstract Art/T30 Gallery/Shutterstock, Inc.

Cover design: Laurie Ingram

Library of Congress Cataloging-in-Publication Data

Print ISBN: 978-1-4514-8457-1

eBook ISBN: 978-1-5064-1892-6

The paper used in this publication meets the minimum requirements of American National Standard for Information Sciences — Permanence of Paper for Printed Library Materials, ANSI Z329.48-1984.

Manufactured in the U.S.A.

This book was produced using Pressbooks.com, and PDF rendering was done by PrinceXML.

To Thomas F. Johnson, for teaching me perseverance, grace, and Greek.

Contents

Part III. Contemporary Challenges

1

Christian Futures: An Introduction

In the Smithsonian Museum of American Art, there is a remarkable display, well worth a trip to the museum by itself. It is a glittering throne intended for Jesus Christ, made from everyday objects, especially aluminum foil. The artist, James Hampton, was a custodian for the General Services Administration of the federal government for most of his adult life, and he labored over this intricate work in a rented garage for many years. On the wall of the garage, he posted a quotation from the King James Bible: "Where there is no vision, the people perish" (Prov 29:18). He called his work with its more than 180 individual components "The Throne of the Third Heaven of the Nations' Millennium General Assembly." He believed that his work was preparation for the second coming of Christ to earth, and that Christ could use this throne for his thousand-year earthly reign, called in Christian tradition the Millennium. In addition to the throne, the complete work involves an altar, offertory tables, pulpits, mercy seats, and other obscure pieces that curators don't understand. He also left a notebook with a secret, as-yet-undeciphered, writing system.

Key to the genius of Hampton's art is the incorporation of ordinary objects. Many discarded objects from the federal office buildings where he worked—electrical cables, cardboard tubes, desk blotters, light bulbs, scraps of insulation—became part of the majestic vision that Hampton drew from Revelation and other biblical texts. Even though Jesus Christ has not yet come to sit on the throne the way that Hampton might have imagined, earth did indeed become heaven, the ordinary became the extraordinary, and the profane was transformed by the hands of the artist into something sacred.

Hampton, the son of sharecroppers in South Carolina, called himself "Director, Special Projects for the State of Eternity" and believed that he had been given a specific task with a direct correlation to the end of time. His labor was helping to bring about God's kingdom on earth. But when Hampton died in 1964, no one knew about this work of devotion that was at once private and universal. Some say that the work was discovered when the garage's owner came to collect the rent, not knowing that Hampton had died, and found the throne and all its accoutrements carefully arranged and glittering.[1]

Hampton's work is a spectacular example of Christian understanding of the future. It demonstrates the themes that have dominated Christian eschatology since its earliest days and continue to inspire, transform, and quicken the imaginations of Christians today. It is a work of profound imagination in conjunction with personal devotion and a close reading of prophetic texts. It transforms revelation into concrete action and the ordinary into the extraordinary.

Hampton's "Throne" articulates a connection to a divine or eternal reality at the same time that it predicts—wrongly, at least so far—an earthly future.

Christian understanding of the future has two roots, and Hampton's throne is one of many branches. One root is the ancient Jewish experience of exile that produced some of the key prophetic and apocalyptic texts from which Christians have drawn for two millennia. The second root is the Christian experience and doctrine of the resurrection of Jesus Christ, an event which encompasses the past, the present, and the future all at the same time.

These two roots have given Christian understanding of the future a peculiar tension between the "already," an immediate sense of God's unfolding will that can be perceived in the past and present, and the "not yet," the future that still waits to be known. Christians have expressed this tension imaginatively, drawing on the received tradition and then engaging and extending it through creative acts (like Hampton's "Throne"). They also have used this tension polemically in order to critique their current social order and to make amendments that they believe align the future more clearly with God's will. And they have used it epistemologically, by which I mean that Christians have used the future in order to tell a story of the whole history of humankind and the entire meaning of the world—a complete story that reveals God's character and intentions.

The polemical, imaginary, and epistemological modes of the future are often intertwined. The polemical finds expression in an imaginative text like Dante's *Divine Comedy*. Asserting a comprehensive form of human knowledge allows someone like Bernard of Clairvaux or Hildegard of Bingen to critique worldly leadership and find it wanting. Longing for social or political transformation leads to works of art like Hampton's "Throne," under construction by an African-American man at the height of the Civil Rights Movement. And so on.

Within these modes, we often find Christians asking how much of the future is under divine control, and how much is in human hands. Christians in different eras and at different times have attributed various degrees of control to God and have given humans considerable power as well. Some Christians, like Hampton, have believed that their actions can bring about a specific kind of future, and others have given complete control to God, who they have argued is entirely sovereign over the future. When Christians have tried to map out the future, they have wondered if God has laid out the entire plan in advance and then recorded it in scriptural texts, or if God has left the future open, at least to some degree, where human action can influence the timing and form of the end. They also have wondered if the end is present now, as in the Gospel of John, which collapses present and future in order to emphasize the radical shift in the relationship between human and divine that Jesus's crucifixion and resurrection introduced.

But that there is an end to human history has been little in doubt in all of Christian history. This study of the end—in whatever form it takes—has been called since the nineteenth century eschatology, from the Greek word *eschaton*—meaning last or end. Eschatology, writes Brian Daley, is "the hope of believing people that the incompleteness of their present experience of God will be resolved, their present thirst for God fulfilled, their present need for release and salvation realized. It is faith in the resolution of the unresolved."[2] Invocation of this hope is written into Christianity's earliest documents and has shaped every era of its history.

For the earliest Christians this was the hope that Jesus's resurrection meant the return of the kingdom to Israel, an event that had been prophesied in Jewish tradition for several hundred years. In the first chapter of the Acts of the Apostles, Luke writes that just before his ascension into heaven, the resurrected Jesus gathers his disciples together to urge them to stay in Jerusalem and await the baptism of the Holy Spirit. The disciples ask him, "Lord, is it at this time You are restoring the kingdom to Israel?" (Acts 1:6 NRSV). Jesus does not give them a yes or no answer. Instead he says, "It is not for you to know the times or periods that the Father has set by his own authority. But you will receive power when the Holy Spirit has come upon you; and you will be my witnesses in Jerusalem, in all Judea and Samaria, and to the ends of the earth." The task for the near future—to be witnesses—is clearer than the farther future—when the kingdom of Israel will be restored. But both are present here: work to do in the present and an unfolding of future events determined by God. The disciples express their longing for a restoration of the kingdom of Israel. Jesus responds with a task: "Be my witnesses."

Then Jesus ascends into heaven, and the disciples suddenly see two people in white robes standing next to them. "Men of Galilee," the white-robed ones say, "why do you stand looking up toward heaven? This Jesus, who has been taken up from you into heaven, will come in the same way as you saw him go into heaven" (Acts 1:11). This moment crystallizes Christian futures: the eyes of the disciples are directed both up to heaven, as Jesus ascends, and forward into the future, because Jesus will come again "in the same way."

Every generation of Christians has had to grapple with the same question that the disciples asked in the first chapter of Acts: is the end now or not yet? They have elaborated this simple question by constructing legends, theories, doctrines, and histories, and telling stories of signs and wonders from the first century to the twenty-first. Each generation has likewise had reason to apply Jesus's words to themselves: "It is not for you to know." Thus the future for Christians has been invested with both fear of the unknown and hope for God's restorative justice.

Fear and Hope

In a scene in the 1985 comedy *Ghostbusters*, the Ghostbusters, a team of four men who claim to have special equipment that allows them to find and destroy ghosts, are trying to convince the mayor of New York City to let them into a haunted space to do their work. They tell him that unless he lets them enter, the city will face terrible consequences. One of the Ghostbusters, Peter Venkman, played by Bill Murray, starts the dialogue from the very biblical tradition that we will trace in this book. Either the mayor allows the Ghostbusters into the building, "or," he tells the mayor, "you can accept the fact that this city is headed for a disaster of biblical proportions."

"What do you mean, 'biblical?'" the mayor asks.

Another Ghostbuster answers, "What he means is Old Testament biblical, Mr. Mayor, real wrath-of-god type stuff! Fire and brimstone coming down from the skies! Rivers and seas boiling!"

Another Ghostbuster chimes in, "Forty years of darkness! Earthquakes! Volcanoes!"

"The dead rising from the grave!"

"Human sacrifice, dogs and cats living together, mass hysteria!"

"Enough!" the mayor says. "I get the point. What happens if you're wrong?"

Venkman answers, "If I'm wrong, nothing happens! We go to jail. Peacefully, quietly. We'll enjoy it! But if I'm right, and we can stop this thing, Lenny, you will have saved the lives of millions of registered voters."[3]

To create this dialogue, Dan Aykroyd and Harold Ramis, both of Jewish religious backgrounds, drew on a reservoir of images from both Christian and Jewish traditions to depict fear of the future—both "Old Testament," as Aykroyd says, and New Testament. The boiling seas (Job 41:31), the dead rising from their graves (Isa 26:19; 1 Cor 15:52) (although in the Bible this is supposed to be a good thing), earthquakes (Zech 14:5; Mark 13:8), fire and brimstone (Isa 30:33; Rev 21:8)—these are all ancient images of the terrifying events of the future and a part of our common cultural inheritance. The humor comes partly from exaggeration and partly from the way that the screenwriters mix in specific cultural references and social fears. Bill Murray's deadpan comment about "dogs and cats living together" is perhaps a joke about contemporary debates over homosexuality that have had their own apocalyptic fervor. The scene works as a piece of comedy because it draws on fears so deeply rooted in our culture, so much a part of a shared vocabulary, they don't need a source to make sense or be mocked.

But Jewish and Christian images of hope have been just as important as images of fear. Every year in the season of Advent, Christians read from the tradition's prophetic texts, like Isaiah 40.

> A voice cries out:
> In the wilderness prepare the way of the Lord,
> make straight in the desert a highway for our God.

Every valley shall be lifted up,
and every mountain and hill be made low;
the uneven ground shall become level,
and the rough places a plain.
Then the glory of the Lord shall be revealed,
and all people shall see it together,
for the mouth of the Lord has spoken. (vv. 3–5)

This text is a poetic evocation of the future, a moment of transformation so complete that it changes the very ground. These prophetic words not only have provided a vision of hope but also a vocabulary for movements of social justice in many different eras and locations of history.

The Bible is full of images like these—a reservoir of human hopes and dreams for a better future—both earthly and heavenly, personal and communal, individual and global. As we look at many perhaps strange (to us) beliefs that Christians have held about the future, we do well to remember that they are rooted in the same fear and hope that guide our own responses to the future. We may not believe that Gog and Magog are waiting behind a magic gate to wreck havoc on us, but we do harbor fears of future terrorist attacks or rogue leaders using nuclear weapons or drastic climate change, all of which have the power to destroy us. The fear is recognizable. Perhaps the hope that is treasured in the ancient tradition is less identifiable in our world. At the present, it may be more difficult to construct and share a unified vision of hope than it is to indulge our collective fears. But hope still plays a crucial role in the Christian tradition; invoked in our liturgies, imagined in our lectionaries, and embodied imperfectly in our communities.

Key Terms

In order to tell the story of how fear and hope have intertwined to create a Christian understanding of the future, we need some basic vocabulary. We already have one key word: **eschatology**—this is the broadest term for Christian understanding of "end things." (Definitions for words in bold throughout this book can be found in the glossary at the end.) Eschatological questions can be personal: What happens to me when I die? They can be social or national: Will the United States of America (or Israel or Spain) play a crucial role in God's plan? They can also be global: What is the fate of the planet on which I live?

The term was first used at the beginning of the nineteenth century, when theologians were dividing up Christian theology into fields. The first usage is credited to a German scholar, Karl Gottlieb Bretschneider, in 1804.[4] Eschatology became the field of knowledge for understanding the future, and for what has been known in the Christian tradition as the "four last things": death, judgment, heaven, and hell. Prior to the nineteenth century, no one had seen reason to separate out eschatology from other areas of Christian theology like christology, soteriology, ecclesiology, homiletics, hermeneutics, and so on. Eschatology was Christian theology. Christian theology was eschatology. But we take these distinctions for granted today. Eschatology does not necessarily correlate to other areas of theology, and some have wondered if eschatology has wandered too far from the rest of Christian theology.

But to begin, eschatology is about ultimate things: the ultimate fate of human kind, the planet, the nation of Israel, and any individual human life. Contemporary biblical scholar and theologian John Dominic Crossan argues that eschatology is central to Jewish and Christian worldviews.

> If your faith tells you that God is just and the world belongs to God, and your experience dreadfully tells you that you are a small, battered people, then eschatology is probably inevitable, and don't let us scholars mystify you on it. Eschatology means if the world belongs to God and is patently unjust, God must clean up the mess of the world. Eschatology is the Great, Divine Clean Up of the world.[5]

Eschatology, then, is not just a question about how the world will end or about where an individual goes when he or she dies. Jewish and Christian eschatology both imply that there is a just ending to the world. There has to be a Great, Divine Clean Up if there is going to be any meaning to the journey that God's people have been on. It isn't simply that the world will end, but that God will enact justice.

Crossan goes on to argue that eschatology, in Christian theology, is never properly about a destruction of the created order. The world is not annihilated.

> No first-century Jew or Christian would think about the end of the world, because that would mean that God has annulled creation, which God would never do. God created the world and stamped every day of it as good, good, very good. The end of the world is not what we are talking about. We're talking about cosmic transformation of this world from a world of evil and injustice and impurity and violence into a world of justice and peace and purity and holiness.[6]

Crossan's point is an important one. While contemporary visions of the end of the world often involve total destruction in some meaningless fashion, the more ancient visions are often centered on transformation of this world into God's kingdom.

Speaking as a theologian, Crossan does overstate his case, however. Not all of Christian and Jewish tradition has been focused on transformation. Eschatology has what historian Marjorie Reeves calls "both a pessimistic and an optimistic expectation concerning history; its end could be conceived either as a mounting crescendo of evil or as the millennium, a Messianic Age of God."[7] In the stories that follow, we will see both impulses at work.

We can break eschatological questions down into two further types: apocalyptic and prophetic. **Apocalyptic eschatology** refers to things that will happen almost entirely by divine action, outside of human control. These events are revealed to humans through special messengers, but humans play little role in their unfolding. In Jewish history, apocalyptic eschatology was first expressed through a literary genre called **apocalypse** by scholars. An apocalypse describes an otherworldly agent revealing to a human one the nature of divine reality and, often, important information about the future. "Apocalypse" comes from the Greek word meaning "revelation." In an apocalypse, the veil between this world and the other world is rent, and humans are allowed to see through to the other side, to eternity. This revelation has a dimension in time: it usually involves a prediction of how and when God will bring about salvation to God's people. But it also has a spatial dimension: it reveals another reality, inaccessible by ordinary human means, a world that appears to exist apart from human time.[8]

The first Jewish apocalyptic texts were written in the period of time when Jews were returning to Israel after exile in Babylon. During the sixth century BCE, the Babylonian king Nebuchadnezzar besieged Jerusalem several times, and many ancient Israelites were sent into exile and captivity in Babylon.

About fifty years later, after the fall of Babylon, they began to return to Jerusalem, where they rebuilt the temple, and write extensively about this period in their history. Stories of the exile and return are important context for the books of Ezra, Daniel, Psalms, 2 Chronicles, 2 Kings, Jeremiah, and several other books that lie outside the traditional canon. They brought back to Israel with them new traditions and stories that had become a part of Jewish culture while in exile.

Among the writings of this post-exilic period, Daniel is the most important apocalypse. The book begins with Daniel, a young man in exile in Babylon, who begins to have unusual dreams and becomes a dream interpreter for the king of Babylon. In the second half of the book, he has an extraordinary and lengthy vision. He sees four beasts rising up from the sea. He sees the throne of God and the presentation of a mysterious figure called the son of man, a ram with two horns, and many other things. Placed in a deep sleep, he is awakened by a man who interprets the dream for him. This vision, the man says, "is for the time of the end" (Dan 8:17). The explanation of the vision, however, is just as puzzling as the vision itself, and leads to more visions and images that readers have been trying to discern since they were first written down.[9]

Apocalypses, like Daniel, often contain journeys into other dimensions in which the human protagonist has the opportunity to see what human eyes ordinarily cannot. These texts are primarily visionary—based on dreams or on things that people see when their eyes are "lifted up." They often contain signs of which humans are urged to be aware. Daniel, for example, prophesies that the end of time will be known by the arrival of a "great protector" but also by a "time of anguish, such as has never occurred since nations first came into existence," and that "many of those who sleep in the dust of the earth shall awake, some to everlasting life, and some to shame and everlasting contempt" (Dan 12:1-2). In other words, the "time of the end" will be known by the arrival of a messianic figure, a time of terrible trial, and the rising of the dead from their graves. These are signs, as we shall see, that become important in the Christian tradition.

From the example of Daniel, we can see that an apocalypse can contain apocalyptic eschatology, but an apocalypse is not only about the future. It also contains rich symbols that resist any simple correspondence to historical reality, and it tells stories that can likewise be interpreted in many different ways. Several other books of the Hebrew Bible contain apocalyptic elements (Isaiah 24-27; Ezekiel 38-39), although Daniel is the fullest example.

Key to apocalyptic eschatology is the idea that the fate of the world, "in its details, its very hour and course, has been fixed from everlasting," as Jewish philosopher Martin Buber explains.[10] There is very little that humans can do—positively or negatively—to affect the outcome, and that may be why, within this kind of eschatology, humans spend most of their time reading signs. The action of God can be swift and brutal according to the tradition of apocalyptic eschatology. Humans would do well to be prepared.

The other kind of eschatology prevalent in both Jewish and Christian tradition is **prophetic eschatology**. Prophetic eschatology describes things that will happen on earth with a mixture of divine and human action. It is not as interested in what is happening in some other dimension, like heaven or hell. It is focused on earthly salvation and earthly transformation.[11]

Prophetic eschatology is found throughout the Hebrew Bible

in texts like Jeremiah, Isaiah, and Ezekiel. It offers both hope and warning to the people of Israel, telling them what to do and what to expect. It is based on revelation, just as apocalyptic eschatology is. But it involves more direct human engagement and the fate of the earth. It can include both long-term and short-term prophecies—sometimes mixed together. In the prophetic tradition, humans are invited to participate in the divine redemptive process, the Great, Divine Clean Up, or what the Jewish tradition has also called *tikkun olam*, the healing of the world.

While the distinction between apocalyptic and prophetic eschatologies can be helpful when attempting to gain a comprehensive view of Christianity's understanding of the future, we shouldn't overread their differences. Biblical writers engaged in both kinds of eschatology, sometimes at the very same moment. The distinction we are making here is not made in the biblical texts themselves. In a later chapter we will look closely at Mark 13, often called the Little Apocalypse, and we will see how prophetic and apocalyptic eschatology merge in words attributed to Jesus. They also merge in the prophet Isaiah, in Revelation, and in many other biblical documents, in both the Hebrew Bible and the New Testament. Both prophetic and apocalyptic eschatologies provide rich linguistic, imaginative, and polemical resources within Christianity.

Both also contain the tension between the now and the not yet, and it is in taking the two kinds of eschatology together that we can perhaps see this most clearly. In the apocalyptic, the now of God's reign exists in images of eternity: the throne of God, the gathering of the angels. God does not wait for the future in this other realm. We are called to look at the present through the lens of the eternal. But prophetic eschatology does not allow us to remain content with the present. Prophetic eschatology always calls us to the not yet of God—the reign of true peace, mercy, and justice that lies outside of the present, toward which God is calling us to act. Through strange, violent, and sometimes beautiful metaphors, eschatological texts invite us to imagine the future as something more fantastic than the ordinary mind can grasp.

The symbolism of eschatological texts, therefore, is never a mere correspondence to a historical reality. It always exceeds that reality. John Collins writes that biblical eschatological texts continue to "engage the imagination long after the events to which they originally referred have faded from memory."[12] Every symbol can be read in multiple ways, gives rise to more than one emotional response, and has resisted any final interpretation for thousands of years, hard as many have tried. Every act of interpretation adds another layer of complexity, more problems to ponder, more puzzles to solve.

For the sake of our work here, we might make a further distinction between a prediction and a prophecy. Biblical talk about the future has too often been interpreted as a set of predictions: words that refer to specific, inevitable events in the future. In contemporary times, we use the word "prediction" to refer to something almost scientific in nature. We make a prediction based on evidence collected from the past that we apply to the future. Thus at the contemporary moment, some Christians read the Bible as if it contains predictions: knowledge collected from the past that tells us about future events. But a prediction is much narrower and less complex than a prophecy. In a prediction, event *y* follows event *x* like points on a timeline. Prophecies, on the other hand, draw on a much wider sense of time. Prophecies make use of something we might call "moral time": time that has been infused with notions of righteousness and wickedness.

Prophecies also draw on eternity, referencing points beyond the timeline. Prophetic time ripens in order for certain events to take place. It can also wane if people don't respond. Prophecy frames time with a view to God's ultimate power and justice. A prophecy is both a statement of the future and a statement about ultimate reality. It evokes the future and, simultaneously, eternity.

Christian eschatology is, as Collins has written, "a resilient tradition." It has helped Christians make sense of time, given them a sense of purpose, and sent them all over the globe fueled by beliefs about their God-given mission. This tradition "continues to haunt our imaginations and remains an indispensable resource for making sense of human experience."[13] Two thousand years after the disciples of Jesus heard those mysterious words about Jesus's return spoken to them by "men in white clothing," we still want to know what they might possibly mean, and in them are embedded two thousand years of interpretation along with some of our greatest fears and deepest hopes. In what follows, we will first look at the tradition's founding texts: Jewish prophets and apocalypses, the Christian Gospels, the letters of Paul, and Revelation. Then we will trace the interpretation and elaboration of these texts through historical developments and trajectories. Finally we will turn to the contemporary moment and ask about the current meanings and potentials of Christian eschatology.

Notes

1. This story comes from Wikipedia without a source: http://en. wikipedia.org/wiki/James_Hampton_(artist). Other information

16

about Hampton comes from the collection notes at the Smithsonian Institute of American Art: http://americanart.si.edu/collections/search/artwork/?id=9897.

2. Brian Daley, *The Hope of the Early Church* (Cambridge: Cambridge University Press, 1991), 1.

3. http://web.archive.org/web/20021219072712/; http://members.tripod.com/Adam_P_B/ghostbusters/script.html.

4. See G. Filoramo, "Eschatology," in *Encyclopedia of the Early Church,* trans. Adrian Walford, ed. Angelo DiBernardino (New York: Oxford University Press, 1992), 1:284–86.

5. John Dominic Crossan, "Opening Statement," *The Resurrection of Jesus: John Dominic Crossan and N.T. Wright in Dialogue,* ed. Robert B. Stewart (Minneapolis: Fortress, 2006), 24.

6. Ibid., 25.

7. Marjorie Reeves, *The Influence of Prophecy in the Later Middle Ages: A Study in Joachimism* (Notre Dame: University of Notre Dame Press, 1993), 295.

8. This definition originated with a group of scholars in the 1970s and has developed into a lively conversation about what is and is not an apocalypse. See John J. Collins, ed., *Apocalypse: The Morphology of a Genre* (Semeia 14; Atlanta: Society of Biblical Literature, 1979); and more recently John J. Collins, "What Is Apocalyptic Literature?," in *The Oxford Handbook of Apocalyptic Literature* (New York: Oxford University Press, 2014), 1–18.

9. Scholars generally date the writing of Daniel to the second century BCE, though the traditions it records may be much older.

10. Martin Buber, *Paths in Utopia,* trans. R. F. C. Hull (Boston: Beacon, 1958), 10.

11. For more on the distinction between prophetic and apocalyptic eschatology, see the introduction in Mitchell Reddish, ed., *Apocalyptic Literature: A Reader* (Nashville: Abingdon, 1990), 19–37.

12. Collins, "What Is Apocalyptic Literature?," 9.

13. Ibid., 13.

For Further Reading

Amanat, Abbas, and Magnus Bernhardsson, eds. *Imagining the End: Visions of Apocalypse from the Ancient Middle East to Modern America.* London: Tauris, 2002.

Ballard, Martin. *Endtimers: Three Thousand Years of Waiting for Judgment Day.* Westport, CT: Praeger, 2011.

Collins, John J. *The Apocalyptic Imagination: An Introduction to Jewish Apocalyptic Literature.* 2nd ed. Grand Rapids: Eerdmans, 1998.

Grabbe, Lester L., and Robert Haak, eds. *Knowing the End from the Beginning: The Prophetic, the Apocalyptic and Their Relationships.* New York: T&T Clark, 2003.

Reddish, Mitchell G., ed. *Apocalyptic Literature: A Reader.* Peabody: Hendrickson, 1995.

PART I

Origins

2

Prophecies and Riddles: Jewish Prophetic and Apocalyptic Traditions

Among students of both Testaments, Jewish apocalyptic remains an unsolved riddle.

—Paul D. Hanson

Five thousand years ago, in Mesopotamia, the people who lived there told the story of a young warrior-king called Ninurta, who was also the god of thunderstorms and floods. Ninurta received word that the plants and stones of the mountains had declared Azag, a mountain-dwelling monster, king, and that the monster was now plotting to take over Ninurta's kingdom. Ninurta marched on the monster but lost the first round when Azag kicked up a dust storm that drove Ninurta's forces back. Ninurta then called on his father for advice. He advised Ninurta to send down a rainstorm to settle the dust. This worked. Ninurta defeated Azag and then released the waters of the river Tigris that had been trapped in the ice of the mountains. The waters revived the people and saved them from destruction.

The story of Ninurta is what scholars have called a "combat myth," common in Mesopotamia in the third millennia BCE.[1] In these myths, a crisis grips the land, usually in the form of a threatening monster. A warrior king is called in to avert or mitigate the crisis. He does battle against the evil force. His victory establishes his power and authority and brings good gifts to the people. Scholars believe that the warrior myths offer the deepest roots of the Jewish eschatological tradition and ultimately the Christian tradition. In Israel, people began to attribute this story not to a warrior-king but to God Godself, who does battle with the people's enemies and attains a cosmic victory over the forces of chaos and evil.[2]

The Day of the Lord

Beginning in the eighth century BCE, a new version of the tradition emerged. This projected the great battle into the future, when God would ultimately defeat the forces of evil. In addition to the victory, God would judge the people of the earth and deliver them to their ultimate fate. The prophet Amos (active during the reign of Jeroboam 786–746 BCE) declared that "the end," when this battle would take place with its subsequent judgment, was at hand. He warned the people that the end would bring about "the day of the Lord," and they had been duly warned.

> Alas for you who desire the day of the Lord!
>   Why do you want the day of the Lord?
> It is darkness, not light;
>   as if someone fled from a lion,
>   and was met by a bear;

or went into the house and rested a hand against the wall,
    and was bitten by a snake.
Is not the day of the Lord darkness, not light,
    and gloom with no brightness in it? (Amos 5:18–20)

Other prophets expanded the concept of the day of the Lord into a cosmic catastrophe followed by the ultimate judgment. The crisis will affect every aspect of life, especially the sun and the stars, which Isaiah prophesies "will not give their light. . . . I will make the heavens tremble and the earth will be shaken out of its place at the wrath of the Lord of hosts, in the day of his fierce anger" (Isa 13:10, 13).

In the next two hundred years after these words were written, the people of Israel did experience an "earth-shaking" catastrophe: the defeat of the kingdom of Israel by the Babylonians and the period of exile in Babylon. This period continued the prophetic tradition, and it told the story both backward and forward, sometimes telling the people that their own behavior brought down the wrath of God and sometimes projecting that wrath into the future as a warning. But the tradition also depicted good news. God's judgment would also bring justice, defeat the people's enemies, and restore the kingdom of Israel.

The tradition further developed to imagine that when God's victory comes, death would be finally defeated, the dead would rise from the earth, the kingdom would be restored, and the people would experience a new beginning and a time of peace and prosperity. In chapters 38–39 of Ezekiel, we see the pattern crucial to Jewish and Christian prophetic texts. First a threat arises. In Ezekiel, the threat is named "Gog," a king in the land of Magog. He threatens the people with destruction, rising up from "the remotest part of the north." God's "wrath is aroused." Like a yet-more-cosmic Ninurta, God will use "torrential rains and hailstones, fire and sulphur" against Gog and defeat him. In a bloody feast afterward, the people will "eat the flesh of the mighty, and drink the blood of the princes of the earth. . . . You shall eat fat until you are filled, and drink blood until you are drunk, at the sacrificial feast that I am preparing for you" (Ezek 39:18–19).

After Gog is utterly destroyed, God then promises to restore the people of Israel:

> Now I will restore the fortunes of Jacob, and have mercy on the whole house of Israel; and I will be jealous for my holy name. They shall forget their shame, and all the treachery they have practiced against me, when they live securely in their land with no one to make them afraid, when I have brought them back from the peoples and gathered them from their enemies' lands, and through them have displayed my holiness in the sight of many nations. Then they shall know that I am the Lord their God because I sent them into exile among the nations, and then gathered them into their own land. I will leave none of them behind; and I will never again hide my face from them, when I pour out my spirit upon the house of Israel, says the Lord God. (Ezek 39:25–29)

The prophecy of Gog (which plays an important role in later Christian eschatology, as we shall see) sets out clearly the pattern for both Jewish and Christian eschatology. There will be a great crisis, greater than the world has ever known. Out of this crisis will come a tremendous battle. This battle will lead to the ultimate victory of God and then to the restoration of God's people. Also layered in the story that Ezekiel tells is the painful exile of the people. They have suffered greatly, the prophet acknowledges, but God has not forgotten them. God's great restoration, the Great, Divine Clean Up, is promised and still to come.

Ezekiel wrote this prophecy in the face of the Babylonian

exile in the sixth century, after the destruction of the temple in Jerusalem. Throughout the entire prophetic text, Ezekiel's vision is connected with longing for political and national restoration. Just before this vision of Gog, Ezekiel is taken to a valley that is full of dry bones. As Ezekiel walks among the scattered human bones, God asks him, "Can these bones live?" God commands Ezekiel to "prophesy to these bones," and as Ezekiel tells the bones of God's intention, there is a noise, a "rattling, and the bones came together, bone to its bone." Breath then comes into the bones, and a great multitude stands before Ezekiel. God tells Ezekiel that this multitude is the restoration of Israel. God says, "I am going to open your graves, and bring you up from your graves, O my people; and I will bring you back to the land of Israel" (Ezek 37:1–12).

The experience of exile and subsequent rebuilding of the temple in Jerusalem around 518 BCE, while Israel was still under Persian rule, created an outpouring of Jewish literature and an expansion of its forms. During this time, Jewish eschatological thinking and writing flourished. Several theories and constellations of beliefs existed simultaneously and were often expressed in the same documents. It is in this period that the distinction between the prophetic and apocalyptic strains of eschatology became increasingly pronounced. Many passages in Isaiah, for example, point to the renewal of the earth through the moral practices of the people, while texts like Daniel emphasize an otherworldly culmination of history.

Through this kind of prophecy, Jewish thought developed the idea of the **messianic age**—a time when life on earth would be especially blessed. This time was prophesied to arise through the coming of a **messiah**, a person who would save the people from their suffering. When this savior comes, God will give the people "new heavens and a new earth." In the renewed city of Jerusalem, "no more shall there be in it an infant that lives but a few days or an old person who does not live out a lifetime. . . . They shall build houses and inhabit them; they shall plant vineyards and eat their fruit . . . for like the days of a tree shall the days of my people be" (Isa 65:17–25). During this time, special rules will apply to human life. The fruit of the earth will be especially plentiful. Sickness and death will be little known. The lion will lie down with the lamb. But the vision is fundamentally earthly, if also utopian. The prophets saw that these things will take place on earth, not in an extra-earthly realm like heaven.

The Resurrection of the Dead

Enfolded into this idea of a messianic age was the notion of the resurrection of the dead. At the end of the present age, an event that the prophets continued to call "the day of the Lord," or simply "that day," would transform and reverse the relationship between death and life. In order to restore Israel once and for all, the past also must be fully redeemed, and thus the righteous dead would need to rise in order to join in the new age. Historian Claudia Setzer reminds us that the resurrection of the dead was not a theory that ancient people had or an argument they made. Instead it was a profoundly communal vision about the nature of righteousness and God's promises. It was often contained in poetic and apocalyptic texts, a way of saying that material reality does not always tell the truth about deeper realities.[3] This does not mean that the resurrection of the dead was "only" a metaphor or that ancient people did not actually believe in it. Instead, resurrection was a powerful, intensely concentrated symbol of the special identity of the people of God and of the power of God to transcend reality as we know it.

Texts from this period vary in their treatment of resurrection. For some, resurrection is only of the righteous, who are then invited to participate in the pleasures of the messianic age. For others, both the righteous and the unrighteous will be resurrected—and this is a matter of ultimate justice. In the general resurrection, the righteous are restored in order to receive their rewards and the unrighteous in order to receive their punishment. The idea of a location for hell or Gehenna was not universal, but it began to be articulated in the post-exilic period as part of a broader conversation about reward and punishment and just recompense.[4] For Jews, resurrection was critical to judgment because a person was a unity: both body and soul.[5] A soul couldn't be judged separately from a body any more than a body could be judged separately from a soul. If divine justice was indeed to take place, it had to take place through the soul *and* the body, in their unity.

We can see how the idea of resurrection had developed from Ezekiel's vision. There the resurrected were a "multitude," but a few hundred years later, they had become more specific beings, morally righteous or morally unrighteous; their resurrection depended not so much on their national identity but on specific acts of justice and mercy, like feeding orphans and widows and caring for strangers.[6]

Often in the prophetic texts, divine judgment is figured as "recompense," which is an image of financial transaction. People will get the reward they deserve. Payment, reward, loss, and compensation are the kinds of images that the prophets often conjure up when speaking of the judgment and the final rendering of God's justice.[7] While there is some individuality allowed in these images, they often also speak of the people of Israel being judged for their collective deeds on the day of judgment. God punishes and rewards the nation for its deeds in relation to its covenant. This judgment takes place in historic time, not beyond it. It is a result of history and takes place within history.[8]

Zoroastrianism

The period of exile in Babylon had brought new eschatological possibilities into Jewish culture. While apocalyptic texts like Daniel show some connection with their prophetic predecessors, they also are quite different.[9] The apocalypses show considerable influence from Persian culture, specifically from Zoroastrianism. **Zoroastrianism** is a religion that developed in Persia and was based on the teachings of a prophet named Zarathustra, who is thought to have lived during the second millennium BCE. Zarathustra taught many things that became integrated into Jewish culture during the period of exile. For example, the Hebrew Bible never mentions demons, but by the time of the New Testament, these spiritual beings, common in Zoroastrianism, had become an ordinary and accepted part of life. Zarathustra also taught that the world would have an end, that this end would be preceded by a final battle with a moral reckoning, and that the wicked would be banished forever.[10] This understanding of history was an important part of canonical apocalyptic texts like Daniel and extra-canonical apocalypses like 4 Ezra, 2 Baruch, and others.

We can't say exactly what Judaism borrowed from Zoroastrianism or vice versa. We can say that Jewish apocalypticism was deeply influenced by Zoroastrianism, and likewise Zoroastrianism by Judaism, while they lived side by side.[11] Among the ideas that Zoroastrianism helped bring into fruition in Judaism, one is especially important. During the Babylonian Exile, Jewish writers and thinkers began to conceive of history as a whole. Especially in the context of writing apocalypses, they began to conceive of history as completed in stages. Daniel, for example, prophesies the four kingdoms, which is close to the periodization of the Persian *Bahman Yašt* in which history is imagined as a tree with four branches.[12] This conception of history as a unity is what Gerhard von Rad has called apocalypticism's "special splendor."[13]

The apocalyptic texts that emerged in the late Second Temple Period (after the second temple was built in Jerusalem around 518 BCE and before it was destroyed by the Romans in 70 CE) emphasized ongoing revelation. They offered a worldview in which God continued to speak to his people and to reveal his plans to them. These plans of God existed "over and above received tradition and human reasoning." They suggested that human events were controlled by unseen, supernatural agents and that human life culminated in a grand *denouement*, divine judgment, in which the righteous at last receive their reward and the wicked are punished.[14]

Greek Influence

At the same time that reward and punishment and the meaning of history were being worked out in relation to resurrection and the messianic age, Jewish culture was also coming into increasing contact with Greek culture. Nikolai Berdyaev has characterized the difference between the two cultures in this way: for Greeks, the world was a cosmos. For Hebrews, it was a history.[15] One version is relatively static: beings are assigned places within a hierarchy. The other version is progressive and narrative, a story about God's particular work with a particular people.

The contact between Jewish and Greek cultures helped to define the concept of the immortal soul.[16] For many Greek intellectuals, the idea of the immortal soul was a clear reason not to fear death. The person was not a unity of body and soul, but more truly a soul wearing, briefly, the cloak of the physical body. Death simply meant the removal of this cloak. This idea took root in Jewish culture but became connected with the question of ultimate justice and righteousness. Might it be that the righteous would go to be with God in the divine realm? How this fit with the notion of resurrection was by no means fully worked out. Some texts, like Pseudo-Phocylides (written somewhere between 100 BCE and 100 CE), have resurrection of the dead and the immortality of the soul side by side, without any attempt to resolve what might seem like a contradiction.[17]

In the first century CE, this made for increasingly elaborate understandings of life after death. A wide variety of inter-testamental texts offered suggestions for how long the dead will remain dead until the resurrection, and where exactly their souls are located in the meantime. In one Jewish text from the first or second century CE, the writer says that the souls of the dead are kept in four hollow places at the end of the earth. The souls of the righteous are separated from the souls of sinners and treated differently. The souls of the righteous have light and are located near a spring of water. The souls of sinners suffer continual torment, even before the final judgment. The book goes on to describe how the righteous will be raised from the dead and will live on the abundant earth, where they will have thousands of children.[18]

Jewish Futures

In the era before the emergence of Christianity, there was no one Jewish belief about the future and the afterlife. Various ideas carried forward into the first century with a complicated mix of earthly and heavenly kingdoms, bodies and souls, catastrophic and restorative futures. At the same time that this expansion of the questions of the afterlife was taking place, apocalyptic texts, with specific revelations about the future, were also being produced in Jewish culture and in the cultures within which Judaism was embedded.

From this overview, we can see that the Jewish context into which Jesus began to speak his own eschatological ideas was rich and diverse. Eschatology had rapidly diversified in the centuries before the birth of Jesus and had gained rich new genres, like the apocalypse, to express eschatological ideas. Judaism was in conversation with all of the cultures around it, predominantly Persian and Greek, and was developing its eschatology alongside, in contradistinction to, and in conjunction with other eschatologies. The experience of exile, return, and life under repressive regimes had shaped Jewish eschatology significantly, and given the Jewish people a passion for ultimate justice and for a day of reckoning when God's kingdom would at last be known through all the earth. The story of crisis and victory inherited from the ancient myths remained central, but it no longer belonged to a mythic past. It was firmly cast into the future and belonged in the hands of God. Jewish tradition developed polemical and imaginative modes. It also increasingly saw human history as a God-ordained unity. This would have long-lasting effects on its Christian inheritors and interpreters.

Notes

1. Richard J. Clifford, "The Roots of Apocalypticism in Near Eastern Myth," in *The Encyclopedia of Apocalypticism*, ed. John J. Collins (New York: Continuum, 1998), 1:3–38.

2. John J. Collins, "From Prophecy to Apocalypticism: The Expectation of the End," in *The Encyclopedia of Apocalypticism*, vol. 1, ed. John J. Collins (New York: Continuum, 1998), 129. We see this myth alive in the Psalms, such as Psalm 96 and Psalm 98.

3. Claudia Setzer, *The Resurrection of the Dead in Early Judaism and Early Christianity* (Boston: Brill, 2004), 12.

4. Ibid., 16.

5. Robert Jewett, *Paul's Anthropological Terms: A Study of Their Use in Conflict Settings* (Leiden: Brill, 1971), 447.

6. Deut 16:14; Isa 10:2; and Jer 49:11 are examples of Hebrew Bible texts that spell out the specific nature of righteousness.

7. David W. Kuck, *Judgment and Community Conflict: Paul's Use of Apocalyptic Judgment Language in 1 Corinthians 3:5–4:5* (Leiden: Brill, 1992), 43.

8. Ibid., 45.

9. Collins, 134.

10. Paul G. Kreyenbroek, "Millennialism in the Zoroastrian Tradition," in *Imagining the End: Visions of Apocalypse from the Ancient Middle East to Modern America*, ed. Abbas Amanat and Magnus Bernhardsson (London: Tauris, 2002), 54–55.

11. See Mitchell Reddish, ed., *Apocalyptic Literature: A Reader* (Nashville: Abingdon, 1990), 33; and Setzer, 10.

12. Collins, 142; and Hans Schwarz, *Eschatology* (Grand Rapids: Eerdmans, 2000), 59.

13. Gerhard von Rad, *Old Testament Theology*, trans. D. M. G. Stalker (New York: Harper, 1965), 2:304.

14. Collins, 157.

15. Nikolai Berdyaev, *The Beginning and the End*, trans. R. M. French (London: Bles, 1952), 197.

16. Colleen McDannell and Bernhard Lang, *Heaven: A History* (New Haven: Yale University Press, 1988), 16.

17. Setzer, 17.

18. This summary is drawn from Adela Yarbro Collins, "The Apocalypse of John and Its Millennial Themes," in *Apocalyptic and Eschatological Heritage: The Middle East and Celtic Realms,* ed. Martin Macnamara (Dublin: Four Courts, 2003), 52–54.

3

Parables and Resurrection: Already and Not Yet in the Jesus Tradition

Eschatology is the mother of all Christian theology.
—Ernst Käsemann

In the wilderness northeast of Jerusalem, at the beginning of what we now call the Common Era, a man appeared with an urgent message about repentance. The Gospels record that he was a strange looking man, with more than a hint of wildness about him. The Gospel of Mark says that he wore camel hair with a leather belt around his waist and that he lived on locusts and wild honey. Like the prophets of the Hebrew Bible, whom he quoted, John the Baptist claimed that "the kingdom of heaven is at hand." The nearness of this kingdom meant that the people needed to purify themselves and turn away from their ungodly ways. As a sign of their repentance, he baptized his followers in the Jordan River. John claimed that an even more eschatological figure than himself was coming after him, one who will "clear his threshing floor and will gather his wheat into the granary; but the chaff he will burn with unquenchable fire" (Matt 3:12). Most scholars believe that Jesus was initially a follower of John and baptized by John, and that many of Jesus's followers were first John's followers. The arrest and subsequent execution of John the Baptist by Herod, who was the local authority in Judea, played an important role in the records that we have about Jesus's life. In the Gospel of Matthew, for example, many steps in Jesus's ministry are marked by the moment they occur in John the Baptist's life and death.

The Kingdom of God

The Roman world in the first century was alive with eschatological expectation.[1] For Jewish people in particular, the sense of crisis, of the need for some all-encompassing change that would overcome the Roman Empire and transform the fate of the Jewish people, meant that apocalyptic texts sprouted and spread. Scholars have identified fourteen between the third century BCE and the second century CE.[2] There was no common agreement about what the much anticipated end would look like, but many agreed that the kingdom of God—envisioned by Ezekiel, elaborated by Isaiah and Daniel in different forms, and further elaborated in many non-canonical texts—was "at hand."

For both John and Jesus, **the kingdom of God** was an essential aspect of their understanding of their work on earth. In fact, many scholars have argued that it was the center.[3] The kingdom of God, or, interchangeably, the kingdom of heaven, was both an ancient and very dense symbol and one that was used in a fresh way by early Christians.[4] Even though the concept of a coming kingdom that would be ruled by God was a very old concept in Jewish thought, the specific phrases "kingdom of heaven" and "kingdom of God" appear far more often in the New Testament than in the Hebrew Bible. This suggests that the concept became central to early Christians, and that as they adapted it to their particular situation, it took on new meanings. It is used to refer *both* to a coming event *and* to an interior, spiritual state. This dual usage—signifying the present and the future simultaneously—sets the tone very early for Christianity's already–not yet understanding of the future. As the career of John the Baptist demonstrates, it had both moral and political dimensions; it could be both polemical and personal. The kingdom of God involves two interrelated concepts: a theocracy—a place and a time when the people are ruled by God and God's law—and a spiritual reality in which one accepts the law of God and God's rule in one's own life.[5]

When the Gospels mention the kingdom of God, they usually speak of it in parables as if it cannot be fully grasped by descriptive or narrative language, and this is in part because it is an "open-ended symbol" that involves political, economic, social, territorial, spacial, national, spiritual, moral, and metaphoric dimensions.[6] Many of Jesus's recorded parables begin with the simple but intricate statement "The kingdom of God is like . . .", and then go on to compare it to a wide variety of personal and agricultural images. "What is the kingdom of God like? And to what should I compare it?" Jesus asks in the Gospel of Luke. "It is like a mustard seed that someone took and sowed in the garden; it grew and became a tree, and the birds of the air made nests in its branches. . . . It is like yeast that a woman took and mixed in with three measures of flour until all of it was leavened" (Luke 13:18–21).

On the surface, these do not appear to our ears to be eschatological images. They are nothing like the four horns of Daniel or the dramatic proclamations of Isaiah. And each of the four Gospels puts a slightly different emphasis on various aspects of Jesus's teachings. Scholars have long noted that the Gospel of John, for example, puts a much stronger emphasis on the immediate reality of the kingdom of God, whereas the Gospel of Mark is more likely to emphasize its impending nature. In addition, we have inherited two thousand years of interpretation of the Gospels, and people have seen in them Jesus as a warrior king, a wisdom teacher, an enigmatic healer and mystic, a prophet who preaches the end of time, a social visionary, a great storyteller, and many other things. The Gospels, with their blend of sayings, events, commentary, and narrative, invite this multiplicity. In the twentieth and twenty-first centuries, scholars have spent a great deal of time using historical documents to determine what Jesus *actually* said and thought. At the end of the day, despite brilliant minds working nonstop on this problem for decades, we still don't know. Rudolf Bultmann is one of many biblical scholars and theologians who has noted that no matter what methods we bring to bear on the Gospels, we end up with at least some "subjective judgment" about who Jesus was and what he was trying to tell us through the words in these texts.[7]

But that does not mean that we can say just anything about who Jesus was, what he believed, and how he acted on earth. We must attend carefully to our sources and to what we know of the historical context, even while acknowledging its limits. The problem comes up because at the beginning of the twentieth century, Albert Schweitzer, the father of the "historical Jesus" movement, pointed out that Jesus probably had strong eschatological beliefs about the imminent coming of the kingdom of God.[8] This is, as Dale Allison puts it, inconvenient for contemporary Christian theology.[9] It makes Jesus look like a failed prophet whose followers then had to compensate for the failure of his predictions about the future.

Even so, in order to understand Jesus's words as recorded in the Gospels and to make any sense out of the tradition that follows, we have to look at the eschatological context in which Jesus taught, thought, and acted. Key to this context is the Jewish eschatological vision that clearly formed Jesus and that he extended. Also key to understanding the teachings of Jesus is to understand how often he employed the future tense. Characteristic of his teaching, as we've received it in the Gospels, are future-oriented statements that seem to point to both an earthly and a spiritual reality, and a contrast between the conditions of the present and those of the future. "Those who exalt themselves will be humbled" (Matt 23:12). "The last will be first" (Mark 10:31).[10] Much of Jesus's teaching was oriented toward the future and toward a time when things will not be as they are now. His sayings suggest that the difference between the current state of reality and the future is divine transformation.

The Little Apocalypse

In the Gospel of Mark, there is a long speech in chapter 13 attributed to Jesus that frequently is called the Little Apocalypse. Chapter 13 echoes, condenses, and recontextualizes Daniel along with other prophetic material from the Hebrew Bible. Versions of the Little Apocalypse are in all the Synoptic Gospels.[11] This is perhaps the clearest demonstration of the Gospels' orientation to the future.

Scholars believe that Mark was written sometime in the first century and that it is the earliest of the four Gospels written by an otherwise unknown author.[12] This Gospel is full of what scholars call "kingdom sayings." Jesus's first words echo those of John: "The time is fulfilled, and the kingdom of God has come near; repent, and believe in the good news" (Mark 1:15). In the midst of healings, miracles, and debates about Jewish law, the Gospel elaborates the kingdom of God through parables: The kingdom of God is "as if someone would scatter seed on the ground" (Mark 4:26); the kingdom of God is "like a mustard seed" (Mark 4:31). Jesus mentions that the kingdom of God belongs to the little children (Mark 10:15) and how difficult it is for a rich man to enter it (Mark 10:23). All of these kingdom sayings are eschatological in some way: they all give us information about the ultimate nature of things, and they are part of the teaching of Jesus about a time and place that is not here and not yet. Jesus's actions—his healings and feedings—must also be understood as eschatological since we are made to understand that with every action he is fulfilling prophecy: he himself is a sign of what is "at hand."[13]

But Mark 13 makes this more complicated. It is a speech almost twice as long as any other in the Gospel, and it is possibly intended as a piece of written rather than oral testimony. Mark interrupts the speech to say "let the reader understand" in verse 14. Some scholars have seen Mark 13 as a kind of prophecy after the fact. They argue that the writer of the Gospel, using Jesus's voice, may be referring to the destruction of the temple in Jerusalem in 70 CE, at least a generation after the death of Jesus, and this catastrophic event may provide the context through which Jesus's own ministry was understood. In Mark 13, Jesus prophesies the downfall of the temple. "Not one stone will be left here upon another; all will be thrown down" (Mark 13:2). But he then goes on to put this event into a greater eschatological context.

The disciples ask him to tell them when the destruction will take place and "what will be the sign that all these things are about to be accomplished" (Mark 13:4). Jesus does not answer them directly. Instead, he tells his disciples to be on guard against false teachers, and that the "signs" of war, earthquakes, and famines are mere "birth pangs" of the world to come.[14] He warns the disciples that they themselves will be persecuted and that they will need the utmost endurance to get through the coming time of trial. Jesus is echoing the tradition in the Hebrew Bible that we have already seen: a time of crisis, persecution, and trial that precedes the "day of the Lord" and the great victory that finally belongs to God. All of this is familiar language, drawn from prophetic texts, and brought into this new situation where the kingdom of God is imminent. The disciples who are listening, or at the very least the Gospel's first audience, are the ones who need this information.

But in verse 10, Jesus adds a new piece of information: "And the good news must first be proclaimed to all nations." Before the kingdom of God can come, the good news must be spread. This verse has been central to Christian understanding of the future. As the concept of "all nations" expanded over the course of Christian history, so did the sense of time and space through which this passage was interpreted. While Jesus appears to be speaking about imminence, this remark gives the disciples work to do—a prophetic and eschatological task to preach the gospel to "all nations." Through the centuries, Christians have presumed that this work belongs to them as well as to the first disciples.

In the next section of the speech, Jesus moves from what we have been calling prophetic eschatology to apocalyptic eschatology: "But when you see the desolating sacrilege set up where it ought not to be (let the reader understand), then those in Judea must flee to the mountains" (Mark 13:14). The "desolating sacrilege" is an expression drawn directly from the book of Daniel, and in the rabbinic tradition it refers to the statue of Zeus placed on the altar of the temple by Antiochus IV Epiphanes in the second century BCE. Daniel says, "From the time that the regular burnt offering is taken away and the abomination that desolates is set up, there shall be one thousand two hundred ninety days" (Dan 12:11). What makes this apocalyptic (in contrast to prophetic) eschatology is that the time is already ordained: 1, 290 days. Everything that happens is exactly according to God's plan. There is nothing for humans to do. In the Little Apocalypse, Jesus advises his followers to flee to the mountains. "For in those days there will be suffering, such as has not been from the beginning of the creation that God created until now, no, and never will be" (Mark 13:19). This time of terrible suffering, as in Daniel, is how people will know that the end is truly at hand.

Continuing in the apocalyptic vein, Jesus then turns to astral bodies, quoting now loosely from several ancient texts, namely Isaiah, Ezekiel, and Joel:

> But in those days, after that suffering,
> the sun will be darkened,
>   and the moon will not give its light,
> and the stars will be falling from heaven,
>   and the powers in the heavens will be shaken. (Mark 13:34–35)

In this unknown time, a time very soon, the rhythms of ordinary life will be disrupted. Things that can be taken for granted, like the patterns of the sun and the moon, will become unreliable. Time—which humans have always marked through the movement of astral bodies—will no longer be counted upon. The "shaking" will be a shaking of both space and time. In this midst of this terrible uncertainty, "they will see the Son of Man coming in the clouds" (Mark 13:26). We have already seen that this shaking of astral bodies is an essential part of Jewish eschatology. It signals the end of the age, the radical transformation of things as they are. It is fundamentally apocalyptic, by the definitions that we have laid out here, because it is out of human hands. It is God's doing—and something that only God can do.

But the Little Apocalypse leaves the apocalyptic here and returns to the prophetic, where earthly life is once again celebrated and anticipated. After talking about the darkening of the sky, Jesus returns to more concrete signs of hope that can only happen if the sun continues to rise and set in its normal rhythms: the green shoots of the fig tree. The natural world is not transformed into terrible uncertainty and fear but into flourishing, into things that are tender and sprouting. The long speech of the Little Apocalypse doesn't end with horror, a darkened sky, and the "abomination of desolation" but with greenness and tenderness, a sign of God in our midst.[15]

In the final section, Jesus returns again to the question of time and seems to answer the disciples' question about when. His answer appears to be both now and not yet. He says, "Truly I tell you, this generation will not pass away until all these things have taken place," and "But about that day or hour no one knows, neither the angels in heaven, nor the Son, but only the Father" (Mark 13:30, 32).

Thus the Little Apocalypse ends with the problem of time that has dogged Christianity throughout its history: both this generation and a day that no one knows, both now and not yet.

Eschatological Hope

Dale Allison reminds us that while Jesus was rooted solidly in "eschatological hope," the kind that was in the air around him, he was not "a cartographer of future states." He did not map out the future for his followers, and while many interpreters have tried to turn the Little Apocalypse into just such a map, their efforts have not been successful. Eschatology, Allison says, was "part of his native religious language, the mythology within which he articulated demand, warning, consolation" and the context within which he interpreted his own life and his followers interpreted his life and death.[16]

Jesus's eschatology included the following elements: a belief that there would soon be a time of great catastrophe followed by a great restoration, especially of the nation of Israel; a belief in the resurrection of the dead; and a belief in a universal, divine judgment. As we've seen in the Little Apocalypse, he also may have had eschatological expectations concerning the image from Daniel 7:13, "I saw one like a Son of Man coming with the clouds of heaven. And he came to the Ancient One and was presented before him," a passage quoted directly in the Little Apocalypse.[17]

Many eschatological texts from the period of the Gospels and the centuries before them speak of a coming time of trial and suffering, a global catastrophe like the one described in the Little Apocalypse.[18] We've already seen the roots of this in the combat myths: the people face a grave crisis to which the great warrior responds, and then experience a transformation or restoration through the work of the warrior. We've also seen this myth projected by the prophets into the future and the human/divine warrior transformed into the solely divine Yahweh who saves the people, restores them, and brings about a time of renewal, while putting an end to the wicked. The stories continue in this pattern: crisis, transformation, judgment, renewal. In the Little Apocalypse, Jesus prophesied this time of crisis using the words of older prophetic texts. In his teaching, Jesus was anticipating the kingdom of God, a restoration that would be earthly, not heavenly, but would involve a great deal of divine intervention. He likely believed that the time of this transformation was ripe and that he himself was a part of its coming into being. And when the crisis had passed, we would be in the eschaton—the time at the end of time—where heaven and earth would not be two separate realms but one continuous realm where people lived free from death and pain.[19]

Resurrection of the Dead

Jesus also believed in a resurrection of the dead—a time when bodies will rise from graves. This tradition goes back, as we have seen, to Ezekiel, where resurrection is linked to national restoration. It is also found in stories of Elijah, who raises the Shunammite woman's son from the dead (2 Kgs 4:18–37). Like Elijah, Jesus too raises the recently dead (Mark 5; Luke 7; John 11). But these personal and individual resuscitations are not quite the same thing as the resurrection of the dead at the end of time. How physical is this resurrection? How much will we be "like the angels in heaven" (Mark 12:25)? Will everyone be resurrected or only the righteous? What is the relationship between resurrection and heaven? The Jesus tradition offers contradictory portraits and doesn't answer any of these questions definitively. Jesus both talks about the resurrection of the dead (Matthew 22) and tells the thief on the cross,

"Today you will be with me in Paradise" (Luke 23:43), two statements that defy systematic or easy reconciliation.

Jesus did not detail his teaching on this—at least not in what the Gospel writers have given us. Claudia Setzer argues that this is because he did not need to. Resurrection of the dead was already a given among the people he was talking to, an important part of their cultural inheritance.[20] It may also have been true that Jesus was focused on more immediate eschatological events, as John Meier has argued.[21] Or, as others have suggested, Jesus was not the literalist that Allison, following Schweitzer, makes him out to be. Bruce Chilton, for example, has argued that Jesus was part of a more esoteric trend in Jewish eschatology that moved toward visions and spiritual understandings of physical phenomena. Chilton argues that Jesus's followers took increasingly literal directions in interpreting his teachings, against Jesus's own teaching and practice.[22] We don't actually know, and as Allison wisely points out, the choices we make about what Jesus believed usually tell us more about ourselves than about Jesus.

Divine Judgment

That being said, a universal, divine judgment was another central idea deeply rooted in Jesus's Jewish heritage. This universal judgment is the one that Crossan calls the "Great, Divine Clean Up." It is rooted in the experience of exile and a longing for a place and time when things will finally be made right, when we will be able to see the wicked for what they are, and when the righteous will be acknowledged. This is the inauguration of the new age, and in prophetic texts it is called the "day of the Lord," when God's enemies are vanquished.[23] In Matthew, Jesus describes this as the day when the "sheep" are separated from the "goats," and his is an intensely moral vision. Those who have fed the hungry, welcomed the stranger, and clothed the naked are the ones who will be acknowledged as the righteous. The sheep are ushered into paradise, and the goats, who turned away those in need, are sent to "the eternal fire prepared for the devil and his angels" (Matt 25:31–46). The vision is drastically either/or: either you are a sheep, or you are a goat. There is no third category.

The Son of Man

The final element of Jesus's eschatology is the figure of the Son of Man. This is another compound symbol that can resonate in multiple directions. We can trace a direct line from the visions of Daniel in which the Son of Man comes "with the clouds" and is given an everlasting dominion to the apocalyptic phrasing of Mark 13, in which the Son of Man again appears "in clouds," this time to gather the elect, and then to the passage at the beginning of Acts when the disciples watch Jesus "lifted up, and a cloud took him out of their sight." They are then told that his second coming will happen "in the same way" (Acts 1:9–11).

While this appears to be a glorification of the image of the Son of Man, Jesus also uses the phrase in humble and simple ways. He uses it in reference to Isaiah's suffering servant; for example, "For the Son of Man came not to be served but to serve, and to give his life a ransom for many" (Mark 10:45). This creates a stark contrast within one phrase that is obscure from the beginning and provides the kind of multi-valence that has had such profound importance for Christian eschatology.

This combination of warrior king and suffering servant eventually gave Christian eschatology and christology their potency. Jesus was and was not the ancient warrior savior. He was and was not the suffering servant of Isaiah. The vagueness of the phrase allowed it to echo on emotional and spiritual planes as well as to simply mean "I," a way for Jesus to talk about himself in the third person. In Greek, the language of the four Gospels, the phrase "son of man" had no meaning. It was a direct translation of a much more eschatologically loaded phrase in Aramaic and Hebrew. For Greek-speaking Christians, however, it could be infused with a very specific meaning that related to Jesus himself.

Eschatological Language and Resurrection

The phrase "Son of Man" is a good example of the fluidity and complexity that Christians used in the first century to make sense of the life and death of Jesus. On the subject of eschatology, the Gospels' stories give us no final, complete portrait of what Jesus himself believed about the future. This leads us to an important question about language. Dale Allison argues that "central to Jesus' teaching and activity was the conviction that God was soon to intervene in dramatic and publicly visible fashion and inaugurate a golden age, 'the eschatological order,'" and his argument is persuasive.[24]

At the same time, as we study Christian eschatological language and teachings going forward, we need to keep in mind the multiple planes on which this language was used and understood. It wasn't only an argument about the nature of time; it also was an expression of the nature of a reality that went beyond the ordinary. As a result, metaphor, imagery, and symbolism played central roles. Biblical eschatology is not, or at least is very rarely, a literal prediction of the future. It *is* a multi-faceted symbolic language that tries to give form to the ineffable. If it were perfectly literal, we would not need parables, visions, symbols, and four-headed beasts to point toward it.

Eschatological language not only answers the question "What does a person believe?" but also helps to construct a person's identity, signaling to them what kind of community they are a part of, what kind of God they worship, and how they are connected to the world and to God.[25] Bodily resurrection, for example, was a highly concentrated symbol, often a part of poetic and apocalyptic texts, that told believers something about their identity: who they were and who they would become. Claudia Setzer describes it this way: "Resurrection is more than a single, curious belief. It functions as a shorthand for an interlocking web of values, a condensation symbol that helps to construct community."[26] Only by understanding this complexity can we understand why the very same text can say quite contradictory things about the nature of belief in paradise or resurrection or heaven. If we try to make literal truth out of eschatology, it loses nearly all of its power. Eschatological language is not symbol *or* truth. What makes it so complex is that it is both literal and metaphoric at the very same moment—it makes meaning in real time about a future that is both symbolic and actual. The complexity of this language is precisely what feeds the tension between the "already" and the "not yet" that makes Christian eschatology such a rich and ongoing tradition.

Thus when Christians began to tell the story of Jesus's resurrection in the first century, they were using a language that was already powerfully invested with meaning. But unlike the prophets of old, they were now claiming that resurrection was not merely a future event. It had become a part of human history. Jesus's resurrection was something that had already happened and a key sign of the eschatological future. They now began to look for Jesus's "coming in the clouds" (Mark 13:26; Rev 1:7) even while they tried to fulfill his commands and follow in his footsteps.

Resurrection creates a distinctiveness in Christian eschatology because it exists in the past, the present, and the future simultaneously. It is radically disruptive to the way that we know human life and death. As theologian John Polkinghorne puts it, resurrection is the "prime source" in Christian theology to argue that the future is open to God's transformation.[27]

Notes

1. See Helmut Koester, "Jesus: The Victim," *JBL* 111 (1992): 3–15; Dale Allison, *Jesus of Nazareth: Millenarian Prophet* (Minneapolis: Fortress, 1998); S. E. Robinson, "Apocalypticism in the time of Hillel and Jesus," in *Hillel and Jesus: Comparisons of Two Major Religious Leaders*, ed. James H. Charlesworth and Loren M. Johns (Minneapolis: Fortress, 1997), 121–36; T. Francis Glasson, *Greek Influence in Jewish Eschatology* (London: SPCK, 1961); and F. Gerald Downing, "Common Strands in Pagan, Jewish and Christian Eschatologies in the First Century," *TZ* 51 (1995): 196–211.

2. Mitchell Reddish, ed., *Apocalyptic Literature: A Reader* (Nashville: Abingdon, 1990), 28.

3. "Kingdom of God," *The Eerdmans Bible Dictionary*, ed. Allen C. Myers et al. (Grand Rapids: Eerdmans, 1987), 625.

4. Scholars believe that the Gospel of Matthew uses the kingdom of heaven, rather than the kingdom of God, out of respect for the Jewish tradition of not saying the name of God, but that there is little discernible difference in the use of this term and how the kingdom of God is used in other Gospels.

5. *Eerdmans Bible Dictionary*, 626.

6. Dennis C. Duling, "Kingdom of God, Kingdom of Heaven," *Anchor Bible Dictionary*, ed. D. N. Freedman (New York: Doubleday, 1992–1996), 4:50.

7. Rudolf Bultmann, *History of the Synoptic Tradition* (rev. ed; New York: Harper & Row, 1963), 102.

8. Albert Schweitzer, *The Quest of the Historical Jesus* (New York: Macmillan, 1961).

9. Allison, 166.

10. Allison, 132. Also Bultmann, 105.

11. Matthew 24 and Luke 21. They all come at approximately the same time in each narrative, right before Jesus's ride into Jerusalem that precedes the crucifixion. The Gospel of John is notably less eschatological and does not have this section in its narrative. There are warnings, but they focus on the present moment.

12. Pheme Perkins, *Introduction to the Synoptic Gospels* (Grand Rapids: Eerdmans, 2009), 57.

13. Mark 1:2-3. Christoph Schwöbel writes, "The imminent coming of the kingdom of God is a center of Jesus' message . . . and the coming of the kingdom of God is so closely related to his person that he is in this person seen as the coming of the kingdom of God." Quoted in John Polkinghorne, *The God of Hope and the End of the World* (New Haven: Yale University Press, 2002), 80.

14. This was a common metaphor among rabbis. See Allison, 145.

15. Paul Galbreath, "Mark 13:24-37," *Interpretation* (October 1, 2008): 423.

16. Allison, 130.

17. NRSV actually translates this as "one like a human being," but the eschatological phrase "Son of Man" took on meaning for early Christians and is used frequently in the Gospels.

18. See for example 1 Enoch, 4 Ezra, 2 Baruch, and the *Apocalypse of Abraham*. We also see this in the Zoroastrian tradition, for example in the *Oracle of Hystaspes*. Likewise, prophecies of a time of trial are found in Daniel, Joel, Isaiah, and Amos.

19. Allison, 156.

20. Claudia Setzer, *Resurrection of the Body in Early Judaism and Early Christianity: Doctrine, Community and Self-Definition* (Leiden: Brill, 2004), 54.

21. John Meier, "The Debate on the Resurrection of the Dead: An Incident from the Ministry of the Historical Jesus," *JSNT* 77 (2000): 3-24.

22. Bruce Chilton, "Resurrection in the Gospels," in *Death, Life-after-Death,*

Resurrection, and the World-to-Come in the Judaisms of Antiquity, ed. Alan Avery-Peck and Jacob Neusner (Leiden: Brill, 2000), 215–39.

23. See Isaiah 2; Amos 5; and Joel 2.

24. Allison, 95.

25. Andrew Cohen, *The Symbolic Construction of Community* (London and New York: Tavistock, 1985). I also follow Setzer, 4–9.

26. Setzer, 144.

27. Polkinghorne, xxiv.

4

Seeds and Sheafs: The Eschatology of the Apostle Paul

What is sown is perishable, what is raised is imperishable. It is sown in dishonor, it is raised in glory. It is sown in weakness, it is raised in power. It is sown a physical body, it is raised a spiritual body.

—1 Corinthians 15:42–44

After Jesus's death and resurrection, the Acts of the Apostles tell us, a Jewish man named Saul was responsible for the persecution of many of Jesus's followers. As he was traveling to Damascus, he suddenly encountered a great light and heard a voice: "Saul, Saul, why are you persecuting me?" The experience changed Saul dramatically, and he became a follower of the one whose voice he believed he had heard.

After his conversion, Saul, whose name was changed to Paul, became one of Jesus's most dedicated disciples, and his letters to the Christian communities that he served have formed the foundation of Christian theology. His eschatology, however, is not something that we can pick up whole from any one of his letters. Each letter was written in a specific context with the needs of a particular community in mind, and so each employs a slightly different language and set of ideas to instruct the community.

Like Jesus, Paul was shaped by a Jewish eschatological context where the features we've just described were central to both his Jewish identity and his emerging Christianity. Like other Jews, Paul anticipated the day of the Lord, when the present age, which he taught was ruled by Satan, would end, and the age to come would bring the anticipated restoration and redemption. As we saw in the Gospels, a time of tribulation, resurrection of the dead, and cosmic judgment were assumed as part of these two ages. But Paul had an added piece of information: the resurrection of Jesus himself from the dead. For Paul, this could only be interpreted as an eschatological event. Jesus had come, as Jürgen Becker puts it, at "the last possible moment in history."[1] And his resurrection signaled the end of the reign of Satan and the beginning of the new era. Thus for Paul that new era was both now—it had already begun in the resurrection of Jesus—and not yet—we continue in the time of labor and birth pangs (Rom 8:22). For Paul, the hour was not about to strike. It had already struck in the raising of Jesus from the dead.[2]

Paul also had a distinct context, and as we look more closely at his eschatological language, we will want to remember that unlike Jesus, Paul spoke to diverse audiences and was often responding directly to the concerns and questions of specific communities. As the context changes, his language and nuances change in ways that can be confusing for modern readers who are looking for a systematic argument that Paul is not constructing.

Parousia

Central to Paul's eschatology was his belief in the **parousia**. *Parousia* is a Greek word which means "coming" or "appearance." It is most often used in the New Testament to refer to the coming or appearance of Christ at the end of time and is used in conjunction with other eschatological phrases like "the day of the Lord." In Paul's first known letter, written not long after his conversion, Paul mentions the *parousia* four times, suggesting that, at least at the beginning of his ministry, his belief in the imminent second coming of Christ was central to his teaching and actions.[3] As Paul himself aged and drew closer to death, he spoke about the *parousia* less often and imagined that he would "depart and be with Christ" (Phil 1:23) rather than Christ coming to him. This does not mean that Paul abandoned belief in the *parousia* itself but rather that he was not as certain that he would see it while he was alive. The *parousia* was a central part of Paul's theology and became central to Christian theology after Paul. Christ would come a second time "at the end of the age," and this second coming, the *parousia,* would signal the beginning of the new age. Paul also used the symbol of the eschatological "trumpet" to talk about this event (1 Cor 15:52; 1 Thess 4:16).

The Day of Our Lord Jesus

Paul brought belief in the *parousia* together with the ancient Jewish belief in the day of the Lord. In his eschatology, the traditional language of the day of the Lord became "the day of our Lord Jesus" (2 Cor 1:14) or "the day of Christ Jesus" (Phil

1:6). This demonstrates the particular direction that Christian eschatology took and its developing distinctiveness from Jewish eschatology. The concept remained very much the same: there would be a "day" that would signal the end of one age and the beginning of another. That day would involve divine judgment and a decisive act to transform the world as it was known. But the word "Jesus" is added to the traditional formula, and with that addition, it came to include the notion of the Son of Man coming on the clouds, the theology of the conquering suffering servant, and other key concepts that propelled Christian eschatology forward.

Paul shared with the writer of the Gospel of Mark a sense of urgency. The age ruled by Satan was very nearly at an end, and when that end came, God's power would be absolute. Paul lived his life, as Peter Brown puts it, "poised between revelation and resurrection."[4] The new age was imminent and required the absolute transformation of the believer. From the resurrection of Jesus, a new community had been born, and that community was the inversion of the imperial society in which it was located. Paul built an image of this community through a series of contrasts. God's power rested not with the emperor but with a crucified criminal. The strong would not inherit the kingdom of God, but the weak would. God did not give us worldly wisdom like that of the philosophers, but foolishness. And God did not use the immortal *pneuma* (spirit), which Greek people already believed to be incorruptible, but the fragile, earthy *sōma* (body) to bring about the final redemption.[5] And victory would finally come through the overcoming of death, "the last enemy"; through resurrection, God's victory is complete (1 Cor 15:26).

While Paul was subverting the empire, he was also inverting the ancient warrior myth. We've seen that in this myth, the people face a crisis and are saved by a man who is stronger and more powerful than they are, a man who is in some way divine. In Paul's inversion, the weakness of Christ—which is an unearthly power—saves. And that "saving" has something to do with overcoming death through the resurrection of the body.

Resurrection of the Body

Paul's belief in the resurrection of the dead was a central part of his Jewish identity, but this idea may not have been as widely accepted in all of his audiences, since he spoke to both Jews and non-Jews. In the passage where Paul discusses what the resurrection of the dead might mean most explicitly, we can see Paul as a skilled apologist writing to an audience that seems inclined to reject the idea. In the first letter to the Corinthians, Paul's audience was largely Gentile. They perhaps did not share baseline beliefs about the resurrection of the dead and the cosmic restoration of the nation of Israel that a Jewish audience might. In chapter 15, Paul appears to think that the Corinthians have either rejected the *body* part of the resurrection of the body, or they have rejected the future part of that resurrection and argued that they are already as resurrected as they will ever be.[6] But bodily resurrection is so crucial to Paul that he insists on its centrality. "If there is no resurrection of the dead, then Christ has not been raised; and if Christ has not been raised, then our proclamation has been in vain and your faith has been in vain" (1 Cor 15:13-14). He adds, "Then we are of all people most to be pitied" (1 Cor 15:19).[7]

But what exactly does Paul mean by resurrection of the body? This is a question that Christian theologians have taken up over and over again, right up to the present moment.[8] If we are going to try to understand what Paul might have envisioned, we might begin with the fact that in ancient Greek society, there was not a division between the spiritual and the physical as we have it today.[9] All "spiritual" realities were also in some way physical. Gods had bodies, as did souls. While modern people are working with a distinction between the material and the non-material, Greek society was working with a "hierarchy of essences."[10] Everything was made from something, but some things were made from heavier stuff than others. In the hierarchy of essences, heavier stuff was lower on the scale of goodness, and lighter was higher. Souls were made from incredibly light, heavenly stuff. And even among souls, there was a hierarchy. Some souls were made of finer stuff than others—this usually had something to do with social class. The spirit, *pneuma*, was a lighter kind of embodiment than *sōma*, but it was still an embodiment.[11]

Paul makes a further distinction between *sōma* (a unity that is closely tied with a person's identity) and *sarx* (flesh), the stuff from which the body was made or, perhaps, the unredeemed aspect of human nature that was at war with the Spirit (Galatians 5). For Paul, it was *sōma*, in some form, that would rise from the dead, but not *sarx*, which he says "cannot inherit the kingdom of God" (1 Cor 15:50). Even *sōma* had to be transformed from one kind of stuff to another kind of stuff. To explain how this might be imagined, Paul uses the metaphor of a seed. A grain of wheat is sown into the earth. There it "dies." From its death comes the sheaf of wheat, something that looks dramatically different from the seed. The grain and the sheaf share an identity, but they are not the same thing. "So it is with the resurrection of the dead," Paul writes. "What is sown is perishable, what is raised is imperishable. It is sown in dishonor, it is raised in glory. It is sown in weakness, it is raised in power. It is sown a physical body, it is raised a spiritual body" (1 Cor 15:42–44).

In order to take on its next form, a seed undergoes a radical transformation. The "bare seed" dies and decays just as the flesh of the human body will. But then it is transformed. When it becomes the sheaf of wheat, it is still in continuity with the seed it once was. But Paul did not place this continuity in either materiality or a kind of formal principle.[12] In other words, the seed is not the same material substance (in Paul's mind) as the sheaf, nor are they the same in form—and yet they share an identity. This has not been an easy aspect of Paul's theology for Christians to make sense of.

Even in Paul's day, it was a complicated argument. Dale Martin suggests that we can make some sense of it by looking closely at the audience that Paul was talking to as he attempted to explain resurrection of the body. As a Gentile audience, the Corinthians might have believed that resurrection of the body was a crass form of popular belief, something like belief in zombies today. People of high social class readily accepted the immortality of the soul, if they believed in any future beyond death. But the physical body had no role to play. They would have imagined resurrection of the dead as the resuscitation of a corpse. As a Jew, Paul was deeply committed to the resurrection of the dead, an ancient belief, and his audience in Corinth contained both these educated people and less educated people for whom resurrection of the dead was a given. His challenge was thus to show that his position on resurrection was "more sophisticated than it appeared on the surface, and to do so without giving up his belief in the resurrection of the body and without alienating the lower classes," who took the resurrection of the body for granted and longed for it.[13]

Thus resurrection of the body is the transformation of *sarx* into "glory," earthly body into heavenly body. At the resurrection, the body becomes something more like the heavenly bodies of the sun, moon, and stars.[14] This was an ancient connection between resurrection and stars (heavenly bodies) echoed in the book of Daniel: "Those who are wise shall shine like the brightness of the sky, and those who lead many to righteousness, like the stars forever and ever" (Dan 12:3). But no aspect—body, mind, spirit, or soul—of a human being is inherently immortal without the saving grace of God. No one is guaranteed immortality. That is something offered to believers at the end of time.[15]

But we notice that this insistence on the transformation of the body from flesh to something more star-like is at least somewhat different than stories in the Gospels about Christ's resurrection. For example, those stories emphasize that after his resurrection, Christ eats and drinks. This suggests some form of more ordinary embodied existence. But Jesus also appears and disappears without physical movement, and is sometimes recognizable and sometimes not. This variety of descriptions suggests that by the time of Paul's writing, there was not a "fixed tradition of the exact nature of the resurrected body of Jesus."[16]

Now and Not Yet

The detailed discussion of the resurrection of the body in the first letter to the Corinthians isn't the only way that Paul discusses the future for followers of Christ, and his view is not consistent throughout his letters. For example, both in his letter to the Romans and in his first letter to the Corinthians, he talks about resurrection as something that is already happening in the lives of believers. They were "in sin," but were now, through the resurrection of Christ, free from this "calamitous situation."[17] This was consistent with his view that the eschatological event, the new age, began with the resurrection of Christ. Some element of the new reality was present *now* in the lives of believers, and was not something for which they would have to wait. At the very same time, believers lived in "anxious longing" for the day that was still ahead of them. And in even further contradiction or at least complexity, Paul writes that if he dies before the *parousia*, he will go immediately to be with Christ (Phil 1:23). We might ask: in what form?

Despite the fact that Paul is centrally interested in ethical behavior and in beliefs about the future that promote good behavior in the present, he does not discuss hell at all. "He lacks the typical apocalyptic relish in vindictiveness and shows scant interest in the posthumous fate of unbelievers," writes Jamie Clark-Soles.[18] Satan appears in his letters as the ruler of the present age but never as the ruler of a future age, and not as the ruler of a realm like hell. "Paul's theology cannot sustain a notion of afterlife that includes Satan's reign over any territory of eternally tormented souls, because this would impinge unbearably on God's sovereignty and Christ's victory on the cross."[19] Instead, God must finally be "all in all" (1 Cor 15:28). Unbelievers will either be convinced in the final acts of the cosmic drama, or they will simply be destroyed (Rom 9:22).[20]

Paul did not create a systematic understanding of Christian eschatology. Anyone looking for specific, definitive Christian teaching on eschatology in the letters of Paul is sure to be disappointed.[21] Like the Gospel writers, he believed that the final act of human history was imminent and that it was tied to the resurrection of Christ. No one would be raised until the *parousia*, the ultimate coming of Christ, and then only believers would be raised. He believed that the resurrection of believers was central to the new era and that believers' faith should be centered on it. Christ, for Paul, was the "measure of all present and future reality" and evidence of the decisive victory of God over the forces of this world, both now and not yet.[22]

Notes

1. Jürgen Becker, *Paul: Apostle to the Gentiles*, translated by O. C. Dean Jr. (Louisville: Westminster John Knox, 1993), 376.

2. M. C. de Boer, "Paul and Apocalyptic Eschatology," in *The Encyclopedia of Apocalypticism*, ed. John J. Collins (New York: Continuum, 1998), 1:355.

3. See F. F. Bruce, *Paul the Apostle of the Heart Set Free* (Grand Rapids: Eerdmans, 2000).

4. Peter Brown, *The Body and Society* (New York: Columbia University Press, 1988), 46.

5. Claudia Setzer, *Resurrection of the Body in Early Judaism and Early Christianity: Doctrine, Community and Self-Definition* (Leiden: Brill, 2004), 67.

6. Dale Martin argues that the first is true in his *The Corinthian Body* (New Haven: Yale University Press, 1995). For the second, see Jaime Clark-Soles, *Death and the After Life in the New Testament* (New York: T&T Clark, 2006), 70.

7. Setzer, 54.

8. N. T. Wright's *Surprised by Hope: Rethinking Heaven, Resurrection, and the Mission of the Church* (New York: HarperCollins, 2008) serves as one recent example.

9. Martin, 15.

10. Ibid., 15.

11. Ibid., 115–16.

12. Caroline Walker Bynum, *The Resurrection of the Body in Western Christianity 200–1336* (New York: Columbia University Press, 1995), 6.

13. Martin, 123.

14. Ibid., 117.

15. Clark-Soles, 79.

16. Martin, 124.

17. Clark-Soles, 73.

18. Ibid., 61.

19. Ibid., 74.

20. This view excludes 2 Thessalonians as authentically Pauline because of its inclusion of a reference to hell in 2 Thess 1:8–9. This is a fact that is still disputed among scholars.

21. Jeffrey Trumbower, *Rescue for the Dead: The Posthumous Salvation of Non-Christians in Early Christianity* (New York: Oxford University Press, 1991), 40.

22. Becker, 376.

5

Alpha and Omega: The Book of Revelation

Look! He is coming with the clouds;
   every eye will see him,
even those who pierced him;
   and on his account all the tribes of the earth will wail.
So it is to be. Amen.
"I am the Alpha and the Omega," says the Lord God, who is and
who was and who is to come, the Almighty.

                                  —Revelation 1:7–8

In the late first century, the island of Patmos, off the coast of modern-day Turkey, was a busy and strategic sea port between the key cities of Rome and Ephesus. When John wrote his famous Apocalypse there, or Revelation as we know it, he was an exile, probably from Ephesus. It was an island of pebbled beaches, dramatic sunsets, a jagged coastline, and a harbor city now called Skela, which was its administrative center. Villages were scattered across the thirty-four-square-kilometer island where fishing and agriculture were important and temples to Artemis, Apollo, and Aphrodite dotted the coast. John probably took up residence in one of these outlying villages. His account of a vision that he received incorporates images of the landscape on which he found himself. He writes of great storms, hail, lightning, and rainbows, all of which were common on this seaworn island. At the center of the island was Mt. Elias, almost 900 feet above sea level, which provided a spectacular view of the mountains of Asia Minor to the east and the islands of the Aegean Sea to the west. One writer in the nineteenth century noticed a connection between Revelation 15, in which John describes a "sea of glass, mingled with fire" (Rev 15:2), and the local landscape, in which the last rays of the setting sun light up the water.[1]

John was likely not in prison on the island but instead free to roam. Drawing on ancient sources, scholars imagine that his exile ended with the death of the emperor Domitian. When Domitian died in 96 CE, the sentences of those he had punished were commuted. John was an elder among a small group of Christian communities in Asia Minor. These were churches that had formed through the travels of the disciples, as they spread throughout the Roman Empire to fulfill the command to "make disciples of all nations" (Matt 28:19). The apostle Paul's home province was here, and he lived in Ephesus for at least a few years during his ministry. The Johannine communities (the communities of the Apostle John) were also likely located in this region.

Christian communities of the first and second centuries were scattered and fragile. Belief in Christ grew up in diverse places and among diverse people of all social classes, but it flourished especially among the poor and uneducated.[2] Among these people, the imminence of a change in the social order and the belief in the resurrection of the dead were an important part of faith. Early Christian communities construc-ted their faith from stories, shared traditions, and the teachings of missionaries and elders. And while scholars agree that Christian martyrdom was not quite as widespread as later Christian documents suggest, still many early Christian leaders were martyred, and those deaths intensified the communities' faith.[3]

John's Revelation, the only Christian apocalyptic text that was eventually accepted into the Christian canon, draws on this sense of persecution and fragility to create its intensity and power. It was not the only visionary or apocalyptic text being circulated at the time. The *Apocalypse of Peter* and the *Shepherd of Hermas*—both influential, but now largely forgotten texts—we will discuss in the next chapter. But the Revelation of John was the one that had the most lasting impact on the development of Christianity.

Because of their geographical proximity and the fact that they were both named John, tradition has sometimes conflated John of Patmos with the Apostle John, but this connection was disputed as early as the third century, when Dionysius of Alexandria wrote that Revelation had, in his view, "no connection, no affinity, in any way" with either the Gospel or the Epistles. "It scarcely, so to speak, has even a syllable in common with them."[4] But Dionysius overstates his case: there are some similarities between the Johannine texts and Revelation. For example, in both, Jesus is Word and Lamb—and only in these.

Even so, contemporary scholars generally agree that the two Johns are probably not the same, in part because the Gospel and Letters of John have significant theological and stylistic differences with Revelation. Revelation combines several apocalyptic traditions, borrowing heavily from Daniel and Ezekiel, but adds new elements as well. The Greek of the text suggests that the writer was not a native speaker and probably was strongly influenced by Hebrew and Aramaic. Some scholars have suggested that the writer was using Hebrew texts and roughly translating them into Greek as he produced his own text. R. H. Charles, who wrote a landmark commentary on Revelation in the early part of the twentieth century, speculated that the writer thinks in Hebrew but writes in Greek for a Greek-speaking audience.[5]

Revelation as Oral Performance

The first audiences for Revelation would not have read the text as a book. They would have heard it read in communities.[6] It is a liturgical document that represents what Christian communities did together in their gatherings, and this performative nature is important to keep in mind as we discuss the book's work in shaping Christian understanding of the future. Revelation depicts a kind of worship service that begins with an invitation and continues with the singing of a hymn. There is a scripture reading and the recitation of prayers, including a psalm of praise and a response in verse. The service closes with congregational singing of a doxology, and the choir sings "Amen" (Revelation 4–5).[7]

Once this oral and performative aspect of Revelation was lost, Christians often read Revelation as a kind of code, a book that could be studied for secrets about the future. But its initial purposes appear to be liturgical. As an oral performance, Revelation might be understood as an attempt to enliven the holy imagination and inspire its audience to "see" beyond the ordinary. This invites a very different reading of the text than the one with which we have become familiar: picking the document apart verse by verse in order to read it predictively, as "future history."

Revelation begins with an announcement: this document contains a revelation from Jesus Christ to his servants about "things which must shortly take place." The announcement was sent by God to Christ, then through an angel who communicated it to John—a chain of revelatory words emanating from Christ himself but reaching the audience through John. The urgency of which John speaks is something that we've already seen as a crucial part of the Christian eschatological inheritance: transformation is coming soon, and this intensifies the need for the audience to respond to what is written. Jesus is "coming with the clouds," John writes, a figure outside time who is the "Alpha and the Omega"—the first and last letters of the Greek alphabet—"who is and who was and who is to come, the Almighty" (Rev 1:7-8).

After this announcement, the text is divided roughly into two parts. The first part is a series of seven letters to the "seven churches of Asia." Each church has a different letter with a specific emphasis for that community. These messages come to the community not from John but from the angel who has directed John to speak. This is a key part of the book as a piece of apocalyptic eschatology: John is a messenger through whom the angel speaks. This is different from both Jesus and Paul, who spoke as messengers but were not mouthpieces for angels. They did not set aside their own identities even as they claimed divine revelation. John did.

Also, unlike many other apocalyptic texts, the Revelation of John does not appear to be **pseudepigraphic**. Scholars believe that many apocalyptic texts, including Daniel, were not written by the person to whom the text was attributed. It was very common for these texts to claim a more ancient source and a more famous figure than the one doing the writing. Thus there were apocalypses written at a much later date attributed to Paul, Peter, and other key figures. But John appeared to have provided his own name and spoken about his actual situation. The angel spoke to each of the seven churches, specifically and directly but we also have a sense that the messages were intended to reach beyond that audience to the broader church.[8] They were both specific and universal.

The second part of Revelation takes John on an otherworldly journey through heaven and the future via a series of scenes rich in complex symbols. John speaks again as himself, and he is invited through an open door into heaven. A voice says to him, "Come up here, and I will show you what must take place after this." "In the spirit," John sees the heavenly throne surrounded by twenty-four additional thrones. He sees thunder and lightning, seven lamps of fire, and "something like a sea of glass, like crystal." Recalling Ezekiel, he sees "four living creatures, full of eyes" who are singing, "Holy, holy, holy, the Lord God the Almighty, who was and is and is to come" (Revelation 4).

Images

Revelation is full of images like these. In every chapter and in almost every verse, John sees something that is not explained. He sees this image of the throne, not as a prediction of the future, but a glimpse into an alternative reality—the reality of heaven—that stands outside time, the reality that "was and is and is to come." From the perspective of this timeless reality, John then sees and hears a series of prophecies and visions told in symbolic language, like those in Daniel. Seven seals are followed by seven trumpets and seven bowls of wrath, a pattern that scholars have suggested is linked to the performative quality of the text. By categorizing visions into sevens, the visions could be more easily memorized and performed as the text moved from hand to hand. The visions of John are bloody and terrifying and stir up some of our most elemental feelings of fear and loathing: death, war, famine, the harming of the earth and the sea, false prophets, and the Whore of Babylon. After just one trumpet, "There came hail and fire, mixed with blood, and they were hurled to the earth; and a third of the earth was burned up, and a third of the trees were burned up, and all green grass was burned up" (Rev 8:7). Nightmare piles upon nightmare, violence upon violence.

Each image in these visions can be read in multiple ways, and many of the images are themselves hybrids. For example, the locusts of the fifth trumpet are described as

> like horses equipped for battle. On their heads were what looked like crowns of gold; their faces were like human faces, their hair like women's hair, and their teeth were like lions' teeth; they had scales like iron breastplates, and the noise of their wings was like the noise of many chariots with horses rushing into battle. They have tails like scorpions, with stingers, and in their tails is their power to harm people for five months. (Rev 9:7–10)

It is a wild, multisensory combination of metaphors—natural and unnatural—that forces the reader either to make obscure meaning of each detail or to surrender to bizarre incoherence.[9] Scholar Michael Gorman explains that this makes Revelation a "perfect storm for polyvalence."[10] Nothing has only one meaning, and everything can be subjected to many different processes of interpretation.

If Paul, as I argued in the last chapter, inverted the warrior myth in his attempt to explain the role of Christ in God's plan, the author of Revelation does not shy away from the image of Christ-as-warrior who defeats evil. In this vision, Christ is the cosmic warrior who answers the crisis at the end of time.[11] Christ appears on a white horse, "his eyes are like a flame of fire, and on his head are many diadems; and he has a name inscribed that no one knows but himself" (Rev 19:11–12). Christ defeats Satan and establishes a "new heaven and a new earth" because the "first heaven and the first earth had passed away, and the sea was no more" (Rev 21:1). A holy city comes down from heaven, and the final chapters are devoted to images of renewal and restoration for those who have endured the time of trial.

At the same time, however, there are hints in Revelation of Christ as the inverted warrior. He is described by the author of Revelation as the Lamb. The Lamb is the one to whom the angels sing their hymn, which John describes as a "new song," though it echoes the Psalms.

> You are worthy to take the scroll
>   and to open its seals,
> for you were slaughtered and by your blood you ransomed
>   for God
>   saints from every tribe and language and people
>   and nation. (Rev 5:9)

The Lamb stands in God's presence, opens the seven seals, welcomes the martyrs, and celebrates their sacrifice. The Lamb is both a figure of sacrifice in which the martyrs share and a figure of victory.

As an apocalyptic text, Revelation was meant for the work of worship, uniting heaven and earth. When participants "performed" the text, they joined heavenly choirs gathered around the throne of God.[12] Christian worship was imagined to be a space and time outside of space and time. Events of the past were compressed with events of the future to participate in an eternal present.[13] But within this eternal context, the text follows the pattern that we've seen from Jewish eschatological texts: crisis—victory—judgment—restoration.

The Future in Revelation

The author of Revelation does not see human action as crucial to bringing about God's future. The future is in God's hands, and God is the ultimate creator of the future. Humans are passive observers, passive sufferers, and passive recipients of God's redeeming work. Even evil has to be interpreted from the perspective of the throne of heaven where God's ultimate good is never threatened. Scholars have argued about whether the kind of apocalypticism presented in Revelation is the kind intended to foment revolution or whether it is fundamentally quietist—that is, does it encourage passivity because the future is so completely in God's hands? Given two thousand years of history and many political revolutions with multiple and overlapping causes, this is a difficult question to answer. On the one hand, Elizabeth Schüssler Fiorenza believes the purpose of Revelation is to "draw its audience away from the magnificent symbols and cultic drama of the imperial cult, to give the imagination of Christians a different political and theological direction."[14] It is clear that Revelation is a polemic if a highly symbolic and coded text. It mocks the emperor and his forces. It creates a grotesque reality from the one that the empire surely wanted people to take for granted. This transformation of Christian imagination from the perspective of God's ultimate good and God's ultimate justice oriented Christians to the Roman Empire differently than other members of that society.[15]

At the same time, action is concentrated so securely in God's hands that Charles Hill argues, "No significant body of Christians ever took it upon themselves to initiate, in a socially disruptive way, the expected transformation of the world" as depicted in Revelation.[16] The righteous celebrated in Revelation are the martyrs, those who have given up their lives for the cause of Christ. They are celebrated for their chastity, but while angels and demons pour out wrath and do battle, images of righteous human action are very few. The question remains open. What action might or might not be required of the readers of Revelation is one of the text's many multivalences. But one thing is clear: humans are rewarded for faithfulness.

The future in Revelation is part of a complete whole, a complete narration that was begun by God and will be finished by God. Revelation 1:8 emphasizes this point: "'I am the Alpha and Omega,' says the Lord God, who is and who was and who is to come, the Almighty." In God, time is a unity. The writer emphasizes this completeness of time several times throughout the text; he condenses the past, present, and future into one sentence. This is the "epistemological" mode of Christian eschatology, in which all of history is interpreted through one lens. Thus we can see in Revelation all three modes of eschatology intertwined: imagination is required to engage the imagery and symbolism of the text. Underlying the text is a polemic about the true nature of reality vis-à-vis the Roman Empire. And the text as a whole attempts to explain all of time from creation to the *eschaton* and beyond.

The Millennium

In Revelation, the kingdom of God is both now and not yet. It exists in an eternal now, to which Christians can have access through, at the very least, worship and messengers like John. And it is yet to come, in the unfolding acts of God. But one area of dispute about Revelation is whether the kingdom of God is an earthly messianic kingdom or an otherworldly kingdom. Scholars have usually tried to place Revelation in one box or the other: either it emphasizes a heavenly kingdom or a coming earthly one. But Adela Yarbro Collins notes that, in fact, Revelation combines these two possibilities into one vision. For example, the author of Revelation seemed to believe that the righteous, or at least the martyrs, will go immediately to heaven to be with the Lord *and* that the kingdom of God will descend from heaven. John wanted to demonstrate that there would be a reversal of the idolatrous and unjust rule of the Romans, but he also wanted to show a heavenly reward for the martyrs. Collins writes that his attempts to reconcile personal eschatology with communal eschatology and immediate reward with future reward are both "rich and suggestive" as well as "paradoxical and unstable." Later Christian writers would usually choose one or the other, but John does not.[17]

In chapter 20, however, John wrote something that has intensified this debate among Christians for centuries. An angel came down from heaven with "the key to the bottomless pit and a great chain." The angel seized Satan, "bound him for a thousand years, and threw him into the pit, and locked and sealed it over him, so that he would deceive the nations no more, until the thousand years were ended. After that he must be let out for a little while" (Rev 20:1–3). This one thousand years with Satan bound became, in Christian eschatology, the **millennium,** the one-thousand-year reign of Christ on earth. Theologically the millennium provided a means for Christians to imagine the unification of heaven and earth, to combine their understanding that God declared creation "good" in

Genesis 1 and their observation of evil and sin in the world. The millennium provided an imaginative resource for tangible redemption of the world, a future hope for the earth.

But as we will see in the next chapter, the millennium was not universally accepted in Christian communities and by Christian thinkers. It has come and gone through various ages of Christian thinking, sometimes deeply invested with imagination and sometimes seeming childish and incomplete. The question of the millennium begins here in the midst of the restless images of Revelation, rooted in Jewish eschatological understanding of God's Great, Divine Clean Up and in Christian understanding of the work of Christ to overcome evil, suffering, and death.

Notes

1. J. C. Fitzpatrick, "A Visit to Patmos," *Christ's College Magazine* (1887): 16.

2. Dale Martin, *Inventing Superstition: From Hippocrates to the Christians* (Cambridge, MA: Harvard University Press, 2004), 242. See also his bibliography in pp. 281–82n20.

3. Claudia Setzer, *Resurrection of the Body in Early Judaism and Early Christianity: Doctrine, Community and Self-Definition* (Leiden: Brill, 2004), 125.

4. Dionysius of Alexandria, *Hist. Eccl.* 7.25.22–27, quoted in Lee McDonald, *The Formation of the Christian Biblical Canon* (New York: Hendrickson, 1995), 224.

5. R. H. Charles, *A Critical and Exegetical Commentary on the Revelation of St. John* (New York: Scribner, 1920), xliv.

6. Lourdes Garcia Ureña, "The Book of Revelation: A Written Text Toward Oral Performance," in *Between Orality and Literacy: Communication and Adaptation in Antiquity*, ed. Ruth Scodel (Leiden: Brill, 2014), 311.

7. This summary is taken from Colleen McDannell and Bernhard Lang, *Heaven: A History* (New Haven: Yale University Press, 1988), 41.

8. Jean-Pierre Ruiz, "Betwixt and Between on the Lord's Day: Liturgy and the Apocalypse," in *The Reality of Apocalypse: Rhetoric and Politics in the Book of Revelation*, ed. David L. Barr (Leiden; Boston: Brill, 2006), 221–41.

9. In the contemporary period, biblical apocalypticist Hal Lindsey has read these locusts as an obvious example of a first-century writer trying to describe a military helicopter. Hal Lindsey, *Apocalypse Code* (Palos Verdes: Western Front, 1997), 42.

10. Michael Gorman, "What Has the Spirit Been Saying? Theological and Hermeneutical Reflections on the Reception/Impact History of the Book of Revelation," in *Revelation and the Politics of Apocalyptic Interpretation*, ed. Richard Hays and Stefan Alkier (Waco: Baylor University Press, 2012), 20.

11. John J. Collins, *The Apocalyptic Imagination: An Introduction to Jewish Apocalyptic Literature* (2nd ed.; Grand Rapids: Eerdmans, 1998), 211–13.

12. Bruce Chilton, *Visions of the Apocalypse: Reception of John's Revelation in Western Imagination* (Waco: Baylor University Press, 2013), 37.

13. This is a paraphrase of David Aune, from his article "The Odes of Solomon and Early Christian Prophecy," *NTS* 28 (1982): 446.

14. Elizabeth Schüssler Fiorenza, *Revelation: Vision of a Just World* (Minneapolis: Fortress, 1991), 122.

15. We should also note, as Erin Runions points out, that the bloody horror and violence of the text often mimics the violence of the Roman Empire and has been used over the course of Christian history to justify violence against perceived enemies. Erin Runions, "Deconstructing Apocalyptic Literalist Allegory," in *The Oxford Handbook of Apocalyptic Literature*, ed. John J. Collins (New York: Oxford University Press, 2014), 235.

16. Charles E. Hill, *Regnum Caelorum: Patterns of Millennial Thought in Early Christianity* (Grand Rapids: Eerdmans, 2001), 2 note.

17. Adela Yarbro Collins, "The Apocalypse of John and Its Millennial Themes," in *Apocalyptic and Eschatological Heritage: The Middle East and Celtic Realms*, ed. Martin Macnamara (Dublin: Four Courts, 2003), 60.

PART II

Historical
Developments

6

Martyrs: Early Christianity

If you have fallen in with some who are called Christians, but
who ... venture to blaspheme the God of Abraham, and the God
of Isaac, and the God of Jacob; who say there is no resurrection
of the dead, and that their souls, when they die, are taken to
heaven; do not imagine that they are Christians.

—Justin Martyr

At the beginning of the second century CE, an intellectual
young man, born to a pagan family in Judea, was on a search for
truth. Justin (later known as Justin Martyr, 100–c. 165) studied
Stoicism, Pythagorianism, and Platonism. He found the
answers that philosophy gave him in his search unsatisfying.
He felt that nothing that he studied gave him a complete
enough picture of the relationship between the human being
and God or a way to understand what God desired from the life
of a human being. Justin wrote that one day, during a time in
his life when he wished "to be filled with great quietness," he
was walking in a field near the sea shore. There he met an old

man. Something about this man intrigued him, and when they began to speak, the old man inquired whether philosophy had brought Justin happiness. Happiness, Justin told him, wasn't the point of philosophy, but truth. The old man told Justin that philosophy was futile. Philosophy was an attempt by humans to reason their way toward God. But revelation was the work of God Godself, a means to open the way toward God. The most compelling way for God to speak to humankind, the man told Justin, was through the prophets. Justin later explained what he learned that day in his *Dialogue with Trypho*:

> There existed, long before this time, certain men more ancient than all those who are esteemed philosophers, both righteous and beloved by God, who spoke by the Divine Spirit, and foretold events which would take place, and which are now taking place. They are called prophets. These alone both saw and announced the truth to men, neither reverencing nor fearing any man, not influenced by a desire for glory, but speaking those things alone which they saw and which they heard, being filled with the Holy Spirit. Their writings are still extant, and he who has read them is very much helped in his knowledge of the beginning and end of things, and of those matters which the philosopher ought to know, provided he has believed them.[1]

This experience "kindled a flame" in Justin's soul, especially the possibility that God might reveal himself to humankind through the prophets, and that the "beginning and end of things" might be known in this way. He became a Christian and gathered around himself a small group of students. He taught and debated Christianity with many dialogue partners, pagan and Jewish as well as other Christians.

Justin's Christianity was risky in the Roman Empire of the second century. At the end of his life, he was denounced after a debate with a Cynic philosopher, put on trial with six of his students, and beheaded. Justin's martyrdom cemented his status among Christians, and his understanding of Christian life and teaching became central to those who carried his faith forward.

Justin Martyr and the Disputed Millennium

Christianity's grasp of the future was one aspect of the faith that appealed to Justin. He believed profoundly in the visionary and revelatory nature of Christianity, and he is the first Christian writer to refer to the Revelation of John. Justin believed that John, the writer of Revelation, was an apostle, and in his *Dialogues*, he gave this version of Revelation 20: "And further, a man among us named John, one of the apostles of Christ, prophesied in a revelation made to him that they who have believed our Christ will spend a thousand years in Jerusalem and that afterwards the universal, and in one word, eternal resurrection of all at once, will take place, and also the judgment."[2]

Justin Martyr admitted that among Christians there were different schools of thought, and he himself was not always consistent. He wrote that he and many others "who are right-minded Christians on all points" were "assured that there will be a resurrection of the dead and a thousand years in Jerusalem," but there were others "who are Christians of pure and pious mind" who did not acknowledge the thousand-year earthly reign of Christ in Jerusalem.[3]

Justin's interpretation of Revelation has been called **chiliasm**. The word comes from the Greek word for "thousand," and it refers directly to Rev 20:4, in which Christ defeats Satan, and Satan is thrown into a pit for a thousand years. This verse was combined with Jewish messianic eschatology to create a place in Christian schemata for a thousand-year reign of Christ on earth before the last judgment.

For Justin, chiliasm was not a test of Christian orthodoxy. It was an interpretive choice, and his own views may have shifted over time.[4] Chiliasm has a mixed history in Christianity. In a report that is attributed to a testimony of Jude's grandsons (and thus to Jesus's grandnephews), the two men were called before the emperor to give account of their faith in Christ. They were asked about the coming of Christ's kingdom and specifically whether it would be earthly or heavenly. An answer that Christ's kingdom was earthly might be threatening to the emperor or other worldly powers. According to written reports from a much later time, they replied that it would be "heavenly and angelic, and it would be at the end of the world, when he would come again in glory to judge the living and the dead and to reward every man according to his deeds."[5] This report, the authenticity of which cannot be verified, suggests that there were Christians very close to Christ who did not anticipate a millennium. They saw Christ's reign as heavenly and coming at the end of time.[6]

The difference between a heavenly reign and an earthly kingdom could orient followers of Christ on earth differently. Both lived in expectation of God's future intervention. But one anticipated a change in earthly conditions, and the other expected an "end" that would transcend earthly time. One appeared to have more immediate consequences for those in power. A competing ruler was a threat. One hovering at the unknown "end of time" was less so.

Resurrection of the Flesh

Justin Martyr's point about the "assurance" of the resurrection of the dead was, in his mind, a greater test of true belief. In his *Dialogues*, he wrote that those who do not believe in the resurrection of the dead do not deserve to be called Christians. Furthermore, he argued, in a rhetorical shift that distinguished him from Paul in the first letter to the Corinthians, there will be a "resurrection of the flesh" instead of a resurrection of the dead or a resurrection of the body. In Justin's writing, we have for the first time the two words "flesh" and "resurrection" put together in the same phrase.[7] We saw how Paul very carefully chose the word "body" and distinguished it from "flesh," arguing for a unity of the body and soul in a person that somehow transcended flesh. This is a difficult position for people of the modern age to accept—that there is a body that is in some sense physical but not fleshly. But the difficulty for Justin was different. He argued that Christianity demands that the *flesh* itself be resurrected. The stuff of which we are made now, in this life, is the stuff that will rise from the dead. The resurrection of Jesus in the flesh made it so.

Justin appeared to have two motivations for making this emphasis in the language of resurrection. He was arguing against people who took Paul to mean that the body that would be raised would be a spiritual—that is, a non-physical—body. Instead of the transformation of the body that Paul claimed, they believed in something more like immortality of the soul, already a common pagan belief. This switch to a spiritual body blurred the distinction between Christian and pagan and gave power to the gnostics, a group of Christians who interpreted the Gospel very differently from those like Justin who claimed to be orthodox Christians. For example, gnostic Christians frequently argued that Christ did not actually become a physical human being. He merely appeared in human form and walked the earth *as if* he were human. Thus he did not actually die and was not actually resurrected.[8] In contrast to this unearthly view of Jesus, Justin emphasized the *flesh* of Jesus and also the flesh of his followers who will be resurrected.

The second motivation was a growing concern with the importance of material continuity in resurrection. This was a concern that would be expressed more and more forcefully over the next hundred years. The body that was resurrected, early Christians insisted, had to be *exactly* the same body as the one that died. Every particle of that body had to have new life. If a martyr's body was scattered or burned, God would have to gather up every bit of that body, every piece of ash and bone, and restore it whole.[9] One reason that early Christians made an issue of this is that pagans frequently accused Christians of cannibalism: they ate the flesh and drank the blood of Christ, and this ritual was easily misunderstood. *Who else's flesh and blood did they eat and drink in their secret rituals?* pagans wondered. But the doctrine of material continuity made cannibalism impossible. How can my body be resurrected whole if your body has become a part of my body? Christians could thus use their belief in resurrection to contest the accusation that they were cannibals.[10]

Early Christians believed that by taking the Eucharist, ingesting it into their bodies, they were already beginning to participate in the resurrection. The flesh and blood of Christ, as it became a part of their own flesh and blood, began the process of transformation before death. Since it was an eternal substance, not ordinary food and drink, Christians became more eternal as they partook.[11]

Historian Caroline Walker Bynum summarizes the position

that developed from Justin Martyr to later Christian teachers like Irenaeus (d. c. 202 CE) and Tertullian (160–220 CE): "The particles of our flesh—nourished and supported in this life by a eucharistic bread that was literally the flesh of Christ—would be reassembled by God at the end of time in such as way that no detail of bodily structure was lost."[12] This is a much more literal understanding than Paul's seed, whose flesh decays but which still becomes a sheaf of wheat. Paul was clear that it was *not* the flesh that became the resurrected body. For these later Christian writers, it was indeed that very flesh.

Irenaeus, writing in the western part of the Roman Empire, reinterpreted Paul to mean not that flesh and blood cannot inherit the kingdom of God but that flesh and blood *alone* cannot inherit the kingdom of God. Yes, flesh was inferior, but it could be made new by the Spirit and with the help of the Spirit it could be resurrected.[13] And it not only can, but must. Irenaeus often referred to the parable of the lost sheep, which to him meant that exactly the sheep that was lost had to be the sheep that was found. This was the flesh of the body that had to be restored to eternal life.[14]

Belief in resurrection of the dead allowed early Christians to define themselves in some important ways. It gave them continuity with Jewish tradition, even as their leaders were increasingly non-Jewish, and allowed them to claim continuity with the God of Abraham, Isaac, and Jacob; it served as a sign to distinguish true from false Christians; it offered a system through which Christians could talk about justice, recompense, and punishment (the righteous would receive their reward, the wicked would be punished); and it demonstrated the power of God to do the impossible, a power that did not belong to "this world." Whenever someone challenged belief in the resurrection of the dead, Christian apologists would counter with the question of whether they truly believed in God's power and might. If so, then with God, anything is possible.[15]

The Millennium and the Blood of the Martyrs

Irenaeus was a bishop in what is now France. He was a follower of Polycarp who received his teachings, tradition said, from John the Evangelist. Irenaeus also followed Justin Martyr on many things, including the millennium.[16] For Irenaeus, belief in the millennium, like belief in resurrection of the dead, was important in the ongoing argument with gnostic tendencies in Christianity. Christians with gnostic tendencies believed that Christ's reign would be spiritual, but the growing orthodox tradition asserted that God cared for both the earthly and the heavenly future of humanity. The earth itself was precious to God and would be restored.[17] Irenaeus and others drew on pictures of the restored land sketched by the prophet Isaiah to depict the millennium earth as one of bounty and joy: flourishing vineyards, mountains with streams of wine, a time when the "wolf will live with the lamb" (Isa 11:6) and "waters will break forth in the wilderness" (Isa 35:6).[18] The millennium offered ancient images of hope that resonated with people across the emerging Christian landscape.

For Tertullian, a contemporary of Irenaeus but from North Africa, this aspect was even more important, and he was more virulent in his expression of it. For Tertullian, imminence—the immediate nature of the second coming—was crucial. This was in part because of Tertullian's experience with martyrdom. Martyrs died knowing that their deaths would bring about the immediate coming of Christ's kingdom. Their physical end was also the end of the world. They died knowing that the time before judgment was short for everyone. At the same time,

Tertullian felt that the righteous needed a reward. The millennium provided an image of reward for those who had suffered that was tangible and satisfying.

Tertullian joined with a group that came to be called the "Montanists" because they were followers of Montanus, a man who claimed that the Holy Spirit had come to speak through him. Montanism was an "effort to shape the entire life of the church in keeping with the expectation of the return of Christ, immediately at hand."[19] Scholars speculate that what appealed to Tertullian most about Montanism was the moral urgency that such immediacy provided. Montanists followed rigid moral codes, including practices of extreme fasting and celibacy, and they claimed a "new prophecy" that told them exactly what was "at hand." The other thing that gave Montanism power was the veneration of Christian martyrdom. Two of the most famous adherents, whose work Tertullian may have edited, were Perpetua and Felicitas—a noblewoman and her slave—who were martyred in the third century. Perpetua kept a prison diary of her experience, which is the first known work written by a Christian woman.[20]

In the part of Africa where Tertullian lived, now Tunisia, a young noblewoman, Perpetua, nursing her first child, and her slave, Felicitas, were taken prisoner for their Christian beliefs. Felicitas was pregnant at the time of their imprisonment. The decree for the deaths of both women came during the reign of Emperor Septimius Severus and was one of many persecutions of Christians in various parts of the Roman Empire. Perpetua's prison diary records her decision to become a Christian, a choice that angered and hurt her father, as well as her life in prison and her visions that depicted the spiritual struggle in which she was engaged. At the end of the document, an eyewitness, who may have been Tertullian himself, described the deaths of the two women at the hands of wild animals and gladiators.

The passion of the martyrs gave their viewpoint considerable power and obviously moved Tertullian. When Tertullian wrote about the resurrection of the dead, he was not thinking about any body but the dead body of the martyr in particular, and perhaps even the dead body of Perpetua. He wrote that the "blood of the martyrs is seed."[21] This is what made resurrection of the dead so critical for him—and specifically resurrection of the *flesh*, "of it indeed, itself, entire."[22]

By the time of Tertullian, resurrection of the flesh reigned supreme. As Dag Øistein Endsjø notes, the less Jewish and the more Greek Christian belief became, the "stronger the emphasis on the resurrection of the flesh." Endsjø sees the popularity of Christianity among non-Jews growing in lockstep with the emphasis on this belief.[23] This suggestion is in contrast with the common scholarly assumption that the Jewish aspect of Christianity emphasized bodily resurrection and the Greek aspect emphasized an immortal soul. In fact, the more Greek Christianity became, the more insistent it became on fleshly resurrection. Endsjø argues that this is because scholars have too often confused the Hellenistic influence on Christianity with the Greek philosophical tradition. But if we look much more broadly at popular belief, we see that Greek people (other than philosophers) would have resonated with the idea of immortal flesh in a way that might likely have made Paul uncomfortable, but that became the orthodox understanding in Christianity.[24]

Tertullian followed Irenaeus and the book of Revelation in claiming that a heavenly Jerusalem would descend from the heavens in the new age. It is not clear if Montanists also believed this, or if Tertullian was adapting it from other sources.[25] For Tertullian, the millennium was necessary because of its moral force. Only the just would rise to enjoy the millennium on earth. Everyone else would wait in a shadowy Hades for the general resurrection and judgment. The millennium was a gift given to the righteous as a reward for their suffering. But he also argued that martyrs went immediately to heaven and did not have to wait for the millennium or the end of time. He cited as proof the vision of Perpetua who "on the day of her passion saw only her fellow-martyrs" in heaven.[26] Heaven gave the martyrs an immediate reward, and the millennium offered the righteous a later but still significant reward for their lives on earth.

A Flowering of Prophecy

Montanism and other prophetic movements grew significantly in the early centuries of Christianity. Early Christianity was ethnically and culturally diverse, and often small Christian communities were geographically isolated. They existed with diverse eschatologies that were intensified by actual martyrdom and local threats of martyrdom.

The rapid development of Christian apocalypticism in the first two centuries of its existence meant that Christians in the Middle East, North Africa, and across the Roman Empire were developing a rich reservoir of images and symbols with which to think about the future. They drew on numerological schemes, lists of signs, "oracular formulae," and the dreams and visions of a variety of seers in order to begin to create what David Frankfurter calls an "enclosed symbolic world."[27] This does not mean that Christian apocalyptic ideas stayed in one place. Christian apocalyptic and prophetic material circulated in fragments and in wholes across communities, where in new contexts they could take on new meanings. But Christian apocalypticism did become its own symbolic universe, with specific associations to specific symbols, that circulated unsystematically to create a "general sense of global instability and breakdown."[28] This enclosed symbolic world pointed to the nearness of the end.

Within fifty years (roughly 75–125 CE), four major apocalyptic documents that claimed to be based on the inspiration of the Holy Spirit emerged.[29] One of them, the *Shepherd of Hermas*, Ireneaus would have included among the scriptures of the Christian canon. Another, the *Apocalypse of Peter*, had a lasting effect on Christianity's understanding of the future. (The other two were Revelation, discussed in a previous chapter, and the *Ascension of Isaiah*.) These documents expressed a general deep appreciation of visions and dreams that was a part of the Near Eastern and Mediterranean context. Dreams were cultivated by fasting, praying, solitude, chanting, and sacrifice.[30] Dreams and visions were intended for communities and were often interpreted by communities. A dream might offer words of consolation and hope. It might deliver a warning. It was a highly respected and ancient form of reception that often spoke directly to the future, and frequently the tellers were female.[31] While sometimes apocalypticism got recorded into literary documents, it also existed as a "broad, intercultural, and multimedia fascination with otherworldly gnosis, secret teachings, and the sacred book of revealed wisdom."[32]

In this context, a few more elaborate apocalyptic documents were written down and passed on. They were popular texts that circulated widely in Christian communities. The *Shepherd of Hermas* was written in Rome in the second century and tells of a series of dreams and revelations that are given by an anonymous prophetess. There are more extant copies of this work than of many canonical New Testament texts.[33] It is an intensely allegorical text with symbols and images that beg interpretation. A beast that appears has four colors and a lady appears to explain the four colors. "The black is this world in which you are living; the color of fire and blood means that this world must be destroyed by blood and fire. The golden part is you, you have fled from this world, for even as gold is 'tried in the fire' and becomes valuable, so also you who live among them are being tried. . . . But the white part is the world to come, in which the elect of God shall dwell. . . ."[34] Texts like the *Shepherd of Hermas* made ongoing revelation possible and could be read again and again with different allegorical interpretations of its signs.

The *Shepherd of Hermas* served as consolation to those who were persecuted and suffering. It reassured its readers that they were the "gold" in a world of "blood and fire." The *Apocalypse of Peter*, which was probably written in Palestine sometime in the early second century, is more a book of warning than consolation.[35] It appears to have been fairly widely known in the second century, referenced by church leaders like Clement of Alexandria and Methodius.[36] Written during a period of persecution for Christians, it is known for its detailed and graphic depictions of hell and the punishment of the unrepentant and Christian enemies.[37] It does not have a corresponding picture of a reign of Christ on earth as a reward for the righteous, but instead depicts the *parousia* of Christ that brings the resurrection of the dead and the final judgment. Christ's kingdom is finally in heaven, not on earth. If nothing else, the *Apocalypse of Peter* demonstrates just how fluid Christian understanding of the future was in the second century. Competing visions of the millennium, the fate of the unrighteous, and the location of Christ's kingdom were all available in different communities and used for a variety of purposes. The *Shepherd of Hermas* and the *Apocalypse of Peter* lost out in the battles over canonization, but they remained important deep into the Middle Ages as they were read and reinterpreted in new Christian moments.

Looking Backward to Look Forward

These movements created problems for the growing establishment of the church. While the passion and feeling of such movements were crucial, it was also difficult to stabilize a situation in which there was a great deal of ongoing prophecy. The Montanists had generations of prophets following Montanus, many of them women, and prophecy movements more broadly often featured women as seers and oracles. In addition to the problem of female power, the documents produced from these various movements contradicted one another. Some church leaders wanted to create a more stable, more male, and hierarchically approved set of doctrines and beliefs, tests of true Christianity against heretical movements.

Hippolytus of Rome (170–235) was a powerful Christian writer, theologian, and orator who looked around at the flowering diversity of Christianity and worried for its future. For two centuries, Christians had anticipated an immediate end to the current age. The anticipated immediacy of that end and the potency of martyrdom had meant that Christian institutions had yet to give much thought to how Christian traditions would be preserved. Hippolytus was extremely critical of Montanism, for example, because "new prophecy" is inherently destabilizing.

With the guidance of Hippolytus, the church began to shift its understanding of time. Historian Jaroslav Pelikan writes that "the church looked increasingly not to the future, illumined by the Lord's return, nor to the present, illumined by the Spirit's extraordinary gifts, but to the past, illumined by the composition of the apostolic creed, and the establishment of the apostolic episcopate."[38] Hippolytus tried to stabilize the church by pushing the second coming off farther into the future and pushing prophecy more deeply into the past, hoping to diffuse some of the power of ecstatic continuing revelation.[39] As far as he was concerned, the last valid written revelation of the Holy Spirit was the Revelation of John. He and other church leaders enshrined the first century as a "golden age" of revelation that had ended.[40]

Even by emphasizing the past, Hippolytus recognized the need for an understanding of the future that was particularly Christian. He created an apocalyptic scenario from various pieces of Christian theology, but without Irenaus's belief in an impending millennium.[41] Instead, reading the Bible as a unity, he decided that the measurement of the ark of the covenant was a "chronological clue." Its "five and a half cubits" translated into five and a half millennia. Thus from the time of Adam to the end of time would be 5,500 years. Since it was widely believed that Jesus had been born five thousand years after Adam, Hippolytus argued that the end of time would come around 500 CE; thus Christians had three centuries yet to wait.[42]

Hippolytus's views were widely influential but not without controversy. He felt that church leadership in Rome had watered down Christian teachings in order to accept a wide number of pagan converts, and he started a rival group. But his chronologies and attempts to conceive of time as a whole, detailed in the Bible from creation to apocalypse, became the foundation for Christian theological readings going forward.

For the early church, the not yet of Jesus's *parousia* was held in tension with the memory of his visible presence. As the faith developed, it had to reckon with a loss of urgency around the *parousia,* but there does not appear to have been widespread disappointment or disillusionment. The fact that, by the end of Christianity's second century, the *parousia* had not come did not signal despair for emerging Christian communities but instead greater imaginative enterprises, increased creativity, and new theological and social battles.

Notes

1. Justin Martyr, *Dialogue with Trypho a Jew,* in *The Ante-Nicene Fathers: The Writings of the Fathers Down to AD 325,* ed. Alexander Roberts, James Donaldson, and Arthur Cleveland Coxe (New York: Scribners, 1905), 1:198.

2. Justin Martyr, *Dial.* 81.4, quoted in L. W. Barnard, *Justin Martyr: His Life and Thought* (Cambridge, UK: Cambridge University Press, 1967), 164.

3. Justin Martyr, *Dial.* 80.2, quoted in Charles E. Hill, *Regnum Caelorum: Patterns of Millennial Thought in Early Christianity* (Grand Rapids, MI: Eerdmans, 2001), 4.

4. Ibid., 136.

5. Eusebius, *Historia Ecclesiastica* 3.20.4.

6. Hill, 130. Hill does want to argue that this report has some authenticity and that it parallels language from other early texts like John 18:36.

7. Claudia Setzer, *Resurrection of the Body in Early Judaism and Early Christianity: Doctrine, Community, and Self-Definition* (Leiden: Brill, 2004), 75.

8. Jaroslav Pelikan provides a helpful overview of basic Gnostic ideas in

The Emergence of the Catholic Tradition 100-166 (Chicago: University of Chicago Press, 1971), 82-94.

9. Caroline Walker Bynum, *The Resurrection of the Body in Western Christianity 200-1336* (New York: Columbia University Press, 1995), 49.

10. Setzer, 90.

11. Bynum, 39.

12. Ibid., 59.

13. Irenaeus, *Against Heresies*; see, e.g., 5.9.2, quoted in Setzer, 128-29.

14. Setzer, 129.

15. Ibid., 76-77.

16. Adela Yarbro Collins, "The Book of Revelation," in *The Encyclopedia of Apocalypticism*, ed. John Collins (New York: Continuum, 1998), 1:409.

17. Bernard McGinn, *Visions of the End: Apocalyptic Traditions in the Middle Ages* (New York: Columbia University Press, 1998), 20.

18. Arthur Wainwright, *Mysterious Apocalypse: Interpreting the Book of Revelation* (Nashville: Abingdon, 1993), 24.

19. Nathanael Bonwetsch (1881), 139, quoted in Pelikan, 98.

20. Brent Shaw, "The Passion of Perpetua," *Past and Present* 139 (May 1993): 3-45.

21. Tertullian, *Apologeticum* 50.

22. Tertullian, *On the Resurrection of the Flesh* 63.1, quoted in Dale Martin, *The Corinthian Body* (New Haven: Yale University Press, 1995), 124. Online at http://www.newadvent.org/fathers/0316.htm.

23. Dag Øistein Endsjø, *Greek Resurrection Beliefs and the Success of Christianity* (New York: Palgrave Macmillan, 2009), 7.

24. Ibid., 12.

25. See Christine Trevett, *Montanism: Gender, Authority and the New Prophecy* (Cambridge, UK: Cambridge University Press, 1996), 96-99; and Hill, 27-31 and 143-59.

26. Tertullian, *De Anima* 55.4, quoted in Hill, 30.

27. David Frankfurter, "Early Christian Apocalypticism: Literature and Social World," in *The Encyclopedia of Apocalypticism*, ed. John J. Collins (New York: Continuum 1998), 1:434. See also McGinn, *Visions*, 33-36.

28. Frankfurter, 433.

29. Greg Cary, "Early Christian Apocalyptic Rhetoric," in *The Oxford Handbook of Apocalyptic Literature*, ed. John J. Collins (New York: Oxford University Press, 2014), 218.

30. Frances Flannery, "Dreams and Visions in Early Jewish and Early Christian Apocalypses and Apocalypticism," in *Oxford Handbook of Apocalyptic Literature*, 106.

31. Ibid., 110.

32. Frankfurter, 416. Frankfurter is not referring to one specific book of revealed wisdom but to the popular idea in early Christianity that a book could contain such revealed wisdom. Many such books circulated.

33. David G. Martinez, "The Papyri and Early Christianity," in *The Oxford Book of Papyrology*, ed. Roger S. Bagnall (New York: Oxford University Press, 2009), 600.

34. *The Shepherd of Hermas*, Vision 4.3.2–5, in *Apocalyptic Literature: A Reader*, ed. Mitchell Reddish (Peabody: Hendrickson, 1995), 258–59.

35. This geographic location and dating comes from Richard Bauckham, *The Fate of the Dead: Studies on the Jewish and Christian Apocalypses* (Leiden: Brill, 1998), 160–258. Others have suggested Syrian or Egyptian origins for this text.

36. Hill, 117 note.

37. Daley, 7.

38. Pelikan, 107.

39. Ibid., 106.

40. Ibid. Not everyone agreed that Revelation should be included in this canonization. This book had a less stable relationship to the canon than any other book of the New Testament. During Christianity's first three centuries, individual communities could select the texts that they wanted to emphasize, include in worship, and teach to converts. This freedom was most notable in the way that churches, particularly in the Christian east, rejected Revelation or treated it with extreme suspicion. Meanwhile it was being widely used in the West and in North Africa. See Bruce Metzger, *The Canon of the New Testament* (Oxford: Clarendon, 1987), 16.

41. Bernard McGinn, "Turning Points in Early Christian Apocalyptic Exegesis," in *Apocalyptic Thought in Early Christianity*, ed. Robert S. Daly (Grand Rapids: Baker Academic, 2009), 85.

42. Bruce Chilton, *Visions of the Apocalypse: Reception of John's Revelation in Western Imagination* (Waco: Baylor University Press, 2013), 25.

7

Time: Origen

It is foolish also of them to suppose that, when God applies the fire (like a cook!), all the rest of mankind will be thoroughly burnt up, and that they alone survive, not merely those who are alive at the time, but also those long dead who will rise up from the earth possessing the same bodies as before. This is simply the hope of worms. For what sort of human soul would have any further desire for a body that has rotted?

—Origen

A wealthy and devout Christian family, living in Alexandria at the end of the third century, made sure their son Origen (184/185–253/254), received the best education possible. He studied the Bible and Greek philosophy under the most venerable teachers in a city that was celebrated for its institutions of learning. But in 202, when Origen was not yet eighteen, his father was arrested during a persecution of Christians carried out under the same imperial regime that killed Perpetua and Felicitas 2500 miles away in Carthage. He was beheaded, the family property was seized, and tradition tells us that Origen's mother had to restrain her son from rushing out to demand that authorities kill him too.

Instead, Origen was appointed to take the place of his teacher, Clement of Alexandria, who had fled during the persecution. He began teaching a wide range of subjects and took up a life of severe asceticism. The Christian historian Eusebius reported that Origen castrated himself around the age of twenty in an act meant to solidify his commitment to a life of learning and holiness.[1] Origen traveled widely and gained a strong reputation throughout the region—so strong, in fact, that the bishop of Alexandria eventually threw him out of the city, apparently out of jealousy. Origen then taught in Caesarea. In 254, he was imprisoned and tortured during another outbreak of persecution and died shortly after being released.

Before his death, Origen wrote prolifically.[2] His commentaries and tracts were copied and distributed throughout the Christian world, and he became arguably the most influential Christian teacher of the third century. He saw himself mostly as a biblical exegete, someone who studied biblical texts and offered, through prayer, interpretations of them. His central contribution to Christian eschatology was that biblical eschatological texts could be read on multiple levels: physical, moral, and spiritual. Origen's readings took a turn away from literal interpretations, and his understanding of time was considerably more complex than previous Christians who awaited the imminent end of the world.

Soul Travel

Origen was convinced that the Bible, which during his lifetime was still in process of canonical formation, needed to be read as a deeply spiritual document. It was best understood through practices of contemplation and prayer. In his commentary on Matthew, of which only fragments remain, Origen took up the question of the Little Apocalypse. Origen argued that these passages of scripture were intended to be read literally only at the lowest spiritual level, where they served as an important warning against false teachers and a comfort during times of persecution. But at deeper spiritual levels, they reveal "various aspects of how Christ will manifest himself spiritually to all humans at the end of time—in glory to those who have been perfected in virtue, judgment to the wicked."[3]

For example, the "famines" at the end of time referenced in Matthew 24 speak of a profound spiritual hunger that precedes Christ's coming; the "clouds" on which Christ comes are the writings of the apostles and prophets; and so on.[4] This was how Origen approached the Revelation of John as well, using symbols to demonstrate moral and mystical progress as the Christian, through ascetic practice, gained closer union with God. Christ's death and resurrection indeed placed Christians in the "last times," but this was not exactly a period in history so much as a spiritual state in which Christians have a lot to do. They must begin "the gradual process of ascent and return to God through an indefinite number of aeons, which is determined by the moral progress of the creature, and not by the fall of this or that kingdom."[5]

In other words, Origen spiritualized time so that Christians could transcend the timeline of history and place themselves on a different map. This does not mean that there is no present and no future but instead that in Origen's view, Christian eschatology must have some relevance for the present life of the believer if it is to have any relevance at all. All eschatology should lead to the work of prayer and self-denial that leads a Christian to God.[6] Past, present, future are not distinct realms of time but one time drawn together in eternity.

This spiritualization of Christian apocalyptic texts helped solve other problems in Christian eschatology as well, such as the resurrection of the body. For Origen, there was indeed a resurrection of the body, but it was clearly a spiritual body, and as a spiritual body, the individual is judged immediately after death. Like Paul, Origen used organic metaphors to argue for a continuity of the physical and the spiritual body.[7] It will be "raised from the earth" and undergo a transformation "into the glory of a spiritual body."[8]

After death, Origen suggested, the soul travels through various realms and undergoes an education specific to that soul's needs. This eternal "school for souls" allowed Origen to preach universal salvation.[9] All souls will undergo purification depending on need, and thus all souls will be saved.

Origen's Spiritual Body

Origen's singular contribution was giving Christians a less literal way to understand their scriptures. He had a less literal understanding of the physical body as well. "River is not a bad name for the body," he wrote, noting that the "body" is never a stable thing throughout all its life.[10] Drawing on 1 Corinthians, he argued that whatever characterizes the body as an identifiable unity on earth will characterize it as such in heaven. Whatever that is, it is not exactly the particles that make up the body at any given moment in its life. "Our hope," he wrote against the pagan critic Celsus, "is not one of worms, nor does our soul desire a body that has rotted."[11] Origen believed that only God was utterly incorporeal and that humans would need some kind of body in the world to come. That kind of body would be one better suited to a heavenly environment, purified and prepared for contemplation.

For Origen there were two critical tensions: one between the "now" and the "not yet," and the other between the individual and the church as a whole. The individual had some access to the kingdom of God now, through contemplative and ascetic practice and through obedience. It was not perfect, but through practice, it could become available. The work of the kingdom of God for the church and for the whole world was something that had to be understood at the level of aeons, and this was difficult for mortals to grasp. The final resurrection would be the "eschatological fulfillment for the whole Church, rather than simply the salvation of individual believers,"[12] and its timeline was not one that can be understood by parsing the kingdoms of this world using Daniel and Revelation, as other Christian exegetes had a tendency to do.

Origen was a powerful thinker, and his work was widely known and even widely accepted, at least until the Council of Nicea in 325. One part of Origen's work that was accepted in the Christian east and remains important in Eastern Orthodox Christianity is the idea that through practice Christians can "walk an ineffable path towards divinization."[13] This means that Christians can become more and more like Christ. Through prayer and fasting and other acts of piety, they are gradually transformed in body and spirit, both throughout their lifetimes and beyond. The ultimate Christian future, in this line of thinking, isn't about the end times, the rise of the antichrist, or when and where Christ will fight a final battle. All of that is irrelevant to the patient practice of prayer and holiness that leads to union with God.

The early martyrdom of Origen's father could have intensified Origen's apocalypticism and his sense of the imminence of the end, as we have seen in other cases, but instead it set him on a spiritual path. That path was ascetic to extremes, but it was not apocalyptic in the sense of Tertullian or Perpetua. Instead Origen forged a controversial alternative interpretation of traditional texts.

Methodius and Responses to Origen

Origen's timing, though, was poor for the wide acceptance of his ideas. Brian Daley notes that from the very beginning, Origen's work was only superficially understood. "No one adopted, in a consistent way, his radically spiritual, internalized reinterpretation of the eschatological tradition."[14]

The decades preceding the Edict of Milan in 313, when Christianity was accepted by the Roman Empire, were an era of violent persecution of Christians, and in the Latin church in particular there was a revival of apocalyptic speculation. The pagan emperor Diocletian (245–311) sought the advice of oracles several times during his reign in attempts to predict the future. When the results failed, Christians were blamed for impeding the oracles, and this led to attempts to purge Christians both from the imperial household and from the broader empire.

Instead of drawing on Origen's complex exegesis, Christians responded using the age-old method of consolation, drawing on images of the millennium and the fall of their earthly enemies. Methodius of Olympus (d. 311), a Christian bishop who opposed Origen on several points, returned to the idea of the fall of the empire as an eschatological event and wrote about a "thousand-year feast" that would precede the last judgment. He described the millennium as a thousand-year sabbath for the faithful, an image later picked up by Augustine. Paradise, in Methodius's view, was not a spiritual condition of union with God in heaven but a this-worldly time and place, a "chosen spot on earth," where the faithful would return.[15] In his *On Resurrection*, he insisted on the resurrection of the flesh and accused Origen of stepping back on this crucial point.

Origen's detractors, like Methodius, objected to the spiritualization and allegorization of basic Christian doctrines, especially the resurrection of the body, as well as his extrabiblical descriptions of the worlds and states beyond death. Origen was accused, after his death, of violating the necessity of material continuity of the bodily resurrection. The body he envisioned was not sufficiently tied to the earthly one for Methodius, nor later for Jerome (347–420). Origen's detractors built a case against him in the following decades, and he was declared a heretic at the Second Council of Constantinople in 553.

Notes

1. This subject is debated by historians. Some argue that this was a story circulated by his detractors. Others, like Peter Brown, argue there is no reason to question Eusebius's account. See Brown, *The Body and Society: Men, Women, and Sexual Renunciation in Early Christianity* (New York: Columbia University Press, 1988), 168.

2. St. Epiphanus estimated that Origen wrote six thousand works, a number that appears in many references to Origen. But many have questioned this number.

3. Paraphrase of Origen's *Commentariorum Series in Matthaeum* 24–25 by Bernard McGinn, "Turning Points in Early Christian Apocalyptic Exegesis," in *Apocalyptic Thought in Early Christianity*, ed. Robert S. Daly (Grand Rapids: Baker Academic, 2009), 96–97.

4. Brian Daley, *The Hope of the Early Church* (Cambridge, UK: Cambridge University Press, 1991), 49.

5. Judith Kovacs and Christopher Rowland, *Revelation: The Apocalypse of Jesus Christ* (Oxford: Blackwell, 2004), 16.

6. Daley, 48.

7. See Caroline Walker Bynum, *The Resurrection of the Body in Western Christianity 200-1336* (New York: Columbia University Press, 1995), 63–71.

8. Origen, *De Principiis* 3.6.6.

9. See Morwenna Ludlow, *Universal Salvation: Eschatology in the Thought of Gregory of Nyssa and Karl Rahner* (New York: Oxford University Press, 2000), 32–37; and Daley, 47–60. Quotation is from *De Principiis* 2.11.6.

10. Origen, Fragment on Psalm 1.5, quoted in Bynum, 64.

11. Origen, *Cels* 5.19, quoted in Daley, 51.

12. Daley, 55.

13. These are the words of Origen's student Gregory the Wonderworker, *Pan* 11.142, quoted in Daley, 60.

14. Ibid.

15. Quotations from Methodius's *Symposium* 9.1 and *De Resurrectione* 1.55.1, quoted in Daley, 62–63.

8

Patriae: Augustine of Hippo

Who can deny that the things to come are not yet? Yet already there is in the mind an expectation of things to come.

—Augustine of Hippo

In 418, Augustine (354–430 CE), the bishop of the North African city of Hippo, received a letter from Hesychius of Salona, himself a powerful bishop in what is now Croatia. Hesychius was concerned about an eclipse that had come after a severe drought. He wanted to know what the learned bishop knew about the end of time and its signs. Augustine wrote back that like Jerome, Augustine's well-known contemporary and correspondent, he believed that the book of Daniel's prophecies were not about the future but about the past. He emphasized Jesus's words that no one knows the hour nor the day. But Hesychius pressed Augustine, saying that he had already read Jerome and did not find Jerome's answers satisfying.

Augustine wrote back that, from his point of view, the world ended for any individual when he or she left it. He told Hesychius that his attempt to discern "proofs" from chosen "signs" was a meaningless enterprise. Biblical passages don't refer to specific times and places, he said. The only true sign, he wrote, was the evangelization of the whole world. The believer was far better off "believing in, hoping for, and loving the One who is coming" than obsessing about the coming itself.[1]

Eschatology and Empire

By the time that Augustine made this assertion and gave this particular eschatological reading of the Bible, a great deal of Christianity's landscape had changed. With the conversion of Constantine in 312, and with the help of Christian writers and thinkers, the connection between the Roman Empire and Christianity transformed the faith's eschatological nature. Prior to the conversion of Constantine, the empire had been eschatological to Christians in the sense that it represented a near ultimate power and evil of "this world," in contrast to the kingdom of God. A Christian empire was unthinkable, even contradictory. But in the aftermath of Constantine, that eschatological story needed to change.

A key figure in transforming the eschatological story of Christianity was Eusebius (260–340 CE), a Roman historian and interpreter of the new era of Christianity. He urged Christians to understand Constantine's military victories as the beginning of a God-ordained golden era of Christianity.[2] For Eusebius, the language of apocalypse provided the means to understand the sudden transformation of Christian fortunes. Christ and Constantine became the "imperial ideal," and the millennium was not the end of human experience but history's unfolding within human experience, more specifically within a Christian empire.[3] Eusebius read Revelation as describing vividly and symbolically the era of Christian persecution followed by the era of Christian flourishing that he himself was witnessing. The New Jerusalem was not at some point in the future but now, unfolding before his own eyes.

Through the influence of Eusebius, standard iconography put images of Christ side by side with images of the emperor. "The power of the state, rightly deployed, conveyed the transcendent power of God," Bruce Chilton summarizes.[4] This was an enduring political and religious philosophy that remained central to Christian understanding in the East, despite the constant pressure of Islam and through the spread of Christianity to the Slavic empires. We continue to see vestiges of it in Russia's post–Cold War assertion of the intimacy between church and state. Church and empire are complementary, not contradictory.

The Sack of Rome

For some Christians, when Constantine moved the capital of the Roman Empire from Rome to Constantinople in 330, this was the coming of the New Jerusalem. But other Christians remained attached to Rome, which was under constant threat. When Rome was sacked by the Visigoths in 410, Jerome, who was living in a hermit's cell near Bethlehem, wrote to Augustine to tell him that the collapse of Rome was the collapse of meaning. This was the third siege of Rome in as many years, and refugees were pouring out of the city. Jerome saw the disaster in eschatological terms. "The world's light has gone out. The head of the Roman Empire has been lopped off, and by the fall of one city the whole planet perishes!"[5]

Augustine didn't see it that way. To Augustine, Rome had always been a borderline pagan city. He believed that Christians had come to accept the myth of an eternal Rome, and that they were mistaken to do so. The old order was undergoing a dramatic change, but God never promised eternity to earthly empires, not even Rome.[6] Augustine believed that "the glory of God's true children" could never be found in an earthly city but "only within the walls of the heavenly kingdom, the true *patria*."[7] In a sermon preached to his congregation, which was troubled by the influx of refugees pouring in from the ruined city, Augustine urged them not to focus too much on earthly events as signs for God's plans.

> Some people say to themselves, "The day of judgment has come, so many bad things are happening, so much the tribulations multiply. Everything the prophets foretold is just about accomplished: the Day of Judgment is at hand." Those who speak this way and who speak from conviction are obviously mentally on their way to meet the Bridegroom. But one war follows another, there is tribulation on tribulation, earthquake after earthquake, famine upon famine, invasion upon invasion: and still the Bridegroom has not come. It is while awaiting his arrival that all those fall asleep who say, "He is coming and the Day of Judgment will find us here." And even while they speak, they fall asleep. Let them be on guard against sleeping; let them persevere in charity until sleep comes. Sleep will find them still waiting.[8]

Over time, Augustine found that arguments over the exact details of the end of time were distracting for Christians both theologically and morally, and he was caustic on the subject of popular belief in "signs" of the end times. To whatever extent belief that the end of time was at hand helped people to feel some urgency for their moral and spiritual well-being, it was good. But beyond that, it became a problem.

Resurrection of the Body

For the first two centuries of Christianity, when people imagined resurrection, they often imagined the body of the martyr and fiercely desired its restoration. If it had been burned, then they wanted those ashes remade into flesh. If it had been dismembered, they wanted it whole. But in the late fourth century of Christianity, with the introduction of monasticism and the passionate asceticism of the monks of the desert, the body that was imagined in resurrection had changed. Instead of the body of the martyr who had given her life in the ultimate sacrifice, the resurrected body was that of the ascetic and the virgin, a body that had been "controlled, lightened, and hardened" by ascetic practice and so became more "impassable" during life, a process that would be completed in the resurrection.[9] This developed into a practice of keeping the relics of saints, in which precious, incorruptible bits of the bodies of saints were kept as evidence that the process of transformation had indeed begun. Asceticism, not martyrdom, became the Christian ideal, and resurrection was imagined through the practice of righteousness.

Like Jerome, Augustine appeared to believe that the resurrection of the body at the end of time would be some kind of reassemblage of parts, even though a "spiritual body."[10] This was because the physical body was central to the identity of the person. In order for that body to continue to be the identity of the person, its flesh had to be transformed completely. In the resurrection, the physical body received beauty, weightlessness, and impassibility. This view of the resurrected body did not harmonize well with Paul's more organic metaphors, and when Augustine used the word "seed," he most often used it in reference to semen, as in the "seed of

Abraham" and the "seed of David." In other words, seed was frequently about the past rather than the future.

Instead of the Pauline metaphor of seed and sheaf of wheat, Augustine preferred the metaphor of vessel for the resurrected body. In Book 22 of *City of God*, he wrote that the resurrected body would be "just as if, after making a vessel of clay, one wished to make it over again of the same clay, it would not be necessary that the same portion of the clay which had formed the handle should again form the new handle, or that what had formed the bottom should again do so, but only that the whole clay should go to make up the whole new vessel, and that no part of it should be left unused." Augustine explained that as long as all the particles of the former physical body were present, it did not matter which transformed particle corresponded to which body part. The essential thing, he explained, was that Jesus's words, "Not a hair of your head will perish" (Luke 21:18), be fulfilled.

Augustine challenged critics of the idea of resurrection of the dead with the mystery of life itself, in which something incorporeal (our spirits) becomes incarnated in our bodies. Is it so hard to imagine, then, that something corporeal (our physical bodies) could become a part of heaven? "What," he asked,

> is to hinder the earthly body from being raised to a heavenly body, since a spirit, which is more excellent than all bodies, and consequently than even a heavenly body, has been tied to an earthly body? If so small an earthly particle has been able to hold in union with itself something better than a heavenly body, so as to receive sensation and life, will heaven disdain to receive, or at least to retain, this sentient and living particle, which derives its life and sensation from a substance more excellent than any heavenly body?

The resurrected body offered a "new and better pattern" than the old body. Augustine drew on Paul to argue that "this corruptible shall put on incorruption, and this mortal shall put on immortality." This will allow the resurrected body to experience purity and happiness and "unbroken peace."[11]

Judgment

While most Christians of Augustine's time believed that some kind of judgment happened immediately after death and a second judgment came at the end of time, they did not have good answers to what happened to the dead between death and resurrection. Augustine had to address this question when, within a very short span of time, both his mother and his son died. He did not write about his son's death, but he did write about his mother's death in a way that betrayed anxiety regarding the fate of the soul. Augustine and his mother were very close, and in his *Confessions*, written after her death, he asked God to "forgive her, I beseech you. Enter not into judgment with her. Let your mercy be exalted above your justice, for your words are true, and you have promised mercy to the merciful."[12]

Augustine's anxiety suggests that he believed in an intermediate (between death and resurrection) state for the soul that involved some kind of judgment, and he wasn't sure how his mother would fare. His doctrine of original sin and his conviction that the fate of the soul rested entirely in God's hands mixed in the *Confessions* with his longing to pray for the dead and influence God's decision. In *City of God*, written much later and with a much more systematic intention, Augustine clarified that prayers for the dead were useful for those whose earthly life was neither so evil that they were obviously condemned nor so good that they would clearly have no need of God's mercy.[13] They must be in some kind of middle waiting place; he called it a "secret storehouse" in the *Confessions*, neither hell nor heaven.[14] For these sinners, Augustine suggested a kind of fire that was not the fire of hell but a purging fire that might purify the soul and allow it to enter heaven.[15]

Our True *Patria*

Late in his life, Augustine wrote *City of God*, his most complete theological treatise, in which he expounded on the ideas nascent after the sack of Rome. Drawing on Paul's letter to the Philippians, "But our citizenship is in heaven, and it is from there that we are expecting a Savior, the Lord Jesus Christ" (Phil 3:20), Augustine continued his argument that Christians would never have a home on earth. In Book 20 Augustine took up the question of Revelation and specifically of the millennium. He was influenced by a man named Tyconius, who, although a member of Augustine's chief theological rivals, the Donatists, nonetheless made an argument about Revelation that Augustine accepted. The millennium had actually begun with the life of Jesus who had "bound" Satan in his many exorcisms, and who already had victory over him. Thus the millennium was not sometime in the future but now, in the life of the church.[16] In fact, the millennium was a kind of timeless reality that could "be applied to the interior life of Christians in all times and places."[17]

Christians entered the kingdom through baptism. This was the "first resurrection" of Revelation 20. The second resurrection would take place at the end of time, but a "thousand years" was just another way of saying "an indeterminate time." This interpretation of Revelation was not meant to dismiss the importance of end things for the Christian but to teach people to look through catastrophe or through their present circumstances for a lasting vision of hope.[18] When the kingdoms of the world collapse, the *civitas dei* remains.[19] The aeons of time imagined by Origen are transformed in Augustine's writings into the endless day—not endless time but freedom from time, "the utterly simple, unchanging present of God's being."[20]

The World's Old Age

Augustine did not abandon eschatological narratives altogether. He was fascinated by the idea of the cosmic week: six periods or ages that would be followed by a golden age, something like Methodius's thousand-year sabbath. He connected this both with what he imagined as the six stages of human life and with the six days of creation. He saw the world in which he lived as in its old age. He noted its "coughing, phlegm, inflamed eyes, anxiety, and lack of energy" as evidence of this.[21]

In *City of God*, he made a list of things that scripture says will happen at the end of time. "We have learned then that these things will come about in or with that judgment: Elijah the Tishbite will come; the Jews will have faith; the antichrist will persecute; Christ will judge; the dead will be resurrected; the good and the evil will be separated; the world will be burned and renovated." But he cautions that these events were not iterated in perfect order, and while his opinion was that they will happen in the order he listed them, he admitted that there was ambiguity on the question.[22] Augustine's clarity about these events came from his reading of the Bible as a unity.

From the scramble of images, interlocking stories, and metaphors that made up Christian eschatology, he singled out those he thought merited being called events.[23] He then drew them together into a single narrative. After Augustine, few teachers in the Christian west would hesitate to use this method of breaking texts into small pieces and using them to create a chain of events—a beast here, an angel there, a day here, ten thousand days there. One scholar has called Augustine's eschatology "an extraordinary flight of the imagination springing from the mysterious depths of biblical truths."[24] But another has said that what gave Augustine lasting influence was his eschatology's "systematic cohesion, its integration into a broad theological synthesis that is both philosophical and scriptural, speculative and pastorally practical, subtly consistent in theory yet passionately personal and experiential in its source and expression."[25]

Not in Human Language

Circulating around the time of Augustine was a popular text called the *Apocalypse of Paul*. In it, the reader accompanies Paul as he ascends through the various levels of heaven. He sees an individual soul, called simply "the soul," arguing for its salvation before various gates leading up to the levels of heaven. This text was widely circulated into the Middle Ages, with readers taking it to offer a picture of life after death and insight into mysteries only hinted at in the scriptures. In the *Apocalypse of Paul*, each soul was judged immediately upon its separation from the body and then went to heaven or hell accordingly.[26] The end of time itself is absent in the text, but similar to Augustine's comments to Hesychius, the end of time is replaced by individual judgment. The *Apocalypse of Paul* depicts the celestial court beyond what is pictured in Revelation and depicts harsh consequences for human sin. Perhaps this is what made the *Apocalypse of Paul* such a popular text: it drew heavily from previous traditions, both Christian and Jewish, and then it extended the older texts into a "fountainhead of ideas and images" that enhanced Christian imagination and began to shift the focus from the fate of Christian enemies to a subtler and more nuanced question about the fate of individuals.[27]

Augustine, who shared theological concerns with the text, objected to the *Apocalypse of Paul* because, in his view, it violated Paul's own injunction in 2 Corinthians 12:4. When Paul was "caught up into Paradise," he "heard things that are not to be told, that no mortal is permitted to repeat." Likewise, Augustine argued that trying to visualize the world beyond in such detail depicted "things which cannot and must not be put into human language." His judgment on this popular text was harsh:

> Taking advantage of which, there have been some vain individuals, who, with a presumption that betrays the grossest folly, have forged a Revelation of Paul, crammed with all manner of fables, which has been rejected by the orthodox Church; affirming it to be that whereof he had said that he was caught up into the third heavens, and there heard unspeakable words "which it is not lawful for a man to utter."[28]

Who, Augustine wondered, would be so foolish as to utter what it is not lawful to utter? In all aspects of Augustine's eschatology, there are examples of his desire to respect the limits of human knowledge, to remain a little agnostic about the future, and not to chase after certainties about the future that are not humankind's to know.

Augustine's Legacy in the West

Some scholars have argued that after Augustine, because of his agnosticism on apocalyptic scenarios, Christian apocalypticism in the West took a long hiatus, or even that after Augustine, Christian apocalypticism was never more than a "marginal attraction" for the faithful.[29] Certainly the fate of the individual soul became an ever more pressing question, but Christian apocalypticism also continued to develop complex narratives about the meaning of history and the future, and many Christians ignored Augustine's advice and continued to study scripture, earth, and sky for signs of the end.[30]

But Augustine made an important contribution in suggesting that the millennium might be read spiritually and symbolically instead of literally. Like Paul, he continued the tradition of seeing the eschatological through the lens of the ethical. If your eschatological beliefs brought you closer to the love of God and honed your inner nature, they were valuable. Christians should "love and long for the coming of the Lord" and be vigilant in their waiting. The end might be coming soon, but if our belief in it damages our own moral development or the moral development of others, then it is of no use. We are better off being agnostic, or as he puts it to Hesychius, we should practice "cautious ignorance" on the timing of Christ's coming, pour our energies into vigilance and preparations, and draw near to God in the meantime.[31]

Augustine's work laid the foundation for later western Christians to reinterpret the kingdom of God as the reign of the Catholic church. Much like the emperors in the East, the church of the West became obsessed with its worldly power, and its power struggles took on apocalyptic tones.

Notes

1. Kevin Coyle, "Augustine and Apocalyptic," in *Augustine and Apocalyptic*, ed. John Doody, Kari Kloos, and Kim Paffenroth (Lanham: Lexington, 2005), 34.

2. Bruce Chilton, *Visions of the Apocalypse: Reception of John's Revelation in Western Imagination* (Waco: Baylor University Press, 2013), 38.

3. Ibid., 39.

4. Ibid., 41.

5. Jerome, *Comment. in Hiezechiel*, prol., quoted in Coyle, 27.

6. Coyle, 27.

7. Ibid., 31.

8. Augustine, *Sermon* 93.6.7 (*PL* 38.576), quoted in Coyle, 32.

9. Caroline Walker Bynum, *The Resurrection of the Body in Western Christianity 200-1336* (New York: Columbia University Press, 1995), 200.

10. Ibid., 95.

11. Augustine, *On Christian Doctrine* 1.19, trans. James Shaw in *Nicene and Post-Nicene Fathers*, First Series, vol. 2, ed. Philip Schaff (Buffalo: Christian Literature, 1887). Revised and edited for New Advent by Kevin Knight, at http://www.newadvent.org/fathers/1202.htm.

12. Augustine, *Confessions* 9.13, trans. John K. Ryan (New York: Doubleday, 1960).

13. Augustine, *City of God*, trans. Michael W. Tkacz and Douglas Kries in *Augustine: Political Writings* (Indianapolis: Hackett, 1994), 21.24.

14. Augustine, *Confessions* 9.7.

15. Jacque LeGoff, *The Birth of Purgatory*, trans. Arthur Goldhammer (Chicago: University of Chicago Press, 1984), 66–68.

16. Craig R. Koester, *Revelation and the End of All Things* (Grand Rapids: Eerdmans, 2001), 7.

17. Ibid.

18. H. I. Marrou, *Augustin et l'augustinisme* (Paris: du Seuil, 1957), 7.

19. Coyle, 39.

20. Brian Daley, *The Hope of the Early Church* (Cambridge: Cambridge University Press, 1991), 132.

21. Augustine, *Sermon* 81.8, quoted in Daley, 133.

22. Augustine, *City of God* 20.30.

23. Brian Daley, "Apocalypticism in Early Christian Theology," in *The Encyclopedia of Apocalypticism,* ed. Bernard McGinn (New York: Continuum, 1998), 2:16.

24. R. W. Southern, "Aspects of the European Tradition of Historical Writing 2: Hugh of St. Victor and the Idea of Historical Development," *Transactions of the Royal Historical Society,* 5th ser. 21 (1971): 159–79 (161).

25. Daley, *Hope*, 131.

26. Anthony Hilhorst, "The Apocalypse of Paul: Earlier History and Later Influence," in *Apocalyptic and Eschatological Heritage: The Middle East and Celtic Realms,* ed. Martin McNamara (Portland, OR: Four Courts, 2003), 73.

27. Ibid., 63.

28. Augustine *Tracates on John* 98.8, trans. John Gibb in *Nicene and Post-Nicene Fathers,* First Series, vol. 7, ed. Philip Schaff (Buffalo: Christian Literature, 1888). Revised and edited for New Advent by Kevin Knight, at http://www.newadvent.org/fathers/1701098.htm.

29. Coyle, 41.

30. Richard Landes, "The Silenced Millennium and the Fall of Rome," in *Augustine and Apocalyptic.* "What Paschoud and others consider so many evaporating puddles of residual millennialism are actually deep and wide-reaching waters of popular belief, and the occasional trace of millennialism in the texts of subsequent centuries, that scholars view as so much flotsam and jetsam of a ship that Augustine sunk in the early fifth century, actually represent the tip of an iceberg of apocalyptic and millennial discourse that pushes up into a medium profoundly hostile to its expression" (152).

31. Daley, 32. On "cautious ignorance" see Roland J. Teske, "Augustine on the End of the World: 'Cautious Ignorance,'" in *Augustine and Apocalyptic*, 193–205.

9

Legends: Pseudo-Methodius and the Antichrist

So be warned, my friend. I have given you the signs of the antichrist. Do not merely store them in your memory. Pass them on to everyone without stint. If you have a child after the flesh, teach them to him forthwith. And if you have become a godparent forewarn your godchild, lest he should take the false Christ for the true.

—Cyril of Jerusalem (313–386)

In 637 CE, five years after the death of Mohammad, Caliph Umar, from the Rashidun Caliphate in what is now Saudi Arabia, traveled to Jerusalem to accept the surrender of the Christians from St. Sophronius, the patriarch of that city. A monk living in what is now Syria felt the crisis profoundly. He knew the emperor was too weak, and that the Church itself was too divided, to stage a strong opposition. The only hope was God's own saving power. He watched as Arab invaders took over churches, confiscated natural resources, and set up their own oppressive governments in the places that they claimed. Sometime in the next few decades, this monk composed a text that profoundly influenced Christian understanding of the future.[1] The monk wrote as if he were Methodius, the bishop of Olympus and the fourth-century martyr who had opposed Origen. In the vision of this monk, now called Pseudo-Methodius, God had taken that more ancient Methodius up to the "mountain of Šenāgar," a mountain local to the monk, to "show him all the generations."[2] The result was a text that was part comprehensive "history" of all of creation and part prophecy of the future that predicted the demise of the Arabs who had taken over the holy city.

Pseudo-Methodius began his narration with Adam and Eve. His purpose was to tell the story of the rise and fall of kingdoms one after another leading to the present moment of crisis and then to prophesy for the future. His apocalypse tried to tell the whole story of human history, to combine knowledge of earth with knowledge of heaven in order to narrate the significance of the present and the imminence of God's action. The need for this comprehensive form of knowledge in the Byzantine Empire was intense. From the fourth through the tenth centuries, there was a "continuum of activity that either produced new apocalypses or so thoroughly reworked earlier traditions or documents that they are now seen as new compilations."[3]

When the capital of Rome was moved to Constantinople in 330, Byzantine Christians saw themselves as the continuation of the Roman Empire. They believed that the Roman Empire was the fourth and last empire in the prophecies of Daniel. Through the apocalyptic narratives they had inherited, they believed that the Last Emperor of this empire would hand over his crown to Jesus Christ in Jerusalem before the day of the Lord.

If the Arabs were to defeat the Roman Empire, then it was not at all clear in this apocalyptic narrative what was to happen next.[4] In Pseudo-Methodius's telling and in the legendary traditions both Jewish and Christian from which he was drawing, the threat of "Ishmaelites" (Arabs) was prophesied from ancient times. They will appear to be victorious until the "king of the Greeks" will arise, like a man arising from a drunken stupor, and he will destroy the "Ishmaelites," restore the land to the Christians, and the kingdom of the Christians will be at peace.

Pseudo-Methodius believed that this period would be marked as well by invasions from the armies of Gog and Magog.[5] According to legend, Alexander the Great had imprisoned the unruly and "unclean" nations of Gog and Magog behind iron gates, perhaps in the Caspian Mountains. They would be unleashed at the end of time, and the Last Emperor would conquer them as well. After a period of peace, the antichrist would then be revealed. The Last Emperor would travel to Jerusalem and lay down his crown on top of the Holy Cross. According to these legends, these were the events that would precede the second coming of Christ, who would then destroy the antichrist in a final battle and usher in the end of time and the final judgment.[6]

To create his narrative, Pseudo-Methodius grafted the legend of Alexander the Great onto biblical traditions and combined those with other, less authoritative texts that circulated in his region. Paul Alexander writes that Pseudo-Methodius's version of "history" would have been preposterous even to his contemporaries.[7] But his reformulation of prophetic traditions was influential throughout the Christian world. The text of Pseudo-Methodius was copied, read, and reinterpreted for a thousand years after its composition.

In the Christian east, the idea of the empire as an instrument of God's will became even more important as that empire was challenged by non-Christian adversaries. Even as early as 637 CE, invasions by both Arabs and Persians made Constantinople a "small Christian enclave in an ocean of Islam."[8] While it claimed the status of an empire in order for its story about God's will to be true, it was in fact already crumbling. As it crumbled, apocalyptic documents attempting to make sense of its past and future proliferated.

The Tradition Expands

During the early Middle Ages, many apocalyptic texts like the the *Apocalypse of Paul*, Pseudo-Methodius, Pseudo-Ephraem, and the *Tiburtino Sibyl* circulated and were copied and re-copied. Because of their extracanonical status, they could be enhanced, changed, and edited by scribes according to the demands of their own cultural moment and the interpretation of their readers. They became influential in political and social thought and gave leaders frameworks through which to interpret the events of history. Kings, rulers, and emperors studied these texts for signs of their own futures as well as for signs of threats and promises.

These Byzantine apocalypses circulated and spread throughout Christendom, and they look strange next to the theological treatises of Augustine that resist the very knowledge that these texts claim. Even so, they were also influential in forming the theology of the church in both the East and the West and were influential in shaping church politics. As Byzantine apocalypses were copied and translated into many regional languages, they were also changed to suit particular circumstances and environments.[9] For example, when Pseudo-Methodius was translated into Latin for use in the western church, scribes enhanced it with many more images from and references to Revelation than the original text contained. Revelation was not widely accepted in the Christian east and was still held at arm's length or spiritualized in the tradition of Origen.[10]

In an environment of almost constant military conflict, eschatology served as a form of theodicy, an attempt to understand why the will of an absolutely sovereign God did not yet rule on the earth. Pseudo-Methodius wrote, "And why does God allow the faithful to undergo these trials? Why, so that the faithful will appear and the unfaithful be made manifest, the wheat separated from the chaff; for this time is a fire of trial."[11] Pseudo-Methodius was able to give meaning to his present moment by imparting to it eschatological significance and moral force. He wrote to "inspire resistance" against the Arabs and to inspire faithfulness and endurance.[12] His message transcended the moment in which it was written, however, and allowed future readers also to interpret their moments as "a fire of trial" in which they were called to faithfulness.

The Last Emperor

Pseudo-Methodius's Last Emperor was a somewhat new addition to the tradition. It was a version of the ancient Ninurta, the semi-divine warrior. But, in this case, he was a "mighty Roman Christian king" who would vanquish Christianity's enemies and enslave them in a slavery "a hundred times more harsh than what they had inflicted on others."[13] This king would create a heavenly kingdom on earth with such "peace and tranquility" as had "never been before, nor would be ever after."[14]

Other texts of the period contributed to this image of the warrior-king: The *Tiburtino Sibyl* (c. 380 CE) and Pseudo-Ephraem (late sixth or early seventh century) also told an eschatological story about great kings and leaders who would rise at the end of time and accomplish God's will. Together they accomplished another important shift. The sun, moon, and stars of traditional apocalyptic texts became metaphors for worldly power. Astral bodies were read as metaphors for emperors and kings. In biblical texts, it seemed relatively clear that the sun, moon, and stars, when they appeared, related to actual astral bodies. But in these texts, they became symbols with a plurality of meanings, and semidivine action substituted for divine action. It was not the coming of Christ, for example, that would bring about the peace and prosperity of the millennium, but the work of the Last Emperor, someone perhaps more like Ninurta than like Christ, without the complexity of early Christianity's inversion of worldly and heavenly power.[15] Action that had once been firmly concentrated in the hands of God, as the mover of the stars and the heavens, was now in the hands of kings and emperors, but these rulers were not ordinary people. They retained mythological dimensions.

The Rise of the Antichrist

These texts also enhanced Christian thinking about a future figure whose importance grew as the narratives developed: the antichrist. The antichrist is mentioned briefly in just a few biblical texts, in which it is not clear whether the antichrist is a future person or a present one, or whether "he" should be understood as a single figure or multiple figures. The word, singular and plural, is mentioned only four times in the Bible, all of them in the letters of John. In tradition, the antichrist is also associated with the "son of perdition" in 2 Thessalonians and with various beasts in both Daniel and Revelation. First John 2:18 encapsulates the complexities of the reference: "Children, it is the last hour! As you have heard that the antichrist is coming, so now many antichrists have come. From this we know that it is the last hour." Antichrists have come and are coming. They are evidence of the last hour, and they are already here. He is singular, and they are plural. Perhaps because of this complexity, it took the eschatological figure of the antichrist a long time to develop, and when he did, several traditions had by then combined.[16] Pseudo-Ephraem has perhaps the fullest description of the antichrist as he comes into his own as a legendary figure:

> But the accursed destroyer of souls rather than bodies, a crafty serpent while he grows up, appears in the cloak of justice before he assumes power. For to all men he will be cunningly gentle, unwilling to accept gifts to place [his own] person first, lovable to everybody, peaceful to all, not striving after gifts of friendship, seemingly courteous among his entourage, so that men will bless him and say he is a just man—they do not realize that a wolf is hidden beneath the appearance of a lamb and that he is inwardly rapacious under the hide of a sheep.[17]

Tradition held that the antichrist would be of Jewish origin, from the tribe of Dan, but later he was understood as coming from within the Christian community itself, and he also made several appearances as a Muslim, which is no surprise given the intense conflict with the expanding Muslim world.[18] Some traditions had him emerging at the end of the reign of the Last Emperor, others as arising "even now." In eschatological stories, some had him being destroyed by Christ's breath (as in 2 Thess 2:8), and others depicted him as thrown into the pit with his father, Satan (as in Revelation 20). Some texts turned him into a false king, others into an inhuman monster. Eventually, he developed a biography, parents, an adolescence, and a career.[19] The antichrist had to develop in a extra-canonical way; writers set aside biblical texts to create an eschatological tradition that became intensely influential even while its warrants were few.[20] But like the Last Emperor, the antichrist was a figure that served the developing Christian eschatological imagination.

Adso's Antichrist

Further to the west of Pseudo-Methodius and for several hundred years after his formative text, imaginative elaboration was taking place on end-times scenarios, specifically the antichrist. Adso (910/915–992 CE), an abbot in a monastery in what is now France, Montier-en-Der, wrote a letter to a woman named Gergerga, the sister of the ruler of the western part of the Roman Empire, Otto I, and the wife of Louis IV, the king of West Francia. In this letter, he aimed to write a full account of the figure of the antichrist, in what has been called the first "biography" of the antichrist. To create this portrait, in the absence of biblical evidence, he drew on the Sibylline Oracles, classical Greek literature, the Venerable Bede, Pseudo-Methodius, and some of the work of the well-known scholar Isidore of Seville (560–636). His conflation of eastern and western texts and his incorporation of various traditions meant that he created a complex and contradictory text with two accounts of the antichrist's career that did not line up particularly well.

From Pseudo-Methodius, Adso concluded that the antichrist would not be found in the church but would be born in Babylon among the Jewish tribe of Dan. He would rebuild the temple in Jerusalem as a key sign of his status as the antichrist. He would convert kings and send messengers throughout the world. "He will perform many signs, great and unheard of miracles," Adso wrote, and then he would "unleash a terrible persecution against Christians."[21]

Adso's work was enormously popular. More than 170 manuscripts from the Middle Ages included his letter, with nine different versions of the text sometimes ascribing authorship to more well-known medieval writers. Bernard McGinn says that we can think of this as just one in a long line of "apocalyptic bestsellers," and it had a long influence on images of the antichrist, even to the present.[22]

Scholarly and Popular Eschatologies

When we go looking for Christian eschatology, we might be tempted to consider only what the theologians have said and to take their words as the truth of the Christian tradition. Theologians have been reluctant to engage popular stories or extrabiblical myths. If we do that, we miss the vivid imaginative engagement of Christians throughout the centuries who used legend, myth, and story to make sense of their own particular time and place, to imagine the future, to embody their fear and prejudices, and to cajole and encourage one another. If we miss that popular engagement, we miss the enduring force of this tradition as its people attempted to shape and interpret the world, to encounter its mysteries, and to try to grasp the future.

At the same time, we should not distinguish intellectual and popular eschatologies too sharply. Adso and Pseudo-Methodius were both educated men whose words had the power to reach the upper echelons of their societies. Christian apocalypticism, McGinn explains, was not a grassroots popular movement, as it might have been in earlier Christian eras when Christianity was a persecuted minority. It did not force "its way like molten lava up through the hardened sediment of institutional and religious forms."[23] Rather, it developed at the level of the institutional elite who needed to be able to interpret the signs of the times and the inherited texts in a way that supported the political and religious establishment. Many of the underlying themes of Christian eschatological literature were political and social in nature, and they were often written to inspire some kind of action. The other-worldly images of eschatology mingled with "this-worldly concerns" in order to become a "lens through which experience and change were viewed."[24] For the religious elite, eschatology became a "universal schema of meaning" within which worthy interpreters could locate specific events and predict the future. Eschatology gave legitimacy to the actions of those who were attempting to influence political and social structures.[25]

Notes

1. Paul J. Alexander, *The Byzantine Apocalyptic Tradition* (Berkeley: University of California Press, 1985), 25. Bernard McGinn dates Pseudo-Methodius somewhat later in his *Antichrist: Two Thousand Years of the Human Fascination with Evil* (San Francisco: HarperSan Francisco, 1994), 90.

2. Ibid., 16.

3. J. H. Charlesworth and J. R. Mueller, *The New Testament Apocrypha and Pseudepigrapha* (Chicago: American Theological Association, 1987), 36.

4. Ironically, the Qu'ran also evokes Gog and Magog during this same period in Sura 21: "till when Gog and Magog are unloosed, and they slide down out of every slope. Then the true promise is nearby."

5. W. J. Aerts, "Gog, Magog, Dogheads, and other Monsters in the Byzantine World," in *Gog and Magog: The Clans of Chaos in World Literature* (West Lafayette: Purdue University Press, 2007), 28.

6. Alexander, 13–33.

7. Ibid., 61.

8. Sidney Harrison Griffith, *The Church in the Shadow of the Mosque: Christian and Muslims in the World of Islam* (Princeton: Princeton University Press, 2008), 24.

9. Alexander, 13.

10. Paul J. Alexander, "The Diffusion of Byzantine Apocalypses," in *Prophecy and Millenarianism: Essays in Honour of Marjorie Reeves* (Harlow: Longman, 1980), 67.

11. Pseudo-Methodius 12.6, ed. Lolos 114, quoted in David Olster, "Byzantine Apocalypses," in *The Encyclopedia of Apocalypticism,* ed. Bernard McGinn (New York: Continuum, 1998), 2:61.

12. Ibid.

13. Robert E. Lerner, "Millennialism," in *The Encyclopedia of Apocalypticism,* 2:330.

14. Ibid.

15. See Alexander, 169, on the Last Roman Emperor.

16. See Wilhelm Bousset, *The Antichrist Legend: A Chapter in Christian and Jewish Folklore* (Atlanta: Scholars, 1999); Alexander, 193–225; and McGinn, who has a wonderful chart on pp. 72–73 that traces the complexities of this tradition in early attempts to describe the Antichrist physically.

17. Pseudo-Ephreum 215, quoted in Alexander, 139.

18. Roberto Rusconi, "Antichrist and Antichrists," in *The Encyclopedia of Apocalypticism,* 2:294.

19. Alexander, 201.

20. Bousset, 224.

21. Adso, quoted in Rusconi, 292.

22. McGinn, 101, 103.

23. Bernard McGinn, *Visions of the End: Apocalyptic Traditions in the Middle Ages* (New York: Columbia University Press, 1979), 32.

24. Caroline Walker Bynum and Paul Freedman, introduction to *Last Things: Death and the Apocalypse in the Middle Ages,* ed. Caroline Walker Bynum and Paul Freedman (Philadelphia: University of Pennsylvania Press, 2000), 4.

25. McGinn, *Visions,* 33.

10

Sketches: Gregory the Great

If we knew at what time we were to depart from this world,
we would be able to select a season for pleasure and another
for repentance. But God, who has promised pardon to every
repentant sinner, has not promised us tomorrow. Therefore we
must always dread the final day, which we can never foresee.
This very day is a day of truce, a day for conversion. And yet we
refuse to cry over the evil we have done! Not only do we not weep
for the sins we have committed, we even add to them.

—Gregory the Great

One cannot blame Gregory (540–604) for turning down the job
of pope when he was appointed by the emperor in 590 CE.
He was a senator's son, who was torn between the active life
of politics and the contemplative life of the monastery. His
native city of Rome was under threat from both Constantinople
to the east and the Lombards to the north. The empire for
which the pope worked had invaded the city several times
during Gregory's lifetime. While technically the pope was still
a bishop under the jurisdiction of the emperor (whose seat was

in Constantinople while still being called the Roman Empire), he had the unfortunate job of trying to run interference between the empire and the troubled but still proud city of Rome. The pope was as much politician as spiritual leader, and the job held multiple risks. Two of Gregory's recent predecessors had been arrested and marched to Constantinople. So when the emperor Maurice wrote to Gregory appointing him pope, Gregory wrote back respectfully declining. In a private letter to a friend, he wrote that the emperor had mistaken him for a lion, when in fact he was an ape.[1] He was appointed anyway.

Gregory stood at the boundary between two different eschatological movements. One was inherently social and political, looking to interpret the roles of kings, popes, and empires within God's plan for the future. The other was personal and individual, giving the question of individual salvation new force and significance. The story of each unique individual human began to find a place in a cosmic drama that extended beyond the boundaries of life.[2] But the questions of worldly power and the futures of kings and emperors, not to mention popes, did not go away.

These two movements did not find easy harmony in the early Middle Ages. Aron Gurevich argues that the problem of collective and individual destinies put early medieval people on "two temporal planes" simultaneously. On one plane they lived out the events of their own lives, and when they died, they faced judgment for the choices, vices, and virtues developed along the way. On the other plane were those events which were "decisive for the fate of the whole world" and over which the ordinary individual had no control whatsoever.[3]

"The Outlines of a World beyond the Grave"

Throughout his life, Gregory wrote extensive treatises for his fellow monks and parishioners. He was a pastoral teacher, and his writings reflect his desire to inspire, comfort, and teach both monks and parishioners. To many early medieval people, the image of God that came most readily was God as an absolute emperor. Humankind was subject to the imperial whims of this God and bidden to be wholly subservient to him. The emperor God demanded absolute righteousness. And yet, of course, even the most faithful person died with some kind of sin still clinging to them. Augustine's teachings had made clear that no human being lived without the taint of sin. How then could a person be saved after death?

That left two possibilities for all but the most pure. One was that some kind of greater purgation was needed after death in order for the ordinary person to be brought into the presence of God. This was something that had been suggested by Augustine and carried forward: some kind of refining fire after death would be necessary. The other was that at some point, maybe on the Last Day, God would simply wipe clean the slate of human sin, as "an emperor on earth was known to pardon criminals and remit arrears on taxes."[4]

God as emperor meant that the human being could do little more than hope for mercy. God could do anything he wanted with the "soiled soul" who appeared in his realm after death. Liturgies from the sixth century reflect this anxiety. They tell the story of a God of absolute power, using images of the "late Roman imperial office."[5] Even the most ordinary person needed to beg for mercy.

Gregory's writings were often directed to mediating this anxiety. In his *Dialogues*, he lays out "almost for the first time," writes Peter Brown, "the outlines of a world beyond the grave," and explores the dynamics of mercy and righteousness. Gregory was not systematic in this endeavor. He often taught and wrote in anecdotes, telling stories about the relationship between the living and the dead.

"Here is what Bishop Felix tells me he knows about a priest who died two years ago after living a holy life," begins one such story. This story tells about how a man who had died with too much sin was able to make it to heaven after all. The priest of Bishop Felix's story brought two loaves of bread as a gift to a man who helped him at the baths where he went frequently, "a place where much steam escapes from hot geysers." The man told him that he could not eat the bread because he was actually a ghost. He had been sent back to earth because of sins he had committed while he was alive, and he was being given a chance to work them off by helping people. He asked the priest to offer the bread to God on his behalf, because that would help him with his penance. Before too long, the priest no longer saw the man at the baths, and assumed that his penance was served and he had moved on to heaven.[6]

Gregory believed that people needed these "authentic testimonies" in order to prepare themselves for life after death.[7] He taught that after death, souls were able to move through various regions as they worked through the consequences of their sins. It was obvious, he wrote, that hell had two regions—a higher region and a lower region. The righteous rested in the upper region awaiting final judgment and passage into paradise. The unrighteous were tormented in the lower region.[8] As simple as this sounds, stories like the one about the priest and the ghost testified that the fate of the dead was considerably more complicated. The man doing penance at the baths was neither entirely "righteous" nor "unrighteous."

He was apparently in neither region of hell but on earth doing penance, and the prayers of the priest helped him to move on in his journey. Gregory's stories were part of a larger anecdotal movement documenting the vague territory between heaven and hell, between death and judgment.

As stories proliferated, a different view of the human being began to develop. Each person became highly individualized, "etched with fine engraver's tools"; their individual deeds, sins, histories, and words created intricate portraits.[9] In the afterlife, the hidden inner being of a person was completely revealed to God, who was the ultimate judge. Gregory wrote, "Let us consider how severe a judge is coming." But then he reminded his readers that it was not only their "evil deeds" that would be judged but "even our every thought."[10] Gregory's audience for this kind of message was largely monastic. He himself was a monk, and he wrote to edify and instruct a monastic community. In some monastic communities, with this kind of focus on every thought of a person, monks began to confess their sins up to three times a day, and thus developed an intimate relationship with their own individual faults, calculating their relationship to righteousness in ever finer detail.[11]

The moment of a person's death was one of intense vulnerability. Death took away all pretensions and social protections. The individual was "stripped of all customary forms of definition: stripped of the body and of an entire social persona." Peter Brown says that the moment of death and the moment of the last judgment were "telescoped . . . in the minds of believers."[12] Both were moments to inspire utter terror with a finality over which the person had no control. Early medieval art depicts monks being plucked off of ladders by demons as they attempt to make their way to heaven, or being fought over by angels and demons at the moment of death. Early medieval Christians did not have many means of mitigating the anxiety that the question of salvation aroused. The outlines of a world beyond the grave remained vague, even as individuals grew more distinct.

The Antichrist among Us

While the fate of the individual soul was debated and monasteries developed practices that helped monks mitigate the effects of sin, Gregory was still intensely engaged in the political affairs of his day. Gregory was convinced that the end of the world was coming quickly. In a sermon early in his career as pope, he "worked his way through the list" of signs that Jesus had offered in Mark 13. Nation was rising up against nation, and he argued the distress of nations was greater than in the past. Earthquakes were destroying cities everywhere; there were incessant plagues. While the sun and the moon had not yet changed as dramatically as Jesus described, any person paying attention could see that that was surely the next sign.[13]

Through his writing, administration, diplomacy, and missionary activity, Gregory worked hard to form a new Christian society in the West. This labor stands at an odd angle with his pessimism about the impending end. This contradiction is an important one in medieval apocalypticism. In the face of impending doom, Christians paradoxically worked to transform their societies, spread the gospel, and expand their kingdoms. On the whole, Gregory was successful in his efforts. He helped broker peace with the Lombards. The emperor Maurice, toward whom Gregory was especially cool, was overthrown, and during his papacy, Gregory was able to improve relationships with Constantinople.

Perhaps because of the intense political battles in which he was engaged, Gregory was especially interested in the figure of the antichrist. Who was the antichrist, and how would he be known? For Gregory, the answer had something to do with politics. Unlike Pseudo-Methodius, Gregory determined that the antichrist was "one of us." The two key characteristics —and Gregory was quick to point out that these were characteristics found in even the most devout believer—were pride and hypocrisy.[14] The antichrist is "the head of all hypocrites . . . who feign holiness to lead to sinfulness," Gregory wrote.[15] Whereas Pseudo-Methodius looked for signs external to the church for the rise of the antichrist, Gregory believed that the antichrist would be a figure arising from within the church. In 595, Gregory was incensed when the bishop of Constantinople declared himself the "universal patriarch." He stopped short of saying that this proved the bishop was the antichrist, but it was precisely the kind of arrogance and hypocrisy by which the antichrist would be known. He saw this as presumption bordering on the diabolical.[16]

Gregory believed that the antichrist was not only a reason to study the world for signs but also a reason for each person to turn inward and examine his own heart. "It is necessary that each of us return to his heart's secret and become very fearful of the harm from [the antichrist's] action, lest when merits are demanded, he falls among the number of such people [i.e., the followers of the antichrist]."[17] The antichrist was a moral problem for the believer. The potential to be deceived was yet another reason to guard one's own heart carefully.

Like many other readers of signs, Gregory was wrong on this point: the end did not come. But in part because of his work in both the inner and outer realms, the interior life of a person and the road to salvation had been sketched in new ways.

Notes

1. John Moorhead, *Gregory the Great* (New York: Routledge, 2005), 3.

2. Peter Brown, "The Decline of the Empire of God: Amnesty, Penance, and the Afterlife from Late Antiquity to the Middle Ages," in *Last Things: Death and the Apocalypse in the Middle Ages*, ed. Caroline Walker Bynum and Paul Freedman (Philadelphia: University of Pennsylvania Press, 2000), 59.

3. Aron Gurevich, *Medieval Popular Culture: Problems of Belief and Perception* (New York: Cambridge University Press, 1988), 145.

4. Brown, 46.

5. Ibid., 48.

6. Gregory the Great, *Dialogues* 4.57.1–7, quoted in Jacques LeGoff, *The Birth of Purgatory*, trans. Arthur Goldhammer (Chicago: University of Chicago Press, 1984), 91.

7. LeGoff, 93.

8. Gregory the Great, *Morals in the Book of Job* 12.13. See LeGoff, 89.

9. Brown, 53.

10. In *Visio Baronti* 22.354, quoted in Brown, 54.

11. Brown, 53.

12. Ibid., 45.

13. Moorhead, 6.

14. Bernard McGinn, *Antichrist: Two Thousand Years of the Human Fascination with Evil* (San Francisco: HarperSanFrancisco, 1994), 81.

15. Gregory the Great, *Morals* 25.15.34, quoted in McGinn, 81.

16. Moorhead, 5.

17. Gregory the Great, *Morals* 29.7.14, quoted in McGinn, 82.

11

Songs: Celtic Sources

The day of the Lord, the King of Kings most righteous, is at hand:
a day of wrath and vengeance, of darkness and cloud;
a day of wondrous mighty thunderings,
a day of trouble also, of grief and sadness,
in which shall cease the love and desire of women
and the strife of men and the lust of this world.

—from *Altus Prosator*

When Patrick (b. 387), the apostle to the Irish, arrived in Ireland in the fifth century CE, he knew he had an eschatological task. He was motivated by Matt 24:14, "And this good news of the kingdom will be proclaimed throughout the world, as a testimony to all the nations; and then the end will come." Ireland was the very ends of the earth as it was known, a pagan country that had never been a part of the Roman Empire, and so belonged to the uncivilized people of the world.

However ignorant I am, he has heard me, so that in these last days I can dare to undertake such a holy and wonderful work. In this way I can imitate somewhat those whom the Lord foretold would announce his gospel in witness to all nations before the end of the world. This is what we see has been fulfilled. Look at us: we are witnesses that the gospel has been preached right out to where there is nobody else![1]

Patrick's mission to the Irish eventually developed into a flourishing Christian culture with distinctive elements. Patrick's sense of the imminence of the second coming became a part of the fabric of Celtic Christianity.

The Four Last Things

In the same year that Gregory was appointed pope, Columbanus (d. 615), a missionary sent to carry Christianity back to the continent from Scottish monasteries, arrived in Gaul. Like Patrick, Columbanus believed that he lived at a moment when "the world already declines and the prince of shepherds draws near."[2] He frequently focused in his sermons on the transitory nature of earthly life. He summarized Christian teaching about the "four last things" (death, judgment, heaven, and hell) this way:

> Here is the way the human being's miserable life runs: from the earth, on the earth, in the earth, from the earth into the fire, from the fire to judgment, from judgment either to Gehenna or to life (everlasting). You have been created from the earth, you tread the earth, you will be laid to rest in the earth, you will rise in the earth, you will be tried in fire, you will await the judgment, and then either torture or the kingdom of heaven will be yours forever.[3]

Even as Columbanus seems to give two parallel sequences, they are, slightly, different. The first sequence emphasizes personal salvation: from the earth back into the earth and then into the fire. In the second sequence, resurrection emerges between earth and fire, and a period of waiting before judgment. Columbanus emphasizes the fleeting nature of human life: it passes briefly, but its consequences are eternal. He hardly answers all the questions an ordinary person might have about these sequences. What does "everlasting life" look like? Where exactly is Gehenna? When will judgment take place? What is a trial in fire?

Over several centuries and a large geographical area, images and ideas to answer those questions accumulated. Historian Benjamin Hudson notes that there was "no uniformity of interpretation of eschatology, either personal or communal."[4] As missionaries spread throughout Europe, the imaginative possibilities of apocalypse and eschatology multiplied. Newly Christian peoples drew on more ancient legends and stories from their own mythologies, combined these with Christian teaching, and expanded the realms of the Christian imagination.

Altus Prosator

Irish and Scottish monasticism was particularly creative in its elaboration of eschatological materials. Located, as one seventh-century monk put it, "at the edge of the world," Irish and Scottish monks invented a language that combined Gaelic and Latin with a sprinkling of Greek and Hebrew.[5] They used this language to write poems with eschatological themes. One example is the long poem, perhaps composed by the founder of the monastery at Iona, St. Columba (d. 597), *Altus Prosator*.[6] The word "prosator" is an example of this invented vocabulary. It is not a Latin word or a Gaelic word but a kind of hybrid meaning "first sower," a metaphor for creator. The title thus means something like "High Creator." *Altus Prosator* retells the story of salvation from Genesis through Revelation in Hiberno-Latin poetry, which is what scholars call this hybrid language. Rendered this way, the entire Bible is condensed and translated into an elaborate poem. The poet writes a complete cosmic and salvation history from the primordial past to the future, writing himself and the reciter of the poem into this history while drawing from Greek mythology and the Psalms. The overall effect is one of awe and wonder, as if the poet has caught a glimpse of the "Most High" at work in all of time and space.

As in Revelation, eternal time and historical time merge in order to paint a picture of reality beyond reality.

> By the singing of hymns eagerly ringing out,
> by thousands of angels rejoicing in holy dances,
> and by the four living creatures full of eyes,
> With the twenty-four joyful elders,
> casting their crowns under the feet of the Lamb of God,
> the Trinity is praised with eternal three-fold exchanges.[7]

The entire Bible is translated through the lens of the throne of God as depicted in Revelation 6, as if the reader stood in this eternal place and so understood all of human history in light of it. But the poem is not entirely about eternity. Creation dominates the first half, and then seven of its twenty-three stanzas are devoted to the second coming and the judgment that follows it.

> We shall stand trembling before the Lord's judgment seat,
> and we shall render an account of all our deeds,
> seeing also our crimes placed before our gaze
> and the books of conscience thrown open before us.
> We will break out into most bitter weeping and sobbing,
> the possibility of repentance being taken away.[8]

Tombs break open, bones gather themselves together, and

"ethereal souls" go to join them. Stars fall and armies hide in caves. The adversaries are devoured by fire, while the righteous "abide in glory from age to age."

The poem is a deep and spiritual reading of the scriptures, not a literal one. At one point, the poet urges the reader to understand astrological signs as "types . . . understood figuratively." His reading of the Bible was based on the monastic practice of *lectio divina*, a form of spiritual reading that immersed the monk in the scriptures so that they might continually speak to the monk's heart and assist in his transformation.[9] The tension between literal and figurative readings has been, as we've seen, a significant one throughout the Christian tradition, and once again, here we feel that tension as the images work on our imaginations. The poet does not distinguish between the literal and figurative. He does not read history as allegory. Instead he maintains the tension so that we can feel the literal nature of our "crimes" and the allegorical nature of "judgment seat" for maximum emotional power.

And, as has so often been the case, the ultimate point of this eschatology is moral. The poem ends by asking its audience who will be righteous at the end of time: "Who can please God in the last time, / the noble ordinances of truth being changed, / except the despisers of this present world?" Little in the poem points to the mercy of God or the gentle humility of the monk. The correct moral deeds are not spelled out, except perhaps in this gesture toward asceticism: "despisers of this world." It is intended to fill its reader with fear and awe, and the poet hopes fear and awe will lead the reader to a transformed moral state.

Cross and Judgment

Doomsday or the last judgment became a central theme in Celtic poetry and art. Irish monumental crosses—an elaborate art form of which many exemplars remain in existence—often featured the crucifixion carved on one side of the cross and the last judgment on the other side. This choice sets the crucifixion in an eschatological context, an elaboration on the inverted warrior of biblical theology. Irish crosses do not depict Christ sitting on throne. Instead Christ is always standing. Scholars believe that this standing position reflects the cross/judgment theology that is central to the crosses' meaning: Christ crucified and Christ coming, as in Rev 1:7: "Look! He is coming with the clouds; every eye will see him, even those who pierced him."[10] These crosses express hope for the ultimate redemption of humanity. They are, art historian Kees Veelenturf believes, more consolation than warning, intended in sculpture form to give their viewers hope for the future with Christ.[11] We can see in them a familiar dichotomy from Pauline theology and from Revelation in which Christ is both lamb and victor, the paradox that drives Christian eschatology forward.

An Irish Eschatological Identity

Prior to the tenth century, a great deal of Irish eschatological literature concerned the fate of the individual—what would happen to body and soul after death—or imaginative excursions to other worlds, the subject of popular legend. But in the second half of the tenth century, Irish attention to the events of the end times sharpened.[12] The *Psalter of the Quatrains* was composed and distributed. In poetic form, it contained a summary of biblical history with fifteen signs that will occur in the week that leads to Doomsday. Other works elaborated on signs of the times and their correspondence to prophecy.[13]

In 1096, the combination of popular belief, imaginative elaboration, eschatological expectation, and existential dread came to a head in Ireland. The particular sequence of events began with a popular belief about an Irish druid named Mog Roith. Stories about this trickster druid placed him in various locations at different times in history.[14] One story had him in Jerusalem around the time of Christ and insisted that he was the executioner who cut off the head of John the Baptist. Irish people believed this action had put a curse on them and meant they would have a special price to pay on Judgment Day.

Another prophecy was added to this one. In this prophecy, which came from the *Vision of Adamnán*, a work dated to the eighth or ninth century, a pestilence was prophesied to come on a Friday near the day when John's beheading was commemorated (August 29). "Woe to harlots and sinners who will be burnt like hay and stubble, by a fire kindled in a bissextile leap year, and at the end of a cycle, and on the feast of the Decollation of John the Baptist," read one prophecy.[15]

Putting together these pieces of evidence, rumors began to circulate that in the year 1096 (a bissextile leap year, a year with an extra moon), the feast day of the beheading of John the Baptist would be the end of the world.[16] Indeed a terrible plague had begun in August of 1095, which confirmed the timing. Many people tried to undertake the "devout penance" required by the *Vision of Adamnán*, with regimens of extreme fasting and penance to prepare themselves for the wrath of God.

And of course, as would become something of a pattern for Christian people going forward, nothing happened. The predictions of specific times and dates, the collation of astrological signs with eschatological texts and with beliefs about the nature of God and his wrath, came to nothing. But what is notable about this heightened expectation is the way that it combined biblical texts, astrological observations, and popular legend to produce a reading of the world that was at once particularly Irish and at the same time universally Christian. Christian teachings mixed with Gaelic culture in eschatological tracts and stories that told of "fantastic trials and fantastic dangers."[17] Eschatology gave meaning to a particular historical and cultural moment.

Notes

1. Patrick, *Confessio,* c. 34, ed. L. Bieler, *Libri epistolarum sancti Patricii episcopi* (Dublin, 1993), 1:76. Translation by James Palmer in *The Apocalypse in the Early Middle Ages* (Cambridge: Cambridge University Press, 2014), 81.

2. Columbanus, *Epistola* 5.4, in *Scriptores Latini Hiberniae,* ed. G. S. M. Walker (Dublin: Dublin Institute for Advanced Studies, 1970), 2:40.

3. Columbanus, *De extremo judicio, Instructio* 9 , quoted in Jacques LeGoff, *The Birth of Purgatory,* trans. by Arthur Goldhammer (Chicago: University of Chicago Press, 1981), 100.

4. Benjamin Hudson, "Time Is Short: The Eschatology of the Early Gaelic Church," in *Last Things: Death and the Apocalypse in the Middle Ages,* ed. Caroline Walker Bynum and Paul Freedman (Philadelphia: University of Pennsylvania Press, 2000), 101.

5. Columbanus, *Ep.* 5.3, Walker (1970), 38.

6. Thomas Owen Clancy and Gilbert Márkus, *Iona: The Earliest Poetry of a Celtic Monastery* (Edinburgh: Edinburgh University Press, 1995), 39.

7. *Altus Prosator,* verse Y, ibid., 53.

8. *Altus Prosator,* verse S, ibid., 51.

9. Ibid., 42.

10. Kees Veelenturf, "Visions of the End and Irish High Crosses," in

Apocalyptic and Eschatological Heritage: The Middle East and Celtic Realms, ed. Martin McNamara (Portland, OR: Four Courts, 2003), 148.

11. Ibid., 173.

12. Hudson, 110.

13. Ibid., 111–12.

14. A druid is a magical figure in ancient Celtic religion and Irish mythology.

15. *Adamnán's Second Vision,* quoted in Veelenturf, 163.

16. Hudson, 116.

17. Ibid., 120.

12

Polemics: Bernard and Hildegard

O wretched slaves of Mammon, you cannot glory in the Cross of our Lord Jesus Christ while you trust in treasures laid up on earth: you cannot taste and see how gracious the Lord is, while you are hungering for gold. If you have not rejoiced at the thought of His coming, that day will be indeed a day of wrath to you.

—Bernard of Clairvaux, *On Loving God*

Jerusalem had been under Muslim control for four hundred years by the time Pope Urban II (1042–1099) surveyed the mythological and political landscape and decided that he had a decisive role to play. Western and eastern Christianities had experienced a final schism in 1054 when the Roman Pope Leo IX declared that all churches in his jurisdiction cede to the Latin rite or close. In response, the patriarch of Constantinople, Michael Cerularius, closed all Latin rite churches in his jurisdiction. It was the last straw in an age-old disagreement and ended in a final, mutual excommunication.

The First Crusade

Just a generation later, Pope Urban II set his sights on Jerusalem in what came to be called the First Crusade. Called to the Middle East by the beleaguered emperor of Byzantium, Pope Urban believed that the Crusade would be the beginning of the regeneration of the Christian church in the East. Medieval European Christians believed that Christianity had already reached the western limits of the world. If Christ's second coming was imminent, Christianity would have to spread back eastward to the lands "lost" to Muslims, Arabs, and Persians. Because the Holy Land was now occupied by unbelievers, the need to reconvert the east was paramount.

Furthermore, Jerusalem was the center of God's plan for the future. Jerusalem was the place where the Last Emperor would lay down his crown. The last judgment, many believed, would take place at the foot of Mt. Tabor, north of Jerusalem. Medieval maps also demonstrated how people had moved out of the Garden of Eden and spread to the edges of the world, but in the last days, they would need to move back toward the center, toward Jerusalem. All of the world would need to converge in order for the last judgment to take place. For this to happen, Jerusalem needed to be in the hands of the Christians. Crusades were thus, in part, a kind of spatial eschatology in action.[1]

The Byzantine emperor Alexios I was attempting to fend off an invasion by Muslims. In addition to helping Alexios, Urban expanded his objectives to the retaking of Jerusalem. In 1099, western troops advanced on Jerusalem and re-took the city. His goals were reconquest, followed by restoration and finally evangelization, each a necessary harbinger for the end of the world.[2] Urban died in 1099, before word of the victory could reach him. But his legacy continued in other crusades as European Christians struggled for dominance in the Holy Land.

Bernard of Clairvaux: Mystical and Political

Urban was a shrewd politician who could unite various forces behind his eschatological vision, but the church that he oversaw had as many interior squabbles as it did exterior battles. Even after Urban's successful crusade, the church's own internal conflicts became deeper. In 1130, a generation after Urban's death, one set of cardinals rebelled against the hasty election of Pope Innocent II, and they elected a rival pope, Anacletus II. He became known as an "antipope," in large part because of the effective use of eschatology as a polemical discourse deployed by his enemies, like the influential abbot Bernard of Clairvaux (1090–1153). Bernard was a man of both the cloister and the world. He had a deeply mystical and contemplative side, and an engaging and charismatic personality that made him a respected political and social figure as well as a man renowned for his holiness.

His eschatological worldview was just as complex as his personality. As an abbot in a contemplative order, it seems clear that Bernard believed that the ultimate destiny of the Christian was union with God. Especially for a monk, that destiny had little to do with worldly campaigns. On the other hand, he was engaged with the politics of his day to such an intense degree that his eschatological beliefs overlapped with the polemics and intrigues of his moment.

Bernard and the Antichrist

Bernard's version of the history of the church, following Gregory the Great, had four eras. He believed that he was living in the third: the era of internal hypocrisy, when the church was rife with falsehood. This was the precipice of the antichrist and of the fourth and final era. In one sermon, Bernard admonished, "I have given you sufficient warning to protect you from the wiles of three kinds of foxes, namely flatterers, detractors, and seducers of the spirit, who are skilled and practiced in representing evil in the guise of good."[3] These were the markers of the antichrist, and he often believed he saw them in his political enemies.

Bernard was a powerful rhetor, and he was not afraid of deploying the emotional resonances of eschatology against his enemies. For example, he often spoke about the antichrist in relation to Anacletus II. Bernard cast his opposition in the heightened rhetoric of eschatology, and this rhetorical strategy helped to gain power for his cause in these intense intra-institutional battles. "Bernard's views on the Antichrist," writes historian Roberto Rusconi, "seem to be the fruit not so much of his conceptions of eschatology as of his practical thoughts on the ecclesiastical politics of his day."[4] Bernard's deployment of eschatological figures and events was not always done in order to teach people about the end of time but instead to infuse the present with urgency and to use eschatology to create meaning in political skirmishes. And yet, his use of eschatological imagery was so effective that its influence far exceeded his own present moment, and so complex that it has left scholars puzzling over it ever since.[5]

The Second Crusade

Scholars have been particularly divided on the question of why, if Bernard's eschatology is primarily rhetorical, he supported the Second Crusade, an ultimately failed attempt to secure western power in the Middle East and stop the spread of the Muslim empire.

In 1145, pilgrims brought back news to Pope Eugene III (1080–1153), a Cistercian like Bernard, that the fragile "crusader states" that had formed after the First Crusade were under intense threat from Muslims. Pope Eugene announced the Second Crusade to aid them and commissioned Bernard to be his spokesperson in uniting the kings of Europe behind the crusade. His vision was for a much more centrally organized crusade than the first, and he looked to Louis VII of France and Conrad III of Germany to unite behind the mission.

Bernard approached Conrad III and hinted to him that his willingness to participate in the crusade had implications for the fulfillment of the prophecies of the Sibylline Oracles. After the First Crusade and the recapture of Jerusalem, there was renewed interest in these and other ancient prophetic documents. Perhaps this was the time to which they applied. Conrad, after all, styled himself as the "King of the Romans" and had ambitions for his family of laying claim to the title Holy Roman Emperor. In urging him to participate in the crusade, Bernard gave Conrad some eschatological context and urged him to think of the last judgment and his standing before Christ.[6]

But Bernard's eschatological interest in this campaign is hard to read. When he was asked to play this role by the pope, his health was poor, and he had every reason to decline politely. Throughout his life, he had maintained that the true monk has little interest in an earthly Jersualem. What difference would the city of Jerusalem make if the true Jerusalem was in heaven? He even resisted attempts by the pope to put Cistercian monasteries in Jerusalem, whereas everywhere else he was a passionate advocate for their expansion.[7] He argued that such projects were a distraction from the true work of monks. He described Clairvaux to a friend as "Jerusalem united to the one in heaven by whole-hearted devotion, by conformity of life, and by a certain spiritual affinity."[8] He did not need another.

Bernard himself, despite his extensive writings, did not spell out his reasons for supporting the Second Crusade. Some scholars have speculated that Bernard's support for the Second Crusade can be understood through his broader eschatology. In Christianity, eschatology has a twofold aspect. There are two kinds of endings: first, personal death; and second, the end of the world. Likewise, there is personal judgment and final judgment. Bernard perhaps perceived mystical union with God as twofold as well. There was the monk's own individual striving after God, and then there was the final reconciliation of God and humankind. After death, Bernard taught, the soul waits without its body for the Last Day, when "it will be finally reunited with a glorified body and be admitted into God's presence."[9] No matter how hard the individual monk works to achieve this union, it awaits the Last Day for this reception of the glorified body and the fullness of God's presence.

Bernard supported the soldiers marching on Jerusalem perhaps because he believed that through them, God was doing a great work that hastened this moment of unification. In a letter to encourage those engaged in battle, he wrote, "The earth trembles, because the Lord of heaven has now begun to loose his own land, the land in which he was seen for more than thirty years, as a man conversing with men. The land, his own, which he honoured with his birth, set to light with his miracles, consecrated with his blood, enriched with his burial. . . . The land, his own, in which the first flowers of the resurrection appeared."[10]

A Change in Orientation

The campaign failed. Conrad and Louis could not coordinate their efforts, and each was defeated separately by Muslim forces. The Second Crusade paved the way for the loss of Jerusalem in 1187. But little is recorded about Bernard's reaction to this failure. Some claim that he was deeply embittered by it.[11] Others note a distinct change in Bernard's eschatological orientation. Maria Wagner looks at the change, in particular, of his understanding of angels and their role both on earth and in heaven.[12] In contrast to his pre-Crusade position, in which angels were extremely active in human life, he began to argue that they had little role at all. Toward the end of his life, he all but renounced a belief in a Last Emperor and the unfolding of end times events in various worldly scenarios. Perhaps we can see a parallel to Paul in this shift. Paul spoke enthusiastically about the *parousia* early in his ministry, but by the end more often mentioned his anticipation of being with Christ in heaven. Bernard, too, came to emphasize the union of the monk with Christ.

Bernard's influence on his time and place was considerable. In many ways, his complex eschatology laid the groundwork for his contemporaries, like visionary and philosopher Hildegard of Bingen (1098–1179) and abbot Joachim of Fiore (1135–1202). Bernard was the "preeminent reformist apocalyptic," and he used eschatology to shape the changes he wanted to make in structures and politics, laying the groundwork for those who would want to do the same in the future.[13]

Hildegard of Bingen

"Two years ago, I saw you in my vision," Hildegard of Bingen

(1098–1179) wrote in her first letter to Bernard in 1147, "as a man able to look at the sun, and not be afraid." In this letter, she asked Bernard for advice, and implicitly for permission, on how to tell about the powerful visions that she experienced. She had been experiencing visions since she was a small child and had even begun attempting to write about them, but she had not yet shared them publicly. She believed that she was being led to do so, but as a woman, she was in an inherently vulnerable position.[14] Bernard wrote back, and eventually, with his help, Hildegard received personal permission from the pope to write and speak about her visions. When she referenced the Bible or Bernard's writings, she added her own visions and interpretations to them, and instead of acting as an exegete of biblical texts, as the tradition had often done, she treated her own visions as allegories and interpreted their symbols in original ways.[15]

"For I looked to the north," she wrote in her visionary theological work *Scivias*, "and behold, five beasts were standing there. . . . One was a fiery dog, but the dog was not on fire . . . one was a lion of tawny color . . . another beast was a sallow horse . . . another beast was a black pig . . . another beast was truly a grisly wolf. . . . All of the beasts were turning to the west."[16] She read these images in various ways, sometimes morally, sometimes politically, sometimes eschatologically. Like other apocalyptic images and symbols, their metaphoric nature allowed this multiplicity of meanings.

In some cases, she read these images as five historical ages. She spelled out what she thought each of these ages and beasts represented. She identified her own time as that of the "fiery dog," a time of ecclesiological immorality that will be followed by the "virile time" of the lion, in which the church would be purified. She saw the time of the tawny lion as a time of great flourishing when clerics would no longer crave worldly goods and "secular princes would rule in justice."[17] But ultimately, Hildegard did not believe that the ages of peace and prosperity could last long. She followed this age with more woe; the sallow horse, the black pig, and the grisly wolf brought the sin of pleasure, the blackness of sorrow, and a time when the kingdoms would be divided by greed. Human nature would not allow purity to reign long upon the earth.

But like Bernard, her visions were not entirely predictive of the future; they were also interpretive of the present. More prescription than description, they sought to influence the direction of the church. Robert Lerner calls Hildegard the "first prophet of social justice in the medieval West."[18] The originality of her voice and images allowed new material to be incorporated into older structures. She used multivalent images that could be read allegorically and were so compelling that people continue to read them prophetically to this day.[19]

Specifically, she used her visions to draw attention to political corruption within the church and to call for higher moral standards among the clergy. Her "prediction" of future rapaciousness among the kingdoms of the earth, for example, can just as easily be read as a diagnosis of the causes of contemporary divisions. Visionary theology allows the question of diagnosis and prediction not to be either/or but both/and. Hildegard's attempts to publicize her visions demonstrate that her work has to be understood in a polemical context, as well as in a mystical one.

Two Resurrections

In the art of the Middle Ages, there was perhaps no image of the resurrection more common than animals regurgitating whole human bodies. Depictions of the last judgment often show people emerging whole from the mouths of animals, arms and legs spewing forth. The twelfth century, Caroline Walker Bynum argues, was perhaps the highpoint in Christian tradition for absolute literalism and materialism in relation to resurrection of the body. "Images found in art, theology, and hagiography all suggest that salvation is reassembly or regurgitation of exactly the bodies we have on earth."[20]

Oddly then, perhaps, medieval people had no problem parsing up the bodies of saints into pieces that could be treasured as relics. Through its scattering, the body of a saint could do miracles in many places at once. Even if this seems contradictory to the principle of unity, it was in fact a confirmation that any part of the saint contained the whole. The body was the person, and the person was the body, even in the form of a finger or a toe or in some other relic.[21]

Belief that marks of sanctity could be found on the body was widespread. People believed, for example, that you could open up the body of a holy person and find the "wound of love" on their hearts, and they often went looking for these signs so that they could report on them during canonization proceedings. Scholasticism, a form of theology that dissected and parsed biblical texts in detail, provided an interesting philosophical foundation for this by drawing on the recently rediscovered philosophy of Aristotle to argue that the whole is embedded in the part. Bonaventure (1227–1274) argued that the whole self is somehow latent in its particles. God can thus reconstruct the whole from any of its parts.[22]

At the same time that saints' bodies were being so carefully examined and then so grotesquely—to our minds—treated and distributed, interest in the afterlife began to move in a direction that was not entirely religious. People began to investigate, for example, the exact nature of decay. The first autopsies were performed in the 1280s as a means to determine the cause of death. Universities began classes in anatomy beginning in 1320, which were based on the examination of cadavers. In the fourteenth century, when a saint whose soul-body was believed likely to produce miracles died, that person's body was boiled after death so that their relics—that is, the bits of their holiness—could be divided up more quickly and distributed. But the same period of time that saw a rise in interest in dividing up the holy bodies of saints for distribution saw a rise in the distribution of dead bodies for other than religious purposes.

While the new disciplines of anatomy and autopsy were beginning to treat the body as an object distinct from the soul, Bernard and Hildegard were developing a split on the spiritual side. For example, Hildegard often used organic metaphors for the soul but inorganic images for the body. Bynum points out that given Hildegard's interest in plants (she was a botanist and herbalist), she might have used organic metaphors for every aspect of human experience.[23] But instead, she reserved images of flowering and greening for the soul only. The body might be recast at the resurrection like a pot recast through fire, but the soul might flourish like a seed growing into a plant.[24]

Likewise, Bernard spoke of two resurrections. The resurrection of the soul takes place now, in the life of a believer, and the resurrection of the body takes place in the future. Bernard argued that the soul was nobler than the body, and that its resurrection, like its fall, was first. Concern for our bodies and for embodied life ought to be utterly secondary to care for the soul. In a series of sermons on Bernard's teachings, fellow Cistercian Herman of Reun emphasized the distinction between the inner and the outer man:

> Hearts and bodies rejoice together because, Christ rising, our inner man is freed from the death of sin and our exterior man is confirmed in the hope of his resurrection, of which he gives us an example. . . . Both are right to rejoice because each co-resurrects with Christ, the inner [man] in fact and the outer [man] in hope. . . . For now [we] rise *in mente* through the word of the son of God and then [we] will rise *in carne* through the word made flesh.[25]

A spiritual resurrection is immediate and available now. The enfleshed resurrection will come later. It gives the Christian a reason to live in hope. These examples suggest that as Christian eschatology developed in the Middle Ages, it began to split the body off from the soul, preparing the ground for belief in an eternal soul that might or might not require a literal resurrection of the body. This would have been literally anathema to earlier generations, but as knowledge about the body grew, this split increasingly made a kind of sense.

Notes

1. Laura Smoller, "Plague and the Investigation of the Apocalypse," in *Last Things: Death and the Apocalypse in the Middle Ages,* ed. Caroline Walker Bynum and Paul Freedman (Philadelphia: University of Pennsylvania Press, 2000), 159.

2. Paul Chevedden, "Pope Urban II and the Ideology of the Crusades," in *The Crusader World,* ed. Adrian Boas (New York: Routledge, 2016), 15.

3. Bernard of Clairvaux, Sermon 65.1.1, *On the Song of Songs III,* trans. Kilian Walsh and Irene M. Edmonds (Kalamazoo: Cistercian, 1979), 179.

4. Roberto Rusconi, "Antichrist and Antichrists," in *The Encyclopedia of*

Apocalypticism, ed. Bernard McGinn (New York: Continuum, 1998), 2:298.

5. Bernard McGinn, *Antichrist: Two Thousand Years of Human Fascination with Evil* (San Francisco: HarperSanFrancisco, 1994), 126.

6. See William of Saint-Thierry, *The First Life of Bernard of Clairvaux,* trans. Hilary Costello (Collegeville: Liturgical, 2015). For a contrasting view, see J. G. Kroemer, "The Eschatology of Bernard of Clairvaux," PhD diss. (Marquette University, 2000), 17–19; and Bernard McGinn, "St. Bernard and Eschatology," in *Bernard of Clairvaux: Studies Presented to Dom Jean Leclercq* (Washington, DC: Cistercian, 1973), 161–85.

7. Peter Raedts, "St. Bernard de Clairvaux and Jerusalem," in *Prophecy and Eschatology,* ed. Michael Wilks (Oxford: Blackwell, 1994), 173.

8. Bernard of Clairvaux, "To Alexander, Bishop of Lincoln," *The Letters of St. Bernard of Clairvaux,* trans. Bruno Scott James (Chicago: Regnery, 1953), 91.

9. Maria Wagner, "The Impact of the Second Crusade on the Angelology and Eschatology of Saint Bernard of Clairvaux," in *The Journal of Religious History* 37/3 (September 2013): 328.

10. Bernard, *Epp.* 343 and 358, *SBO* 8, pp. 312 and 435, quoted in Raedts, 179.

11. This is an argument made in Kroemer, "The Eschatology of Bernard of Clairvaux."

12. Wagner, 335.

13. E. Randolph Daniel, "Exodus and Exile: Joachim of Fiore's Apocalyptic Scenario," in *Last Things,* 126.

14. Hildegard of Bingen, "Letter to St. Bernard of Clairvaux (1147)," at http://www.cengage.com/music/book_content/049557273X_wrightSimms/assets/ITOW/7273X_05_ITOW_Hildegard.pdf.

15. Robert E. Lerner, "Millennialism," in *The Encyclopedia of Apocalypticism* 2:341; and Charles M. Czarski, "Kingdoms and Beasts: The Early Prophecies of Hildegard of Bingen," *Journal of Millennial Studies* 1/2 (Winter 1999): 1.

16. Hildegard von Bingen, *Mystical Visions,* trans. from *Scivias* by Bruce Hozeski (Santa Fe: Bear, 1986), 3.11.1–6, 346–47.

17. Lerner, 341.

18. Ibid.

19. See, for example, a contemporary popular Catholic eschatology, Reid J. Turner, *The Five Beasts of St. Hildegard: Prophetic Symbols of Modern Society* (Self-published, 2014).

20. Caroline Walker Bynum, *The Resurrection of the Body 200-1336* (New York: Columbia University Press, 1995), 223.

21. Ibid., 205.

22. Ibid., 241.

23. Ibid., 158.

24. Ibid., 176.

25. Herman of Reun, *Sermones festivales*, ed. Edmund Mikkers et al. (CCCM 64; Turnhout: Brepols, 1986), sermon 24 (p. 97) and sermon 25 (pp. 102–3).

13

Patterns: Joachim of Fiore

"But," he said, "the God who once gave the spirit of prophecy to
the prophets has given me the spirit of understanding, so that in
God's Spirit I very clearly understand all the mysteries of Holy
Scripture, just as the holy prophets understood who once wrote
it down in God's Spirit."
— Ralph of Coggeshall, writing about Joachim of Fiore

Near midnight at the feast of Easter in the mid-twelfth century,
in the abbey of a Cistercian monastery in southern Italy, an
abbot awoke with a profound spiritual vision. Joachim of Fiore
(1135–1202) had been studying Revelation for a commentary
that he hoped to write, but the more he wrestled with the text,
the less he understood it. The symbols were too difficult and
too entangled. He had all but given up when this new vision
came to him. His vision was that Revelation offered the key
to understanding the harmony of all scripture and even all
history—past, present, and future. The reason he had not been
able to discern its meaning was because he was thinking too

small. This new insight allowed him to think in a way that was comprehensive and intricate at the same time and thus opened up new vistas of prophetic knowledge. Most especially, it allowed Joachim to see God's patterned development of human history.

A New Exegesis

Joachim, like others of his day, treated texts like later scientists might treat the anatomy of an animal. He picked them apart in order to apprehend them in the most detailed way possible. Joachim studied scripture as well as the work of philosophers, prophets, and astronomers. Using his insight into Revelation as the book that provided what he called the "concord" between the Old and New Testaments, he mapped these onto known historical records and created an elaborate typology of history, which could in turn be used to read the future. Joachim's innovation was to take biblical texts, the random collection of Christian hopes and legends, and a vague belief in a God-ordained pattern to history and turn this into a discipline that produced a "coherent and articulated philosophy of history" such that Christianity had not seen before. He was, Morton Bloomfield claims, the "first systematic thinker about the nature and meaning of history."[1]

Joachim's two influential works, *Exposition of the Apocalypse* and *Concord of the New and Old Testaments*, used Revelation as the linchpin to understanding God's pattern for historical development. This allowed the informed reader to interpret the past and anticipate the future. We've already seen how important the two ages theory was to both Jewish apocalypticism and Pauline theology. The present age is the age of Satan. It is the age that is always on the verge of ending and whose demise has been preached by the prophets since time immemorial. The second age is the age of Christ's victory, whether this is imagined as a one thousand-year millennium or as an eternal paradise. But Joachim added a third age and took Satan out of the picture. His three ages were the ages of the Father, the Son, and the Holy Spirit. The first age ran from the creation of Adam and Eve until the birth of Christ. The age of the Son lasted from the birth of Christ until Joachim's own time. The third age was just beginning, the age of the Holy Spirit. Each age overlapped the other by a few hundred years, so Joachim found in the Old Testament key events which signaled the beginning of the age of the Son, just as there were events in the history previous to Joachim's own time that portended the age of the Holy Spirit.

In addition to each age corresponding to a particular member of the Trinity, each age also corresponded to a particular way of life that was blessed by God above others. The first age was the age of the married. The second was the age of the clergy. But the third age would be the age of the monk. Monasticism would prove to be the way forward. He called each form of life a *status*, and each was an organic entity "sprouting from each other overlapping, and progressively moving step by step from the world of the married and the promise that the Hebrews would conquer the land of Palestine, to the ultimate virginal monastic contemplatives whose 'conquest' would be the complete peace and silence in which to contemplate God."[2] Each age involved liberation, journey, and conquest, but in the last age, these would be the work of the soul. The meaning of each age became progressively more spiritual and less literal and material.

The seven seals of Revelation provided the "fullness of history," and Joachim looked for *concordia* between the two testaments that allowed him to determine patterns for the third age.[3] Using the *concordia*, a reader "could look back from a 'mountain peak' and, by seeing the road that had been traveled, discern the main shape of the road that still lay ahead. To reveal the concords and interpret them was the task that God had given Joachim."[4] He had been given the gift of spiritual understanding, and he must help to cultivate this in others.

A Progressive Understanding of History

Even though history became progressively more inward, it also involved external events. Like many previous readers of Revelation, Joachim saw that the book's symbols mapped well onto events of his own day, and he believed that the book revealed the end of the age of the Son. The antichrist, he argued following in Gregory's footsteps, would be a universal pope who would have dominion over the whole earth. His research suggested that this person had already been born and was on the earth. He rejected the apocryphal teachings about the antichrist and was not interested in the legendary imaginings of some of his predecessors. Using his patterns of history, he tried to reconcile the biblical use of both antichrists and antichrist.[5] There were antichrists like Herod, Nero, and Muhammad. But there would eventually be one antichrist, the "Seventh King," who would be the greatest of them all. He believed that the antichrist's precursor was Saladin, the Muslim warrior who had recaptured Jerusalem in the siege of 1187. The antichrist would arise from within the church and partner with Saladin or someone like him, and together they would take over the church. If the inward journey involved liberation and conquest, Joachim saw that the outward journey included exodus and exile, and this included those who worked to reform the church and all the righteous.[6]

But there was still hope for the church, and that hope was not in the past but in the future. It was not a matter of recovering past practices or celebrating the martyrs of history. History, Joachim saw, had a progressive movement. This is an aspect of Joachim's thought that was fundamentally anti-Augustinian. In Augustine's view, the world, in its old age, accumulated woes until the saving coming of Christ. But in Joachim's thought, God was still at work shaping and transforming the world.[7] So monasticism had the work of reforming the church and bringing it to perfection in the age of the Holy Spirit. The inner journey that monks took was not a journey undertaken for the salvation of the individual soul but on behalf of the whole church.[8]

Joachim's Influence

Marjorie Reeves points out that Joachim did not have only one theory of history. He was continuously working out the details of several that overlapped and intertwined. With three ages and two *tempora* and multiple patterns of five and seven, he was trying to untangle events from one another and assign them their proper place on his map.[9] Joachim allowed that one symbol in Revelation could have multiple meanings and apply at different moments, or several different symbols could all apply to the same event. Joachim's map was something like a topographical map where certain points have height and depth that others did not.

Joachim's map itself did not have a great deal of staying power. As events occurred, the map itself outlived its usefulness. But Joachim made several key contributions nonetheless that had a great deal of influence on Christian understanding of the future. One was his break from Augustinian theology that opened the church up to reform based on eschatological reasoning. Augustine had placed eschatology in the realm of mystery. A person could have opinions about it, but those opinions should not be used to direct the church as a whole. In Joachim's theory of ages, the monk could criticize the clergy based on a progressive theory of history and an understanding of eschatology.

Another legacy of Joachim's three stages was the sense that time was always in transition. If history is always moving, then we are always at a moment of change. Joachim enhanced the sense that Europeans were "living at a turning-point in time."[10] This sense of transition, crisis, or forward motion has accompanied European Christianity to the present. The present is merely a transition. The real unfolding of time is ever so slightly ahead of us. Frank Kermode asserts that an "end-dominated age of transition has passed into our consciousness, and modified our attitudes to historical pattern."[11] Following Joachim, we try to see the process from the perspective of the end, from Joachim's traveler's mountain top.

The Spiritual Franciscans

One group of reformists within the church picked up Joachim's ideas and gave them immediate application. This group is often called the Spiritual Franciscans. During his lifetime, Joachim did not see the fruit of his work on reformation of the church. But with the arrival of Francis of Assisi (1181–1226), many of Joachim's followers saw Joachim's schema at work. Francis was an exemplar of the monk on an inward journey, facing exile and renunciation but also transforming the church as he transformed himself.

Today we rarely think of Francis as an eschatological figure. To us, he is the radical reformer whose chosen life of poverty, tender care for animals, and gentleness have made him the beloved figure found in garden statues. The prayer attributed to him says nothing about the end of the world but instead offers moral instruction. But in the thirteenth century, Francis's critique of the church was so powerful that it could only be eschatological. His reform movement, which began during Joachim's lifetime, seemed to herald Joachim's third age. He himself did not claim an eschatological place in the scheme of things, but after his death, some of his followers claimed that he was the angel of the sixth seal of Revelation. M. H. Abrams called the Spiritual Franciscans the promoters of a "militant program of radical political, as well as moral and religious, reform, which has had a recurrent influence on revolutionary thinking."[12] Francis introduced a new kind of religious order, one in which devotees were called friars or mendicants instead of monks. Friars were more itinerant than monks had been traditionally, and they gained a reputation for a greater commitment to poverty.

Those who combined Joachim's and Francis's work, the Spiritual Franciscans, put considerable pressure on the church hierarchy and acted as inspiration for future church reformers.[13] These were friars, and they claimed the distinction of being the harbingers of Joachim's third age. In the early part of the thirteenth century, these reformers pinpointed Emperor Frederick II Hohenstaufen (1194–1250) as the antichrist, per Joachim's description. "What other Antichrist should we await," wrote an unnamed monk in Cardinal Ranier of Viterbo's circle, "when, as is evident in his works, he is already come in the person of Frederick? He is the author of every crime, stained by every cruelty and he has invaded the patrimony of Christ, seeking to destroy it with Saracen (Muslim) aid."[14]

Frederick died before his identity as the antichrist could be confirmed. But the conflict continued to intensify, although now Frederick became the "precursor" to the antichrist, or in a gruesome imitation of Christ's resurrection, his return from hell was predicted. In turn, Frederick's circle began to use antichrist language to refer to the popes, calculating Innocent IV's name so that it equaled 666, the number in Revelation used to refer to "the beast," who, in this amplified tradition, was equivalent to the antichrist.[15] This demonization of one's opponents in eschatological terms was, of course, an ancient tradition. What was different with the Spiritual Franciscans was the brazen way that they named their opponents, not concealing their rhetoric behind elaborate symbols but instead using those same symbols to reveal the true evil.

Another legacy of Joachite Franciscans was the use of Joachim's work against the clergy. As we saw, Joachim claimed that the age of the clergy was coming to an end, and the age of the monks was on the rise. This provided the new religious orders that arose following Francis with fodder to criticize the more established clergy. But by claiming to be the true coming of the third age, these mendicants also opened themselves up to attack by clergy when their "human failings" were revealed.[16] One Franciscan follower of Joachim, for example, wrote a book called *Introduction to the Eternal Gospel*, in which he claimed that the second *status* of Joachim was ending and that in the third *status* the established church would be destroyed. It would be replaced by a spiritual church headed, of course, by the Franciscans.[17] This infuriated the clergy, who used such writings to claim the Franciscans heretical and made *them* the forerunners of the antichrist. And so the rhetoric went.

Peter Olivi's Antichrist

In the late 1200s, one particularly powerful Spiritual Franciscan came to the fore. Peter Olivi (1248–1298) was a mendicant, an apocalyptic propagandist, a Scholastic theologian, and a charismatic leader.[18] Olivi's attempts at clerical and ecclesiastical reform made him increasingly apocalyptic. He came to believe that the only hope of reform would come through events of an apocalyptic nature. He saw the forces of good and evil within Christian society coming to a head in the year 1300. To Joachim's schema, Olivi added a "mystical Antichrist" who was not a person but a group active among his contemporaries within the church. Olivi's image of the antichrist developed in such a way that it held together many of the previous contradictions that such a figure carried. He was Christian and non-Christian, clergy and lay, individual and collective. He was a tyrant and a heretic all at the same time.[19]

The key to Olivi's image of the antichrist, however, was wealth. The Spiritual Franciscans had created a deep divide in the increasingly wealthy church about the nature of that wealth. Following Francis's example, they preached poverty as a mark of righteousness. By corollary, wealth was, at best, a marker of moral failing and at worst, a sign of the antichrist. Olivi himself preached a strict level of poverty for friars. Working within the tradition but also innovating, Olivi articulated a vision of a papal antichrist that was to be influential deep into the Reformation. His antichrist was the enemy of poverty and the friend of wealth. From Olivi forward, whenever a pope or a cardinal flaunted his wealth, this image of the antichrist lurked for critics and reformers.

Notes

1. Morton Bloomfield, "Recent Scholarship on Joachim of Fiore and His Influence," in *Prophecy and Millenarianism: Essays in Honour of Marjorie Reeves* (Harlow: Longman, 1980), 23.

2. Ibid., 134.

3. See Marjorie Reeves, "The Seven Seals in the Writings of Joachim of Fiore," *Recherches de théologie ancienne et médiévale* 22 (1954): 211–31.

4. E. Randolph Daniel, "Exodus and Exile: Joachim of Fiore's Apocalyptic Scenario," in *Last Things: Death and the Apocalypse in the Middle Ages*, ed. Caroline Walker Bynum and Paul Freedman (Philadelphia: University of Pennsylvania Press, 2000), 132.

5. Bernard McGinn, *Antichrist: Two Thousand Years of the Human Fascination with Evil* (New York: Harper Collins, 1994), 138.

6. Daniel, 137.

7. McGinn, 137.

8. Ibid., 136.

9. Majorie Reeves, *The Influence of Prophecy in the Later Middle Ages: A Study in Joachimism* (Oxford: Clarendon, 1969), 5–6.

10. Ruth Kenstenberg Gladstein, "The Third Reich," *Journal of the Warburg and Courtauld Institutes* (1955), quoted in Frank Kermode, *The Sense of an Ending* (New York: Oxford University Press, 1967), 14.

11. Kermode, 14.

12. M. H. Abrams, "Apocalypse: Theme and Variations," in *The Apocalypse in English Thought and Literature: Patterns, Antecedents, Repercussions*, ed. C. A. Patrides and Joseph Anthony Wittreich (Manchester: Manchester University Press, 1984), 349.

13. David Burr, *Spiritual Franciscans: From Protest to Persecution in the Century after Francis* (University Park: Pennsylvania State University Press, 2001). McGinn says that it is not proper to speak of an actual

party of Spiritual Franciscans until the end of the thirteenth century, but we use the term here to help us trace a trajectory. McGinn, 159.

14. Quoted in McGinn, 154.

15. Ibid. This was a common move among twentieth-century apocalypticists as well, who calculated the names of Ronald Reagan, Saddam Hussein, and others to 666. See Paul Boyer, *When Time Shall Be No More* (Cambridge: Harvard University Press, 1992), 276.

16. McGinn, 158.

17. Ibid.

18. Ibid., 159.

19. Ibid., 161.

14

Circles: Dante Alighieri

The glory of the One who moves all things
permeates the universe and glows
in one part more and in another less.
I was within the heaven that receives
more of His light; and I saw things that he
who from that height descends, forgets or can
not speak; for nearing its desired end,
our intellect sinks into an abyss
so deep that memory fails to follow it.

—Dante Aligheiri

"When I had journeyed half of our life's way, I found myself within a shadowed forest, for I had lost the path that does not stray," Dante Alighieri (1265–1321) wrote in the opening to his epic poem the *Commedia*.[1] In the woods, Dante (the narrator of the poem) met his hero, the poet Virgil, who offered to take him on a journey "through an eternal place," where Dante could also undergo a journey of personal transformation.

The poet Dante was, like his narrator, in his own dark wood.

Dante had been a powerful political figure in his native city of Florence. He was one of six governing priors in a deeply divided city. One intense point of contention was the amount of authority that Rome should have in Florence. Dante was among those seeking more autonomy, and when the opposing group took power in 1302, Dante was exiled. He spent the rest of his life as an outsider and a wanderer, never returning to Florence.

While the conditions of Dante's exile are radically different from those of John of Patmos, exile stimulated and elaborated Dante's vision. The root of Dante's vision, like John's, was longing—longing for his enemies to be vanquished, longing for a true homecoming, longing to see his people made whole and no longer suffering, longing for love to be complete, longing to see his now-dead beloved Beatrice. Unlike John, Dante was a classically trained poet with the intricacies of Italian, his native language, at his command. Also unlike John, Dante did not tell readers that his vision was a direct message from God. He created a three-part *commedia*, an elaborate and dramatic fiction, in which a single soul, Dante, is taken on a journey through hell, purgatory, and heaven, with Virgil as his guide through hell and purgatory and Beatrice taking him through heaven.

Dante's Circles

Dante imagined hell as an inverted cone; each circle encloses less space than the one above it. Purgatory is a pillar, also of narrowing circles, but it ascends rather than descends. Paradise is like the orbits of planets moving outward from the earth. Dante detailed this spatial eschatology, populating each circle of each realm with politicians, figures from the Bible and from Greek mythology, his own friends and family, and poets.

Dante did not claim direct divine revelation, but he did articulate a journey of the soul that was at once intimate and cosmic. The placement of individuals in the eternal topography was more important than prophecies and timelines. But Dante did try to situate his version of eternity within classic Christian teachings about the last judgment. In Canto VI of *Inferno*, Dante encountered an old friend, Ciacco, who was in one of the upper levels of hell for the sin of gluttony. After Dante and Ciacco discuss the outcome of Florentine politics, Virgil tells Dante that Ciacco will now sleep until "the blast of the angelic trumpet" (*Inferno* 6.95). Then he will regain his body and return to hell. Dante asked Virgil if, at the resurrection, "after the great sentence"—that is, the last judgment—Ciacco's suffering would be lessened or greater. Virgil answered,

> Remember now your science
>   which says that when a thing has more perfection,
>   so much greater is its pain or pleasure.
> Though these accursed sinners never shall
>   attain the true perfection, yet they can
>   expect to be more perfect then than now. (*Inferno* 6.106–11)

According to Virgil, the resurrection is a step toward perfection, and perfection increases feeling. This is an interesting contrast with Augustinian eschatology, which held that the resurrected body is likewise more perfect but less subject to emotion. It is perhaps a hint that Dante's poetry was a step toward Romanticism that would, by the nineteenth century, highlight and celebrate human feeling as akin to divine feeling. From this passage, we also understand that in cosmic or eschatological time, Dante's journey took place on the "long road between death and the general resurrection."[2]

The Soul's Journey

Dante's "fiction of judgment" is paradoxical. It claims to known the unknowable, to imagine the unimaginable, and to give words to the ineffable. The authority the poet claims in his poem is extreme. He condemns his enemies, by name, to hell. He claims to know exactly the nature of right and wrong, heaven and hell, and in between. And by what authority? This is not clear. He "repeatedly transgresses the limits inscribed by the biblical apocalypse tradition," Claudia Rattazi Papka writes.[3] This tradition often stops in its tracks to describe the limits of its own seeing. We know that Augustine followed Paul on this, objecting to texts like the *Apocalypse of Paul*, which claimed sight of "things which cannot and must not be put into human language."[4] John of Patmos also saw the Book of Life opened, but did not tell his readers what was written there (Rev 20:11–15). But Dante did not stop. Because he was writing a sort of fiction, he did not limit his imagination and claimed more territory than his canonical predecessors. This does not mean that what he wrote was false. It simply claimed a different and subtler kind of authority that drew its power from language itself.

The purpose of the soul's journey was love, not knowledge. Dante was put on this journey by his lost love, Beatrice, because, Virgil told Dante, Beatrice feared that bitterness, acrimony, and loss were causing Dante to lose the way of love. "Love," Beatrice told Virgil when she commissioned him, "prompted me, that Love which makes me speak" (*Inferno* 2.72). She would have Dante learn that love is the force that "moves the sun and the other stars" (*Paradiso* 33.145). And in order for love to be made perfect, there would have to be a resurrection. Humans need bodies in order to love fully.

Purgatory

In Dante's hell and purgatory, there are no physical bodies.[5] The work of purgatory, as Dante had it, was to prepare the self for the full restoration of paradise, and the fullest form of paradise was an embodied one. In order for that preparation to take place, the person, in the form of a "shade," had to endure purgatory. Purgatory was an idea in Christian understanding that had only recently gained a name and an official doctrine. Pope Innocent IV (1243–1254) first gave the concept a name. To the bishop of Tusculum, he wrote, "We, following the tradition and authority of the holy Fathers, call that place [of purification] purgatory."[6]

As Innocent's words indicate, the idea was not entirely new. Innocent himself drew on 1 Corinthians 3:13–15: "Fire will test what sort of work each has done. . . . If the work is burned up, the builder will suffer loss; the builder will be saved, but only as through fire." Augustine had spoken of purgatorial fires and imagined that souls would need to go somewhere and do something to be purged of sin before entering paradise. And the idea had percolated in popular culture for a long time, becoming codified through scholastic elaboration of hierarchies and orders—what Jacques LeGoff has called the "spatialization of thought."[7]

Purgatory became defined as a "transitory fire" that cleansed certain kinds of sins.[8] It was a place in the afterlife where souls went to become ready to enter paradise, and throughout the Middle Ages, imagination about the kinds of punishments that took place there flourished. Each now-thoroughly-individualized soul underwent a specialized program in the afterlife that could address his or her specific sins. Sin itself was broken into pieces so that each individual piece could be addressed separately. There were purgatorial programs for greed and lust, for jealousy and gluttony, that usually involved some kind of quasi-physical persecution. Liars had their tongues cut out, gluttons were forced to drink poison, and so on.

Purgatory also increased the traffic between the living and the dead and, as such, created an entirely new economy for churches. People came to church to help to pray their dead out of purgatory. Masses in the name of a specific person, for which a priest was paid, helped the dead person pay off some of his or her debt; prayers helped too, and medieval people, especially the wealthy, often made bequests to a priest or a mendicant to pray on their behalf after their deaths. The doctrine of purgatory also increased anxiety, however. While it did increase hope for the otherwise potentially damned, it also required the living to do a great deal on behalf of the dead.[9]

Shades and Bodies

Purgatory involved a very complex relationship between the material body and the soul, a problem that had long existed in Christianity, as we have seen. By the twelfth century, "person" was used to refer to a unity that included both body and soul. Caroline Walker Bynum calls the journey of the soul, as imagined in the Middle Ages, a "somatomorphic" one in which the body undergoes some kind of change but also retains some kind of continuity.[10] The concept of the self, Bynum says, was one "in which physicality was integrally bound to sensation, emotion, reasoning, and identity—and therefore to whatever one means by salvation."[11] Medieval people could not imagine a "soul" wandering through the afterlife without some kind of physical form.

The soul-body of purgatory Dante called a "shade." The physical forms that Dante saw in purgatory were not complete, and their state of being was temporary. They were vessels in the process of being melted down. In Canto 21 of *Purgatorio*, the pagan poet Statius confesses his love for Virgil, the poet who is Dante's guide. When Statius realizes that he is in the presence of Virgil, he falls at his feet. "Brother," Virgil said, "there's no need— / you are a shade, a shade is what you see."

In his answer to Virgil, Statius gives a hint of the difference between the physical "reality" of purgatory and that of paradise. "Now you can understand," he says to Virgil, "how much love burns in me for you, when I / forget our insubstantiality, / treating the shades as one treats solid things" (*Purgatorio* 21.131–36). The difference between the reality of purgatory and the reality of paradise is love. Love, in the *Commedia*, is the ultimate reality, and love is what transforms those in purgatory into the fuller body-soul form of paradise. In paradise, the saved regain "the beloved and whole body of earth, expressing the person in its every detail and sensual experience."[12] For Dante, the reason that we must regain our bodies in paradise is because we need them to experience and express love. Love is the meaning, the *telos*, of human existence and of the journey that the soul Dante had undertaken. Dante's own metaphor for this was the caterpillar and the butterfly. The body in paradise is the butterfly's body, the one that flies to God after its life as a worm (*Purgatorio* 10).

The Beatific Vision

As an exile, restoration was Dante's greatest longing. He longed for the dead Beatrice, and so restored her to fuller-than-human glory in paradise. He longed for the lost Florence so he created a holy city through which he traveled with Beatrice as his guide. But the end of his journey was not, finally, restoration. He longed for Florence, but did not return. He and Beatrice did not settle down, even in his imagination, to a happily ever after. Instead Dante's vision, in the end, turned away from Beatrice and Florence toward the divine. As Dante reached the Empyrean, the highest part of heaven, Dante's vision, which had been so steady through all the realms of the other world, faltered.

> As the geometer intently seeks
> to square the circle, but he cannot reach
> through thought on thought, the principle he needs,
>
> so I searched that strange sight: I wished to see
> the way in which our human effigy
> suited the circle and found place in it—
> and my own wings were far too weak for that.
> But then my mind was struck by a light that flashed
> and, with this light, received what it had asked.
> Here force failed my high fantasy; but my
> desire and will were moved already—like
> a wheel revolving uniformly—by
> the Love that moves the sun and the other stars.
> (*Paradiso* 33.133–45).

The final vision was the failure of vision. The final seeing was to have one's own will and desire revolving like the planets with the motion of love.

What Dante described in the final canto of *Paradiso* is what scholars have called the **beatific vision**—the ability to see God through no will or work of one's own. The beatific vision was a crucial part of the eschatology developing in the Middle Ages to answer at least one of the persistent questions about life after death and before the last judgment: When does a soul purged of sin meet God? The idea was largely introduced by Augustine in the fifth century. In *City of God*, he wrote that in heaven "we shall rest and see, see and love, love and praise. Behold what will be, in the end to which there shall be no end."[13] Dante envisioned this at the end of *Paradiso*, when all the righteous are absorbed with seeing and feeling the love of God.

In some ways, what Dante proposed here was a soul that could have a full experience of God without a bodily form. Dante did believe that we have to have our bodies to love, but he ended the *Commedia* with a mystical insight into the nature of all reality—one that feels to the poet like trying to square a circle, so different was it from the ordinary and known life.

The beatific vision—the opportunity for the purged soul to see God—was a development of the late thirteenth and early fourteenth centuries and was in some ways the outcome of the doctrine of purgatory. It revealed the conflict between the ancient doctrine of resurrection of the dead and the question of the afterlife. If the purged soul had the opportunity at the end of its suffering to see God, and if this vision of God can come to a soul on its own without a body, then what did the body add to blessedness? What remained incomplete? "Theologians, poets, and visionaries imagined the soul that achieved beatitude as if it already in some way possessed, or expressed itself in its body," Bynum writes.[14] That soul did not need to await the resurrection.[15]

After Dante, in the fourteenth century, people began to speak about the relationship between the soul and the body like the relationship between lovers. They were connected by desire. The body was something like a "beloved bride, rewarded with gifts particular to her because of her experience and merit on earth."[16] A soul in the afterlife yearned for its body like one lover might yearn for another. The soul was embodied in its journey through the afterlife but in a metaphoric fashion that was different from the discussion of substances that had dominated earlier Christian thinkers. Corpses were now imagined as separate entities that were enlivened and animated by souls. Bodies now rose whole from the grave, not reassembled or disgorged. The body, as per the scholastic theologian Thomas Aquinas, was an expression of the soul, its "overflow, the gesture that manifests the soul's intention."[17] But the soul was more primary.

Notes

1. *Inferno* 1.1–3. All translations are from Dante Alighieri, *The Divine Comedy*, trans. Allen Mandelbaum (New York: Knopf, 1984).

2. Harvey Stahl, "Heaven in View: The Place of the Elect in an Illuminated Book of Hours," in *Last Things: Death and the Apocalypse in the Middle Ages,* ed. Caroline Walker Bynum and Paul Freedman (Philadelphia: University of Pennsylvania Press, 2000), 204.

3. Claudia Rattazi Papka, "The Limits of Apocalypse: Eschatology, Epistemology and Textuality in the *Commedia* and *Piers Plowman,*" in *Last Things,* 233.

4. Augustine, *Tracates on John* 98.8, trans. John Gibb in *Nicene and Post-Nicene Fathers,* First Series, vol. 7, ed. Philip Schaff (Buffalo: Christian Literature, 1888). Online at http://www.newadvent.org/fathers/1701098.htm.

5. Caroline Walker Bynum, *The Resurrection of the Body 200–1336* (New York: Columbia University Press, 1995), 300.

6. Quoted in John F. Clarkson et al., eds. *The Church Teaches: Documents of the Church in English Translation* (St. Louis: Herder, 1955), 347.

7. Jacques LeGoff, *The Birth of Purgatory,* trans. Arthur Goldhammer (Chicago: University of Chicago Press, 1984), 3.

8. "Transitory fire" is a phrase from ibid., 102.

9. Ibid., 17.

10. Bynum, 319.

11. Ibid., 11.

12. Ibid., 302.

13. Augustine, *The City of God against the Pagans* 22.30, trans. R. W. Dyson (Cambridge: Cambridge University Press, 1998), 1182.

14. Bynum, 279.

15. This argument was not universal. A key moment of transition was the *visio dei* controversy of the fourteenth century when Pope John XXII preached that all souls would have to wait for final blessedness until after the last judgment. His view was strongly dismissed by contemporaries. See Alexa Sand, *Vision, Devotion, and Self-Representation in Late Medieval Art* (Cambridge: Cambridge University Press, 2014), 73–74, for a clear explanation of the controversy and its implications.

16. Ibid., 319.

17. Ibid.

15

Visions: Julian of Norwich and the Black Plague

All shall be well, and all manner of thing shall be well.

—Julian of Norwich

Rumors of a destructive plague began to spread in Italy in the summer of 1347. By then, the plague that had killed 15 million Chinese had spread along the Silk Road to Constantinople. It reached Italy in the spring of 1348. The writer Giovanni Boccacio described the symptoms in his famous book the *Decameron*.

> Here the sickness began in both men and women with swelling in the groin and armpits. The lumps varied in size, some reaching the size of an ordinary apple and others that of an egg, and the people commonly called them *gavoccioli*. Having begun in these two parts of the body, the *gavoccioli* soon began to appear at random all over the body. After this point the disease started to alter in nature, with black or livid spots appearing on the

arms, the thighs, everywhere. Sometimes they were large and well spaced, other times small and numerous. These were a certain sign of impending death, but so was the swelling. No doctor's advice, no medicine seemed to be of any help.[1]

The plague spread quickly and devastatingly. It killed a third of the human population in Europe, and perhaps as many as 200 million people worldwide.

Making Meaning from Disaster

For Christians, the plague raised questions that seemed to have no answers. The ritual of last rites, in which the priest offered the dying person one last absolution of sin before they crossed over to the other side, had become a way to offer protection to the soul on this perilous journey. But the waves of plague meant that millions of people could not receive last rites. There simply was no time and no capacity. Priests were among those most hard hit by plague and died in large numbers. The whole society reeled with the problem of how to make sense of so much suffering and death. Was it the wrath of God? Was it a sign of the end of the world?

As people struggled to reconcile these events with their religious beliefs and assumptions, they dipped deeply into the well of eschatology. The imagery of plague became what historian Laura Smoller has described as an "an endless web of free associations in which earthquakes, snakes, and toads served simultaneously as metaphors for corruption, apocalyptic signs, and natural causes of disease."[2] Signs were read as both supernatural and natural at the same time. On the one hand, medieval authors seemed to be attempting to bring the disease under the control of human knowledge. They explained it in terms of vapors and bad airs and humors. On the other hand, their explanations seemed to draw them ever more into a language that had been pre-established, a language of "eschatological signs, portents, and free associations" that all pointed toward the end of time.[3]

The groundwork for the association between plague and eschatology had of course been laid long before. Mark 13, Matthew 24, Luke 21, and Revelation 16 and 18 all interpreted plagues eschatologically. As the plague spread and survivors tried desperately to deal with literal piles of putrefying bodies, there was little time to explain it, eschatologically or otherwise. But in the period after the plague receded, spiritual as well as material explanations were offered, usually combined. This meant that as the fourteenth century continued, scholars and theologians began to develop an almost proto-scientific investigation into both the plague and the possibility that it portended the end of the world. The anticipated "end" gave them reason to study nature carefully in an attempt to anticipate divine action.

For example, in the mid-fourteenth century, the medical faculty of the University of Paris wrote a treatise that began by blaming the plague on the "triple conjunction" of the planets Saturn, Jupiter, and Mars on March 20, 1345. The triple conjunction caused "moist vapors" to rise from the earth. These were then "corrupted" by Mars and Jupiter. The arrangement of the planets further caused winds, especially warm, moist southerly winds, to blow, as well as earthquakes. Earthquakes caused more corrupted vapors, and so on.

They went on to say that more pestilence could be predicted should the winter be warm and wet with southerly and easterly winds—the directions from which pestilence came. They noted that there had been further signs, such as a preponderance of falling stars. The sky "had in fact taken on a distinct yellow and red tone from the scorched vapors . . . and there had been frequent lightning, thunderings, and intense winds from the south, carrying great amounts of dust with them."[4]

Anyone familiar with Christian eschatological discourse can read the signs of this document: falling stars, earthquakes, plague, and skies doing unusual things. This was the end of time. While the medical faculty was attempting to offer a natural explanation for the terrible calamity that had befallen them, they were doing so within a system of signs that all pointed to the impending end.

Nature and theology were not two separate entities. Nature was understood as God's other book beside the Bible, and it could be read for signs just as the Bible could be read for signs. "The earth," as Smoller explains, "was never just the earth, but . . . the arena in which God's plan of salvation unfolded."[5] The stars were not just the stars. Study of them was a prerequisite for the study of theology in medieval universities. Eschatology gave people reason to examine the earth carefully, and eschatology was already a comprehensive form of knowledge that included the study of texts, stars, and a variety of earthly events.

But the development in the aftermath of the plague took things a step further. By reading the signs of the earth, people might be able to predict divine action. Many resisted the development of this "scientific apocalypse," as Laura Smoller shows. Matthew Paris, a pre-plague chronicler, had already begun to "explain" England's unexpected earthquakes in apocalyptic terms, because he could not explain them naturally. England lacked the underground caves and deep cavities that, he argued, generate earthquakes.[6] Thus if England experienced an earthquake, it could only be because of divine action. Paris had his share of objectors who believed that this way of explaining and anticipating undermined God's omnipotence and power, God's ability to do anything at any moment with no explanation at all. Attempts to predict and explain disaster were both continuous with the tradition of studying the world for "signs" of the end and discontinuous with it, both new and very old at once.

All Shall Be Well

For most Christians who had lost loved ones in the plague, the far bigger question was not why, but what had become of their beloveds' souls in the afterlife, especially those who had died without the benefit of last rites. It seemed they had entered the difficult, even literally tortuous journey of the afterlife without special protection. On the east coast of England, a small group of people developed a special office specifically to pray for these and other dead. These were anchorites, and they located themselves in churchyards and attached themselves to churches, where they devoted themselves entirely to prayer. Parishioners supported them with food and aid, and while anchorites were small in number and located in a fairly small geographic area (perhaps numbering around fifty over 150 years until the Reformation), they had a lasting impact on western Christianity specifically through the person of Julian of Norwich.[7]

Julian of Norwich, an anchorite who entered her anchorage at St. Julian's church in the busy river port city of Norwich around 1393, wrote a book called *A Revelation of Love*, the first known book written by a woman in the English language. While this book did not apparently travel far during her lifetime, it resurfaced in France during the Reformation and again in the nineteenth century until she became known as one of the greatest theologians of the English language, according to Thomas Merton.[8] But her theology developed largely outside the scholarly halls of the medieval church. She wrote for people she called her "even Christians," that is, ordinary people who were struggling with questions of an eschatological and ultimate nature. In the churchyard of St. Julian's in Norwich, she both worked on her book and received people from her neighborhood and beyond to talk with them about spiritual concerns.[9]

The theology recorded in A Revelation of Love was based on one extended visionary episode and then a long practice of prayer and contemplation that followed it. She wrote that when she was "thirty winters old and a half" and living with her mother, she became so ill that she thought that she would die. After she received last rites, she received a series of visions that became the basis of her life's work. We might say, then, that her theology is deeply rooted in an eschatological experience. She was taken to the very end of her life, the very outposts of her understanding, and reached a place where "holy church" had given her its very last gift. From this place, her visions began.

Norwich had been devastated by two plagues in Julian's lifetime. The first had come when she was six years old, in which as much as eighty percent of the population died. The second plague came in her late teenage years and killed eighty percent of the children. The loss was of a magnitude that is difficult to imagine, and while Julian does not mention the specific circumstances of plague and loss, her book is an attempt to grapple with suffering, death, and evil. In one scene in A Revelation of Love, the plague seems evoked when Julian sees a child rising from a putrid pile of rotting flesh.

And in this time, I saw a body lying on the earth, that looked gross and fearful and without shape and form, as if it was in a bog of stinking mire. And suddenly out of this body sprang a full fair creature, a little child, fully formed, swift and alive and whiter than a lily, and it glided quickly up to heaven. The bog of the body signifies the great wretchedness of our deadly flesh, and the littleness of the child signifies the cleanness and pureness of our soul (64.25–29).[10]

Julian's perception of the pureness of the soul can be contrasted with other societal impulses. The plagues had convinced many that God was waging a great war against humanity because of sin; Julian looked at the same circumstances and saw the "marvelous compassion that our Lord has for us in our woe and the courteous promising of clean deliverance" (64.35).

When Julian turned to the future in her writing, it was not to predict divinely ordained disaster. She critiqued the obsession with heaven and hell so common in her day as a problem rooted in lack of trust. She wrote that she asked Christ, who was showing her many things, to show her hell and purgatory. But in spite of her request, she was not "able to see anything of this" (33.6–7). In the tradition that we have been following, so many Christian seekers have been taken on vivid journeys through heaven and hell that this refusal is astonishing. In fact, it even seems to throw Julian off balance. She spends the rest of the chapter in which she has reported this lack of seeing repeating to her reader that just because she was not able to see hell and purgatory did not mean that she departed from the church's teaching. But emphasis on the love, "courteousness," and grace of God did indeed undermine—or at least put in tension—teachings on damnation and tortuous purification.

Julian's eschatology centered on one saying of Christ in her visions that she dwelt on extensively. Christ said to her, "I may make all things well, and I can make all things well, and I will make all things well, and I shall make all things well." She examined the verbs in this saying, wondering what "may," "can," "will," and "shall" each meant in turn. Her theology hinged on the ability of God's love to make all things well, but from where she stood, in the midst of sin and woe, she could not imagine how this was possible. Julian did not offer a Joachim-like pattern for history. She did not even see a patterned afterlife, like Dante's. Her book contained no predictions of specific events and few allegorical details of the kind that Hildegard put forward. But Julian saw the future as a time of fulfillment when God's work would be completed. She echoed Augustine in saying that the secrets of salvation are known to God alone. Julian called this God's "privy counsel."

But as Julian meditated on Christ's saying that "all shall be well," she wrote,

> There is a deed that the blissful Trinity shall do on the last day, as to my sight. And what the deed shall be and how it shall be done, this is unknown to all creatures who are beneath Christ, and shall be until the time when it is done. But the goodness and the love of our lord God will that we know that it shall be. At the same time, the might and the wisdom of Him, by the same love, conceals and hides what it shall be and how it shall be done (32.19–24)

Julian reiterated an ancient idea, what Dominic Crossan called the "Great, Divine Clean Up," that God would act in final restoration. Julian envisioned a deed so deep and secret and so powerful that it had the capacity to wipe out sin and suffering forever on the last day. Trusting in this was crucial to faith, even if no one could know precisely how it would be done.

"All shall be well" was not an eschatological program of the kind that many Christians found increasingly persuasive in the period after her life and writing. Instead, it was an assertion rooted in contemplation and prayer. The meaning of "all shall be well" was not precisely tied to events but was an orientation of prayer. Prayer is trust. Trust is prayer. When Christians oriented themselves to trust in God, they had to conclude that through some mystery, the future was in God's hands.

Notes

1. Giovanni Boccaccio, *Decameron*, introduction, trans. David Burr; online at http://www.history.vt.edu/Burr/Boccaccio.html.

2. Laura Smoller, "Plague and the Investigation of the Apocalypse," in *Last Things: Death and the Apocalypse in the Middle Ages*, ed. Caroline Walker Bynum and Paul Freedman (Philadelphia: University of Pennsylvania Press, 2000), 163.

3. Ibid.

4. Ibid., summarizing the document on 173.

5. Ibid., 183.

6. Matthew Paris, *Chronica Majora* 4.630, quoted in Smoller, 164–65.

7. Carole Hill, "Julian and Her Sisters: Female Piety in Late Medieval Norwich," in *The Fifteenth Century* 6, ed. Linda Clark (Rochester: Boydell, 2006), 165–87.

8. Thomas Merton, *Seeds of Destruction* (New York: Farrar, Straus & Giroux, 1964), 275.

9. We have a record of only one of these visits from Margery Kempe. See Margery Kempe, *The Book of Margery Kempe*, ed. Barry Windeatt (Essex: Pearson Education, 2000), 119–20.

10. Julian of Norwich, *A Revelation of Love*, from *The Writings of Julian of Norwich*, ed. Nicholas Watson and Jacqueline Jenkins (University Park: University of Pennsylvania Press, 2006), 325. Translations are my own.

16

Maps: Christopher Columbus

Who would doubt that this light, which comforted me with its
rays of marvelous clarity . . . and urged me onward with great
haste continuously without a moment's pause, came to you in a
most deep manner, as it did to me? In this voyage to the Indies,
Our Lord wished to perform a very evident miracle in order to
console me and the others in the matter of this other voyage to
the Holy Sepulchre.

—Letter from Christopher Columbus
to King Ferdinand and Queen Isabella of Spain

In 1490, in the Lisbon workshop of Bartolomeo and Christopher
Columbus, the two brothers developed a map that Columbus
was to use for his voyage to the "West Indies." It was a map
of the world as Bartolomeo and Christopher knew it to be,
complete with patterns for celestial navigation. On one side of
the map was Spain and on the other side was Japan, a place
that the Columbuses called "Cipagnu." They believed that the
mistake that previous sailors had made was to sail east instead
of west to reach the Indies. They believed that the Indies were

just a few thousand nautical miles off the west coast of Spain and that Christopher's trip would be much shorter than others, but they also knew that he would be traveling literally through uncharted waters. What monsters and dangers lay in those waters, where medieval maps had always marked, "There be dragons," the brothers could not know.

The two Columbus brothers had been influenced by an Italian map-maker named Paolo dal Pozzo Toscanelli. Toscanelli had argued that the "stretches of unknown sea" to the west were much shorter than had previously been believed and that traveling west was a wise, if untested, choice.[1] Ironically for those of us living on this side of Columbus's voyage, Columbus believed that the world was smaller than the one that had been passed down to him from antiquity but was of essentially the same shape and kind.[2] He believed that he had the fairly easy task of filling in missing pieces. Pauline Moffitt Watts explains, "The world was commonly depicted as a disk divided into three parts: Europe, Asia, and Africa. This disk was circumscribed by a band of oceans, the impassable sea whose unknown expanse had been feared since antiquity."[3] This tripartite construction came from Genesis 9:19 in which the three sons of Noah were said to have peopled the earth after the flood. This geography was not a neutral one based on scientific fact. It was fundamentally a religious and eschatological conception of the nature of reality that contained a story about both the beginning and the end of the world.

Fulfilling Prophecy

To make the map he would use for sailing, Columbus relied on several sources besides Toscanelli, nearly all of them religious in nature. There were the "mathematical arts" that he believed he had learned from the "patriarchs and prophets" of the Bible; there were the scriptures, which revealed the nature of time and space; and commentaries on the scriptures and extrabiblical apocalypses like Pseudo-Methodius that helped him to understand the divine plan. He also collected and annotated many classical works from antiquity. And there was astronomy, which, in addition to being useful for nautical mapping, held secrets and signs about the end of time. Columbus was largely self-taught, and he collected these materials through a specific lens: his own role in the divine plan.

These sources taught him that somewhere in the northern parts of Asia, the tribes of Gog and Magog were imprisoned behind walls that had been constructed by Alexander the Great. Drawing on Pseudo-Methodius, Columbus believed that these tribes would be "loosed upon mankind when the end of the world was imminent."[4] He believed that when this time came, there would appear an emperor-messiah who would bring about the conversion of all the peoples of the world to Christianity and the final recovery of the Holy Land from the infidels, but also the advent of the antichrist. Columbus was torn between his desire to explore the routes west and his desire to go to the Holy Land, where he might help in the work of unseating the Muslim conquerors and abetting the end of the world. In all of his letters to Ferdinand and Isabella before he embarked west, he linked his own eschatological fate to that of the monarchs, who also believed they had a fundamental role to play in the unfolding divine plan for the end of time.[5] He was obsessed with the march into Jerusalem that Isabella and Ferdinand were planning, and he did not want to be left out. Because of some entitlements that his wife

Isabella had received through her own inheritance, Ferdinand called himself the King of Jerusalem already.[6]

Yes, Columbus was an explorer and a beneficiary of new technologies in sailing in what every school-aged child has learned to call the "age of exploration." Yes, he hoped to develop a trade route that would benefit Spain. But an often overlooked and, to us, incongruent aspect of his driving passion was a vision for the end of time, in which he believed God had given him a special role. He came to believe that he had fulfilled many prophecies, and throughout his life, he collected these prophecies into a book that he called the *Book of Prophecies*. This book included both scriptural references and bits and pieces from other sources that together created a picture of his special place in the divine plan.

Columbus had long been absorbed with islands. A common medieval belief was that the Garden of Eden was on an island in the ocean that had been separated from the mainland by the waters of the great flood. When he landed on the coast of Cuba, he believed that he may have found the "New Heaven and the New Earth" described in Revelation, or perhaps the island where God had hidden the Garden of Eden. But as he came to understand that the island on which his ship had landed was full of people, something that did not quite resonate with his understanding of the Garden of Eden, he became absorbed with the idea that his role in the end of time was to bring every tribe and nation to Christianity—the same "sign" that had been central to Augustine from Matt 24:14, "And this good news of the kingdom will be proclaimed throughout the world, as a testimony to all the nations; and then the end will come." To his *Book of Prophecies*, he added this from Augustine: "God will prevail, it is said, against them and he will wipe out all the gods of the peoples of the earth and they will adore him, each one from its own place, all the peoples of the islands."[7]

As his life continued, he gave more and more divine attribution to the spiritual and eschatological aspects of his voyages. In 1500 he wrote to Prince John of Portugal, "God made me the messenger of the New Heaven and the New Earth of which he spoke through St. John in the Apocalypsis, after having spoken of it through Isaiah; and he showed me where to find it."[8] His ultimate goal, however, was "not simply to reach the east by sailing west, or even to bring about the conversion of the Indies, but rather to see a crusade to Jerusalem, where history would reach its culmination."[9] In a letter to Ferdinand and Isabella, he wrote that the previous knowledge accumulated by scholars had been of little use to him in his successful voyages west. The only useful thing was prophecy. "What Isaiah said was completely fulfilled and that is what I wish to write here in order to remind Your Highnesses of it so that you may rejoice when I tell you by virtue of the same authorities that you are assured of certain victory in the enterprise of Jerusalem if you have faith."[10]

Columbus believed that if Isabella and Ferdinand led a crusade on Jerusalem, they could further the coming of the end of the world with his blessed help and participation. We can see here a slight shift from the kind of eschatological belief of the Middle Ages. In the Middle Ages, Christians worried about the coming of "God's wrath," in part because it could be so utterly unpredictable. They saw themselves at the whim of an almighty God, and looked anxiously to the world around them to try to read the signs of this God's feelings and activities. Bernard had looked around and perhaps seen the hope of the Last Emperor in Conrad III and so helped to inspire the Second Crusade. But Columbus, Ferdinand, and Isabella imagined themselves as even more active participants in bringing about the end of the world. They believed that they had been assigned discernible roles. They studied ancient texts for words that would refer directly to them, and then Columbus set sail as a result. Whereas in the past, figures like the Angelic Pope or the Last Emperor or the antichrist were semi-mythological figures and had done all the heavy lifting in apocalyptic scenarios, Columbus imagined himself, neither pope nor emperor, as an essential end-times actor.

Ironically, Columbus was instrumental not in bringing about the end of the world but in actively shaping the new one that we all share. Like other Christian students of the future that we have encountered, Columbus was utterly wrong and strangely right at the same time. Ferdinand and Isabella did not undertake the crusade to "free" Jerusalem that Columbus had urged them to make. After the Edict of Expulsion of the Jews in 1492 and the war to drive out the Moors from Spain, Isabella died. But Columbus did expand Christianity's understanding of the world. The Great Commission, given in Matthew 28 to "go and make disciples of all nations" had become a dramatically different task than had previously been understood.

From Prophecy to Economics

Even while Columbus spoke the language of religious prophecy to explain his discoveries, these narratives were quickly complemented with narratives of economics. What could the peoples and resources of the Americas give to the empires that Columbus, and soon other explorers, served? While missionaries began to arrive for the conversion of what was considered the remaining peoples of the earth, traders became obsessed with all that the "New World" had to offer a cramped and stifled Europe. We cannot say that these two narratives—the eschatological and the economic—were in competition with each other. Europeans simultaneously extracted resources, rhapsodized about the Edenic quality of the land they had "found," and projected this land into apocalyptic scenarios based on a longstanding Christian lens.

A key difficulty for these traders and explorers was how to make sense of the peoples Europeans encountered on the American continents in light of their received stories about the world. Who could these people possibly be in relation to the Bible and its already comprehensive narrative?[11] Eventually, most Europeans settled on a narrative of conversion. Europeans saw that the "evangelization of large and apparently receptive native populations on a land that until then had been the domain of devilish ideology meant that the eschatological times were near."[12] To believe that the eschatological time was near was a strong tendency of Christians in every era, as we have seen. It was not so much that the times signified the fulfillment of Christ's prophecy as that Christians brought this interpretation to events as they encountered them. Either the native peoples of these lands were dwellers in Eden, pure and innocent "savages" who had not been ruined as we were by original sin, or they were diabolical devil worshipers who must be destroyed so that God's people could thrive in this new land.

Through a slight shift of the same lens, primitive innocents became pagan cannibals who, like the Jews and Muslims in Spain, must convert or be destroyed. Driven by eschatological beliefs, a root violence led directly to all varieties of conquest, slaughter, and exploitation for personal gain. A deep irony of this encounter is that while Europeans read it through an eschatological narrative about the coming end of the world, they indeed played a "world-ending" role for thousands of native people who were destroyed intentionally or unintentionally by disease and conquest.

A Christian Utopia

Some Christian missionaries mingled these two perspectives —the primitive innocent and the pagan cannibal—into a third possibility: native peoples were indeed morally superior to Europeans, but they still required conversion to Christianity to create a final Christian utopia.[13] The Franciscans, who began to arrive in 1520, developed a distinct eschatological narrative about the peoples of the Americas. Conversion was important, yes, but it was important because they believed that together with the native peoples, they could construct the much-looked-for millennium. Instead of looking backward toward Eden or the Lost Tribes of Israel, the Franciscans looked forward to the eschatological promises of Revelation, toward the New Heaven, the New Earth, and the New Jerusalem. Speaking specifically of Franciscans in Mexico, Georges Baudot argues that "the missionaries seemed to be the only ones who wanted to get well acquainted with the natives of Mexico."[14] These missionaries became fascinated with the differences in human cultures and began to document them, forming the basis for a new approach to the question of humanity. This fascination that the Franciscans developed with the peoples of the Americas ultimately gave us the legacy of the disciplines of anthropology and ethnography.[15] But initially, they both studied and converted the peoples of America in order to understand how to bring about the kingdom of God on earth.

We cannot underestimate how for Europeans these voyages and encounters were remapping the world and transforming the very foundation on which they believed they had stood. The transition from the Middle Ages to the era we call "modernity" involved dramatic shifts in the understanding of time and space, and radically different accounts of the relationship between divine and human action. But as in the Middle Ages, Christians had a drive for a total vision, a complete story. In a vastly expanded world, the work required to attain that total vision, and the complete conversion, for example, of all the world's people, was greater than had been previously thought.[16] From the need for a total vision came an intensified eschatology through which all of time and its meanings could be known. In contemporary scholarship, we've come to call this the "master narrative" of European civilization, and we can see that eschatology played an important role in giving time a completeness, "the sense of an ending," as literary critic Frank Kermode put it.[17]

Notes

1. Pauline Moffitt Watts, "Prophecy and Discovery: On the Spiritual Origins of Christopher Columbus's 'Enterprise of the Indies'," *The American Historical Review* 90/1, suppl. to vol. 90 (February 1985): 81.

2. Ibid., 83.

3. Ibid., 77.

4. Ibid.

5. Alain Milhou, "Apocalypticism in Central and South American Colonialism," in *The Encyclopedia of Apocalypticism*, ed. Stephen J. Stein (New York: Continuum, 1998), 3:4–5.

6. Arthur H. Williamson, *Apocalypse Then: Prophecy and the Making of the Modern World* (Westport: Praeger, 2008), 71. Isabella received rights to the French county of Brienne, which had "regency" over Jerusalem, a nominal claim at best.

7. Watts, 94.

8. Columbus, quoted in ibid., 102.

9. Laura Smoller, "Plague and the Investigation of the Apocalypse," in *Last Things: Death and the Apocalypse in the Middle Ages,* ed. Caroline Walker Bynum and Paul Freedman (Philadelphia: University of Pennsylvania Press, 2000), 186.

10. Columbus, in *Scritti,* ed. Cesare De Lollis (Rome: Ministero Della Pubblica Istruzione, 1892–1894), 80 and 82; quoted in Watts, 96.

11. Georges Baudot, *Utopia and History in Mexico,* trans. Bernard R. Ortiz de Montellano and Thelma Ortiz de Montellano (Niwot: University Press of Colorado, 1995), xv.

12. Milhou, 10.

13. Ibid.

14. Baudot, 71.

15. Ibid., xv.

16. Robin Barnes, "Images of Hope and Despair: Western Apocalypticism, ca. 1500–1800," in *The Encyclopedia of Apocalypticism,* ed. Bernard McGinn (New York: Continuum, 1998), 2:143.

17. Frank Kermode, *The Sense of an Ending: Studies in the Theory of Fiction* (New York: Oxford University Press, 1967).

17

Urgency: Martin Luther

For my part, I am sure that the Day of Judgment is just around the corner. It doesn't matter that we don't know the precise day . . . perhaps someone else can figure it out. But it is certain that time is now at an end.

—Martin Luther

In June of 1520, Pope Leo X issued "The Threat of Banishment and Burning the Papal Bull of Excommunication" against troublesome friar Martin Luther (1483–1546). In December of that year, Luther responded by collecting the papal bull, a book of church law, and other books written by his enemies and burning them at a public place in his home city of Wittenberg. He reportedly cried out, "Because you, godless book, have grieved or shamed the holiness of the Father, be saddened and consumed by the eternal flames of Hell."[1]

Luther's Revelation

At the same moment that these dramatic activities were unfolding, Luther was at work with his collaborator Lucas Cranach on an illustrated version of Revelation. This was the only book of the Bible that Luther chose to illustrate, and his choice was, at least in part, to use the images of the book to further his polemic against the papacy. Using woodcuts, he and Cranach dressed up one of the beasts and the Whore of Babylon in the papal tiara.

But despite giving his conflict eschatological meaning and furthering his polemic, Luther was not easily won over by the Revelation of John. "My spirit cannot fit into this book," he wrote, because "Christ is not known or taught in it."[2] There were other books of the canonical Bible that he also did not like—Hebrews, James, and Jude. Taken together he believed that these books violated the principle of salvation by grace and faith alone (*sola gratia* and *sola fide*). He believed that among other problems, Revelation depicted people who had earned salvation through martyrdom. For prophecy and eschatology, he turned instead to Daniel.

Luther shared with Revelation, however, a perception of crisis, the sense of the world on a precipice.[3] Indeed the need for an end in Christianity was as obvious to Christian theologians as the Reformation progressed as "that there is a Sun in the firmament," as one seventeenth-century reformer put it.[4] And just as obvious was that the end was soon. One of the greatest proponents of this sense of eschatological crisis was Luther himself.

Over time, Luther's appreciation for Revelation grew. He read church history through its pages: The angel with the censer in Revelation 8 was Athanasius and the Council of Nicea.

The angels with plagues were the Montanists and Origen, and anyone who preached righteousness through works.[5] He came to see much of his own time revealed in its ancient words. Revelation, for example, makes clear that the church will suffer conflict and struggle. He came to believe that the two beasts of Revelation 13 revealed the "final two abominations that Christians would have to bear."[6] The first was an external abomination: the rise of "Mohammedism." He argued that the Mohammedan kingdom was indicated by the prophecies of Gog and Magog, whom Satan had sent to do battle against Christians once he had been loosed from his thousand-year bondage. The internal abomination was the papacy. The papacy was the antichrist, the masterful perverter of the Gospel. He believed that these two forces were working together as signs of the end of time. In 1453, a generation before Luther's birth, the Ottomans had conquered Constantinople; and in the sixteenth century, as a part of the Ottoman Empire, they were advancing across Europe, threatening Vienna in 1529, just five hundred miles south of Luther's center of operations in Saxony. Luther prayed for God to strike down both the "Turks" and the pope, but he also believed that their convergent evil was a sign that this was indeed the end of history.

Polemics and Convictions

On the one hand, we must understand Luther's eschatology as thoroughly polemical. His desire to describe the pope as antichrist came about during his conflict with the pope over indulgences. In the Middle Ages, it became common practice for people to pay to the church a small amount for the reduction of the punishment that they would receive for their sins after death. This was called an "indulgence," and indulgences could also be small acts of kindness or gifts given to the church as well as monetary payments. But in the late Middle Ages, the practice came under intense scrutiny, not least by Luther. In 1521, he published a pamphlet with Cranach called *Passional of Christ and Antichrist*, in which they depicted a cartoonish pope. In one scene Christ enters Jerusalem on a donkey while the pope enters with a pompous procession. In another, Christ throws the moneychangers out of the temple while the pope invites them back in. This use of Christ and antichrist imagery was directed at a reformation of the church that seemed to belong not to the end of the world but to the future, where a more moral and Christ-like community could be formed.[7] This aspect of Luther's eschatology might be described as prophetic rather than apocalyptic, aimed at the transformation of this world rather than the brink of the next.

On the other hand, Luther did appear to believe whole-heartedly that his era was the final era. As early as 1520, when he was not yet forty years old, he wrote to a friend, "I am so oppressed that I have virtually no doubt that the pope is really and truly the antichrist for whom, by the commonly accepted view, the world is waiting."[8] The antichrist is nothing if not, as the apostle John had written so many years before, a sign of "last hour" (1 John 2:18). At first, Luther thought Pope Leo X (1475–1521) was the antichrist, but the pope's death in 1521 transformed Luther's thinking. With further study, it became clear that the antichrist was not an individual, but the papacy itself, an institution, not a person.[9] Beginning with Luther, the idea of the papacy (occupied by whatever individual pope) as antichrist spread emphatically through all of Protestant Europe and fueled the Reformation in image, text, and deed.

Luther became convinced that his own age was the decisive one, when the struggle between God and Satan had become radically clarified and in which God's will would now be thoroughly known. "For my part," Luther wrote, "I am sure that the Day of Judgment is just around the corner. It doesn't matter that we don't know the precise day . . . perhaps someone else can figure it out. But it is certain that time is now at an end."[10] In this passage, Luther merely expressed certainty of finality, but later he grew even more pessimistic. "I wish that I and all my children were dead," he wrote in 1533. "For things are going to get still more awful in this world. Whoever remains alive will see that it will become worse and worse."[11]

Luther's Chronology

Even though Luther did not settle on a day when the end would take place, he did create a chronology through which divine will and God's patterned work of history could be observed. Luther began with the idea that the Bible teaches that creation would last for six thousand years. He believed that he stood approximately at the year 5500 (four thousand years from the birth of creation to the birth of Christ, and fifteen hundred years after the birth of Christ). Each period of God's history was roughly two thousand years. This then was the third and final age. Technically, given this kind of math problem, the world should still have had five hundred years to go to complete the final age (1500–2000 CE), but Luther was convinced that God would shorten the final age "for the sake of the elect."[12] Reformation historian Robin Barnes understands Luther's schema of history to indicate a "deep need for certainty in a universal order" and a "deep desire for prophetic reassurance" that grew as Luther aged.[13]

The Spread of Luther's Eschatology

Luther himself did much to vivify and popularize criticism of the Catholic church using eschatological imagery, but the invention of the Gutenberg printing press in 1439 and its increasing use in the sixteenth century for popular polemic meant that these images spread widely and quickly. Vivid tracts depicting in visual form the understanding of the evils of the papacy influenced people across Europe. The tiara-crowned Whore of Babylon riding on a seven-headed beast through a Babylon-Rome or a pit of monsters out of which the papacy rises became key symbols. The rise of these eschatological depictions was connected to Luther's production of a German-language Bible and his passionate belief that people must have access to the scriptures for themselves. Throughout the sixteenth century, we find images of reformers attacking the antichrist with stacks of printed books or breaking down the walls of Rome with them.[14] As the scriptures came into the hands of the laity, they often came laden with eschatological images that interpreted the meaning of the words for them, instructing them about God's unfolding plan for history.[15]

By the mid-sixteenth century, a kind of "siege mentality" had taken over Luther's followers and those in other break-off groups that had experienced similar foment.[16] They were steeped in the idea that the end of the world was just around the corner. While Luther preached that his followers had no reason to dread the coming judgment and should instead welcome it with joy, this did not necessarily undermine fear.

Previous generations had been taught to fear the coming wrath of God. Luther preached that by faith alone, the saved could greet the judgment fearlessly. But the sense that world events were intensifying in such a way as to bring about the end grew into a frenzy in the mid-sixteenth century. What Barnes calls "radical outpourings" spread through the Reformation landscape. The preacher Thomas Müntzer (1489–1525), who had once been an associate of Luther but had broken with him, helped to foment the German Peasants' War of 1525. Müntzer believed that Luther's approach was too academic; he wanted a revolution that would usher in the millennium.[17] Anabaptist leaders of various kinds preached that the end of the world would come in 1528 and 1530. An Anabaptist uprising that began in 1534 in Münster ended in a massacre in 1535. Collections of Luther's post-1530 prophecies appeared, which his followers saw as divinely inspired.[18] Foment spread.

In the decades after Luther's death, his followers intensified their apocalyptic rhetoric, and with that intensification came a sense of hopelessness in this world. Everywhere, Lutheran Andreas Musculus (d. 1581) observed, there were signs of "universal breakdown."[19] The Germans, who through Luther had been offered the true light of Christ, had proven themselves to be just as full of vice and division as any of the other peoples of the earth. Moral and social decay was everywhere among them. And still the end did not come.

Calculating the End

Gradually, this feverish certainty of the end became a search for greater understanding. Followers of Luther began to study the relationship between history and prophecy more carefully, looking for correspondence and ways to understand God's plan. The concept of history with which they worked became increasingly literal and linear, and historical time—what it meant, how it would end, how God acts or does not within it—became a "genuine obsession" among Luther's heirs.[20] Increasingly complex periodization and chronologies were hallmarks of the moment, and chronologists were working to determine the exact dating of Christ's birth, for example—which, using the six-thousand-year schema, they could then use to calculate the end of time. To these descendants of Luther, history became a third text, alongside scripture and nature, that humans could read to discern the meaning of God's will and work for the future. But instead of one unifying map of history emerging from all of this feverish energy, multiple versions competed for attention. The result was "dizzying confusion."[21]

Because of the growth of printing, theologians and preachers of an increasingly popular variety had wide access to tools and resources to create their own eschatological schemata. Apocalypticists of all kinds could now not only draw on a far greater variety, but they could also print and distribute their own ideas far more easily. Thus a "truly eclectic" apocalypticism began to emerge in northern Europe.[22] The search for universal knowledge became an individualized pursuit. Lutheran bishops recognized that this flourishing apocalypticism was not in their favor. As Lutheran clergy withdrew from Luther's emphatic "end-of-the-world" talk, groups that disagreed splintered off, and these groups continued the search in their own small apocalyptic units for the correct calculation of time's end.

Notes

1. Online at http://www.luther.de/en/bann.html.

2. Martin Luther, quoted in Bernard McGinn, *Antichrist: Two Thousand Years of the Human Fascination with Evil* (New York: Harper Collins, 1994), 204.

3. Robin Barnes, *Prophecy and Gnosis: Apocalypticism in the Wake of the Lutheran Reformation* (Stanford: Stanford University Press, 1988), 2.

4. George Hakewill, *An Apologie of the Power and Providence of God in the Government of the World* (1627), 441, quoted in Bryan Ball, *A Great Expectation: Eschatological Thought in English Protestantism to 1660* (Leiden: Brill, 1975), 157.

5. Craig Koester, *Revelation: A New Translation with Introduction and Commentary* (New Haven: Yale University Press, 2014), 49.

6. Barnes, 41.

7. See McGinn, 203–5.

8. Luther, quoted in Jaroslav Pelikan, "Some Uses of Apocalypse in the Magisterial Reformers," in *Apocalypse in English Renaissance Thought and Literature,* ed. C.A. Patrides and Joseph Wittreich (Manchester: Manchester University Press, 1984), 85.

9. Arthur H. Williamson, *Apocalypse Then: Prophecy and the Making of the Modern World* (Westport: Praeger, 2008), 43.

10. Luther, *Preface to Daniel,* quoted in Gerald Strauss, "The Mental World of a Saxon Pastor," in *Reformation Principle and Practice: Essays in Honor of Arthur Geoffrey Dickens,* ed. Peter Newman Brooks (London: Scholar, 1980), 169.

11. Luther, quoted in Barnes, 49.

12. Barnes, 51.

13. Ibid., 52.

14. Pierre Eskrich (Cruche), *Histoire de la mappa-monde nouvelle papistique* … (detail) (Geneva, 1567), reprinted in N. Z. David, "The Sacred and the Body Social in Lyonis," *Humanities in Review* 1 (1982): 66.

15. Barnes, 55.

16. Ibid., 4.

17. Bruce Chilton, *Visions of the Apocalypse: Receptions of John's Revelation in Western Imagination* (Waco: Baylor University Press, 2014), 77.

18. Robin Barnes, "Images of Hope and Despair: Western Apocalypticism, ca. 1500–1800," in *The Encyclopedia of Apocalypticism*, ed. Bernard McGinn (New York: Continuum, 1998), 2:155.

19. Ibid., 154–55.

20. Barnes, *Prophecy*, 101.

21. Ibid., 114.

22. Ibid., 4.

18

Taxonomies: Isaac Newton and John Donne

At the round earth's imagined corners, blow
Your trumpets, Angels, and arise, arise
From death, you numberless infinities
Of souls, and to your scattered bodies go,
All whom the flood did, and fire shall o'erthrow,
All whom war, dearth, age, agues, tyrannies,
Despair, law, chance, hath slain, and you whose eyes
Shall behold God and never taste death's woe.

—John Donne, from Holy Sonnet VII

In 1680, the first comet was spied through a telescope. Gottfried Kirch, an astronomer in Berlin, discovered the comet, later called both Kirch Comet and Newton's Comet. Sir Isaac Newton (1642–1726/7) had been working on planetary orbits since the 1660s, and the 1680 comet allowed him to demonstrate his theories and predict the orbit of the comet. The theory allowed scientists to predict the orbits of other planetary bodies and created the foundation for Newton's theory of gravity. This was a key development in modern mathematics, physics, and astronomy, and certainly of far greater importance than Newton's own interpretation of this event. But for Newton, the comet was not just a planetary body. Newton was developing a theory of the cosmos that was engaged with questions of prophecy, biblical studies, and a comprehensive understanding of history.

A Search for Universal Knowledge

In the seventeenth century, eschatology and astronomy had yet to fundamentally part ways. In fact, astronomy was one way that people could ask a question, writes Robin Barnes, that "grew more and more pressing: how could proper insight into the fundamental truths of the universal scheme be gained?" The sources to which people could turn for knowledge that could be transformed into eschatological narratives grew: astronomy, astrology, alchemy, ancient prophecies, new prophecies, medicine, biblical studies, proto-geology. The desire to solve the problem of divine will and the meaning of human history "spurred on the crucial debate over method in philosophy and science."[1]

This framework became increasingly technical. By the seventeenth century, apocalypticists were at work on minute calculations about how and when and where particular events would take place. One man, John Napier (1550–1617), working at St. Andrews University in Scotland, used a combination of biblical studies and mathematics to develop algorithms so that predictions of eschatological events could be more precise. He in turn influenced Joseph Mede (1586–1639), a naturalist whose book *Key of the Revelation Searched and Demonstrated* was widely influential, including on Isaac Newton.

Mede's *Key of the Revelation* was a taxonomic approach to Revelation based on what Mede called "synchronisms." He carefully delineated the symbols of Revelation and systematically mapped them onto synchronic events, "so that it may prove, as it were, a Thesean clew to those who are involved in this sacred labyrinth, and a Lydian stone to discover the true, and to refute every erroneous interpretation."[2] He searched through Revelation and then layered images on top of one another so that the time, inherent within them, could be made visible.

While he calls his method "self-evident," it is difficult for the contemporary reader not to get lost in the overlapping symbols, images, and time-frames purported to reveal themselves so naturally.

> My first synchronism shall be that of the remarkable quaternion of prophecies displayed in equal intervals of time. First, Of the woman living in the wilderness for a time, times, and a half, or (as it is there more fully expressed) for 1260 days. Secondly, Of the seven-headed beast restored, and endued with power for forty-two months. Thirdly, Of the exterior court (or of the Holy City) trodden down by the Gentiles for the same number of months. Fourthly, and lastly, Of the witnesses prophesying in sackcloth for 1260 days.[3]

In other words, the woman in the wilderness of Revelation 12 spends the same amount of time there as the seven-headed beast of Revelation 13 who endured for forty-two months, which is the same as the number of months that the Holy City was defiled by Gentiles in Revelation 11 and the same amount of time as the witnesses also of Revelation 11 preached. And so on. After working his way through seven "synchronisms" twice as well as some corollaries, interpretations, and expositions, Mede concludes that the end of the world should fall, roughly, around 1716.

As a professor at Cambridge and a polymath of wide interests, Mede gathered a broad following. While the role of eschatology in the development of natural philosophy is rarely recognized today, in the seventeenth century they were hard to distinguish. Barnes argues, "The rise of the new natural and mathematical philosophy" was directly related to "the search for insight into the ultimate plan of the universe."[4] Mede was using some of the methods of this new philosophy with its taxonomic approach to texts to read Revelation again, as if for the first time.

Newton's *Observations upon the Prophecies*

Isaac Newton followed Mede closely. An English mathematician and physicist, Newton has been immortalized for his role in the scientific revolution of this era. But far less widely known is that Newton spent a good deal of time researching a set of observations on Daniel and Revelation in order to understand the mysteries of these prophetic texts. He corresponded at length on the subject of his findings with philosopher John Locke. As with Columbus, Newton's ideas about nature, history, and the nature of the cosmos were formed in the cauldron of Christian eschatology. His study of apocalyptic eschatology might be considered "a point of intersection for his . . . diverse interests, be these mathematics or alchemy, astronomy or ancient religions, chronology or bible study." His means of investigating prophecy were similar to his ways of organizing other areas of inquiry. He sorted and collated a vast amount of data and then drew conclusions about what he had found there.[5] Newton believed that the "Apocalyps," as he called Revelation, was a key to "guide and direct [the Church] in the right way." All prophetic scripture, not unlike the theory of gravity, was a reliable guide for predicting the future.[6]

In his own study called *Observations upon the Prophecies of Daniel and the Apocalypse of St. John*, which he did not publish in his lifetime, he took a more strongly correspondence-oriented approach than Mede. He was opposed to symbolic readings of scripture and argued repeatedly that the literal meaning of scripture was in all cases to be preferred. Yet, unable to sustain literal readings when it came to prophecy, he developed a correlation theory of the language of prophecy. For example, where scripture offered a natural sign, the reader was to understand a political one. This allowed him to find a "middle way" in which the allegorical would not conflict with reason, and he would still be able to read prophecy without resorting to mystical explanations.[7] For example, here is his description of how to read prophecies that involve the sun, moon, and stars:

> In the heavens, the Sun and Moon are, by interpreters of dreams, put for persons of Kings and Queens; but in sacred Prophecy, which regards not single persons, the Sun is put for the whole species and race of Kings, in the kingdom or kingdoms of the world politic, shining with regal power and glory; the Moon for the body of the common people considered as the king's wife; the Stars for subordinate Princes and great men, or for Bishops and Rulers of the people of God, when the Sun is Christ.[8]

Thus, when we read in prophecy about the sun or the moon or the stars falling or turning to blood, we should be looking for signs in the "body politic or ecclesiastic." Since sacred scripture is not interested in individuals, as he asserted, we must look for vaster correspondences on the level of civilizations and whole races.

Very often in his reading of prophecy, natural signs corresponded to political conditions. Meteors were signs of war. Deserts indicated spiritual dryness. With this correspondence theory of language as a kind of codebreaker, Newton then undertook to tell the history of the kingdoms of the world so that they further corresponded to the four metals, four beasts, and ten horns of Daniel.

He believed that the millennium was literal but not imminent. "I, and as many as are Christians, in all things right in their opinions, believe both that there shall be a resurrection of the flesh, and a thousand years life at Jerusalem built, adorned and enlarged," he wrote in the *Observations*.[9] But doing his own calculations, he did not see how this was prophesied to occur until sometime well after the year 2000, and he was skeptical of people who attached dates to prophecy. "The folly of Interpreters has been, to foretel times and things by this Prophecy, as if God designed to make them Prophets."[10] He believed that there was reason to continue to "look into these things," as he believed that a great deal of prophecy still referred to the future. "It is to us and our posterity that those words [of prophecy] mainly belong," he wrote.[11] But, as some scholars have pointed out, Newton's theory that the millennium would not come for several hundred years, without an impact on the present, largely made his commentaries irrelevant and consigned them to the dustbin of history.[12] His inheritors did not continue to read his work on Revelation, to which he had devoted such careful study.

John Donne and the Taxonomy of an Apocalyptic Sermon

Like Newton, the poet and churchman John Donne (1572–1631) argued that Revelation was best read in such a way that the "figurative sense is the literal sense."[13] In other words, scripture, properly interpreted, is literal, even when it is figurative. Like Newton, Donne proceeded by corollary, pointing out correspondences that then led to proper interpretations.

In the spirit of his age, in which taxonomy was so important, for example, he used the images of Revelation to categorize things. In a sermon on Rev 4:8, he broke the image of the four beasts around the throne of heaven into parts and examined each part individually: the eyes, the wings, their particular actions. "Their persons and their action will be our two parts of this text. In each of which we will have three branches," Donne preached. He meditated at length on the numbers four and six, broke each part of the four creatures into small parts, and then read each part morally.[14] For example, he saw the four creatures as exemplifying four character traits that a minister of God should cultivate: courage, hard work, clear sight, and humanity. And even while it was broken down into individual parts, the image as a whole should lead the believer to contemplate the unity of the Trinity.

Donne took the text of Revelation and broke it into small pieces and then, like a student of anatomy, picked up each individual bit and studied it carefully. He believed that unlike the other animals of the earth, whose "inferior natures are possessed with the present," "man is a future creature." A Christian is a person on a journey, a person whose journey ends "beyond the sublunary maze of the phenomenal world, in the world to come."[15] The human destination is not death, but judgment—a condition that takes place in the beyond.

At the same time, unlike his contemporaries, Donne was less sure about the use of Revelation to predict the future. It couldn't really be understood until its prophecies had been fulfilled.[16] He noted that for every symbol of Revelation, a person could find thirty interpretations. Instead, Donne looked for unity and wholeness, for moral readings instead of predictions. "He that seeks proof for every mystery of religion," he said. "Shall meet with much darkness, but he that believes first, shall find everything to illustrate his faith." His eschatology contained a resurrection of the dead at the sound of the last trumpet and an acceptance of God's mysteries in the moral formation of a believer.

By the time Newton, Donne, and their contemporaries were finished working over Revelation, Christian eschatology had become its own area of specialized research. While for Newton and Donne Revelation remained a "key" to unlock the whole meaning of history, eventually their work of breaking prophetic scriptures into smaller and smaller pieces meant that eschatology broke off from other fields of theological specialization—christology, ecclesiology, soteriology, hermeneutics, and so on—becoming a field unto itself. This is one of the ironies of the story of Christian eschatology: that a search for universal knowledge led to an island of arcane speculation.

Notes

1. Robin Barnes, *Prophecy and Gnosis: Apocalypticism in the Wake of the Lutheran Reformation* (Stanford: Stanford University Press, 1988), 265.

2. Joseph Mede, *The Key of the Revelation, Searched and Demonstrated Out of*

the *Naturall and Proper Charecters of the Visions: With a Coment thereupon, According to the Rule of the Same Key*, online at http://www.ccel.org/ccel/mede/key.ii.html.

3. Ibid.

4. Robin Barnes, "Images of Hope and Despair: Western Apocalypticism, ca. 1500–1800," in *The Encyclopedia of Apocalypticism*, ed. Bernard McGinn (New York: Continuum, 1998), 2:165.

5. Sarah Hutton, "The Seven Trumpets and the Seven Vials: Apocalypticism and Christology in Newton's Theological Writings," in *Newton and Religion: Context, Nature, and Influence*, ed. James E. Force and Richard H. Popkin (Dordrecht: Kluwer Academic, 1999), 165.

6. Yahuda Newton MS 1, fol 4r, in *Trauato sull apocalisse*, ed. Maurizio Mamiani (Turin: Bollati Bolinghieri, 1995), 10.

7. Reiner Smolinski, "The Logic of Millennial Thought: Sir Isaac Newton Among His Contemporaries," in *Newton and Religion*, 259.

8. Isaac Newton, *Observations upon the Prophecies of Daniel and the Apocalypse of St. John* (1733), online at http://psalm139.com/file/newton.pdf, 14–15.

9. Ibid., 171.

10. Ibid., 251.

11. Ibid., 173–74.

12. Michael Murrin, "Newton's Apocalypse," in *Newton and Religion*, 220.

13. John Donne, *The Works of John Donne: Sermons*, ed. Henry Alford (London: Parker, 1839), 1:325.

14. John Donne, *The Sermons of John Donne*, ed. Evelyn M. Simpson and George R. Potter (Berkeley: University of California Press, 1962), 8.1:37–60.

15. John Donne, *The Works of John Donne*, ed. Henry Alford (London: John W. Parker, 1839), 6:259; quoted in C. A. Patrides, "'Something like a Prophetick Strain': Apocalyptic Configurations in Milton," in *Apocalypse in English Renaissance Thought and Literature*, ed. C. A. Patrides and Joseph Wittreich (Manchester: Manchester University Press, 1984), 207.

16. Joseph Wittreich, "'Image of that Horror': The Apocalypse in King Lear," in *Apocalypse in English Renaissance*, 176.

19

Anxieties: John Calvin, Increase Mather, and Second Advent Theologians

God's patience is nigh out of date.

—George Wither (1625)

"To His Highnesse The Lord Protector of the Common-Wealth of England, Scotland, and Ireland. The Humble Addresses of Menasseh Ben Israel, A Divine and Doctor of Physick, in Behalf of The Jewish Nation," wrote Rabbi Menasseh Ben Israel (1604-1657) to Oliver Cromwell in 1655. Ben Israel, living in the Netherlands, intended his letter to address the exclusion of Jews from England since 1290. Ben Israel believed that it was time for Jews to return to England so that they could prepare there to return to their true home in Palestine. He wrote that this time for return was "very near at hand." His reading of biblical prophecy had led him to see that the exclusion of Jews from England was, in fact, inhibiting the culmination of history because the return of the Jews to Palestine could not take place until the "People of God" were "first dispersed into all places and Countreyes of the World."[1]

Ben Israel had broad support among Protestants. They took Ben Israel's prophetic logic and extended it: first the establishment of a Jewish kingdom in Israel, and then the coming of Christ to establish his kingdom. Ben Israel understood that his messianic expectation was matched by his Christian audience's expectation of the second coming, and he used this common prophetic tradition to make his argument. The idea that Jewish restoration would precede Christian restoration grew strongly in prophetic readings of scripture after 1600.

John Calvin's Sovereign and Unknowable God

But that Protestant support for what came to be called Zionism had arrived through strange means. It began with a figure who eschewed passionately the idea that a true believer could know the future will of God: John Calvin (1509–1564). Unlike Luther, Calvin felt that humans should not waste time on speculation about the work of an absolutely sovereign God. They had too much important moral work to do in their own lives. If, as Calvin argued, God was absolutely sovereign and human depravity was likewise total, what could humans know of the workings of so far superior a being? Calvin was always "careful to talk about the workings of Divine Providence with a reserve that acknowledged their mystery."[2]

One of these unfathomable mysteries was who would finally be saved and who would not. Humans, in and of themselves, could make no good choice. Therefore God must make these choices for them. Calvin proposed that there were among all of humanity an "elect," and these were the saved. Calvin believed that scripture taught that salvation was pre-ordained by God, and was "without any respect to human worth."[3] The end result was that salvation depended entirely on God's mercy and on nothing else.

Calvin, biographers have noted, was a person who projected a "sense of foreboding ... pervasive and unappeasable."[4] The world, for Calvin, was a place of uncertainty in which "we cannot be otherwise than constantly anxious and confused."[5] All of our low-level human anxieties, the ones that follow us around in our days, are finally about death and judgment and are rooted in lack of faith. And we have good reason to be anxious about death and judgment because, as one biographer notes, Calvin's concept of God's justice was so "high" even angels could be condemned.[6]

At the same time, scripture tells us not to fear. When we are anxious about the future, we "do not concede the care of the world to God."[7] Calvin's final solution for anxiety was a paradoxical one: since the believer has no control over anything and God's sovereignty is absolute, the believer must release the future to faith.

Beyond this, Calvin's view of the eschatological future was simple: Christ will return. Somehow Christ's reign will be realized on earth. Calvin never commented on Revelation, and he seemed to be suspicious of the millennium's "carnal" leanings. He criticized Christians for being "more impressed" by the raising of the body than of the raising of the soul.[8] Given the great complexity of salvation as it had been laid out in the Middle Ages, Calvin vastly simplified this system. He rejected purgatory as unnecessarily complicated and a cause of corruption in the church. He taught that judgment came immediately at the moment of death, and there was nothing the living could do about the fate of any particular soul, nor really about the fate of their own souls.[9] The only mention of eschatology in the Anglican Forty-Two Articles of Religion that had been adopted as a Calvin-influenced broad Protestant consensus in 1553 was belief in the resurrection of the dead and the last judgment.

But the legacy of Calvinism did not carry this simplicity forward. Protestant fascination with eschatology intensified in the late sixteenth century. Calvin's agnosticism did not fully serve the English Reformation's purposes, and as we have already seen with Mede, Newton, and others, Revelation was a central object of fascination. Bernard McGinn notes that "nowhere was Revelation more avidly studied and more vociferously debated than in Reformation England."[10] This fascination was transported when English reformers crossed the Atlantic Ocean to establish colonies on the American continent.

The Conversion of the Jews

At the age of eighty-three, the year before his death, the American-born Puritan minister Increase Mather (1639-1723) wrote in his diary, "I desire nothing more than the conversion of the Jews."[11] What had made the conversion of the Jews a key sign for Mather?

The first thing is Mather's literal reading of biblical texts. He frequently reminded his New England audiences that the "literal interpretation of Scripture ought never to be rejected for an allegorical one except necessity compel thereunto."[12] He was especially emphatic on this question when it came to reading eschatological texts. Israel meant Israel—a literal, not a figurative place. If the will of God for the end of time was to unfold, Israel would have to be restored. One problem was that the actual land of Palestine had been largely unknown to both European Christians and European Jews for hundreds of years. Palestine was a "remote and impoverished backwater that had been under the rule of . . . the Muslim Ottoman Empire since 1517." Before that, yes, Christians had fought crusades and established monasteries, but for Europeans, it was largely a place of the imagination. If the meaning of scripture was to become "plain," as Mather and others insisted it must, Jews must return to Palestine, and there they must also acknowledge Jesus as the Messiah.

Christian interaction with Judaism over the course of its 1500 years in Europe had been highly fraught. As Christianity became less Jewish, as early as Justin Martyr in the second century, Christians appropriated Jewish prophetic and eschatological texts, claimed, as Justin Martyr did, that God had abandoned his chosen people because they rejected Christ, and took on Hebrew prophecies as their own. Jewish communities throughout Christendom had been subjected to violence, isolation, prohibitions on the ownership of property, inquisitions, expulsion, pogroms, and many other forms of prejudice and abuse.

But in the 150 years after the death of Calvin, with all of the eschatological turmoil of England as it transitioned from being a Catholic to a Protestant nation and the further eschatological turmoil of establishing the American colonies, the "question of the Jews" had become central. Jewish conversion to Christianity was linked to what Mather called his "chiliastical" position—that is, he believed that the Bible taught a coming millennium. Mather's 1669 book *The Mystery of Israel's Salvation* was a comprehensive attempt to argue for literal readings of scripture, including a literal restoration of Israel. He saw a connection between the conversion of the Jews, the defeat of both Catholic and Muslim enemies of the true church (that is, the Protestants), and "the glorious day for the elect upon this earth."[13]

While he was unsure if conversion of the Jews would happen first, followed by possession of "the Land promised unto their Father Abraham," or the reverse, he was certain that with these "late days," both were signs of the coming end of time promised by God. "The consummate salvation of Israel" would be completed in "the great battle of Armaggedon."[14]

He laid out a connection between the conversion of the Jews and the hoped-for millennium in this order:

> I take these things for Principles, and no way doubt but that they are demonstrable. 1. That the thousand apocalyptical years are not passed but future. 2. That the coming of Christ to raise the dead and to judge the earth will be within much less than this thousand years. 3. That the conversion of the Jews will not be till this present state of the world is near unto its end. 4. That, after the Jews' conversion there will be a glorious day for the elect upon earth, and that this day shall be a very long continuance.[15]

In other words, the conversion of the Jews was a sign that the millennium was very near. The idea of the conversion of the Jews became closely linked to their return to Palestine, and this is where the tentative alliance between Protestant and Jewish desires began to form.

"Prophesy Can Never Be Enough . . . Beaten Upon": Second Advent Theologians

The seventeenth century for English Protestants in both England and in the American colonies was a time of intense religious fervor, when religious beliefs pressed on every aspect of life. When these Protestants read in their Bibles that Jesus and Paul taught the imminence of the second coming, they did not wonder how the founders of their faith could have been so wrong. Instead they marveled at how much nearer the time must be now.[16] The second coming, wrote one seventeenth-century theologian, "belongeth unto us now living, as it did unto others in time past."[17]

A key sign for these "Second Advent theologians," as Bryan Ball calls them, was the extreme sinfulness of their present day. Thomas Hall argued that the following were signs of the end of the world: "The Drunkennesses of the Dutch, the Lust of the French, the Italians' Ambition, the Spaniards' Treachery, the Laylanders' Witchcraft, the Covetousness of the Jew, the Cruelty of the Turk and the Monsters of Münster."[18] He agreed that while such sin was plentiful among other nations, it was also "rife amongst us." In the same commentary, he continued his list, decrying how the Devil had "appeare[d] amongst us with open face: Arians, Arminians, Socinians, Anabaptists, Familists, Separatists, Mortalists, Perfectists, and (a compendium of all of these in one) Quakers."[19] He and many others also continued the still more common tradition of condemning the pope in eschatological terms. The locusts of Revelation 9 are the "Pope's Cleargie, as Abbots, Monkes, Friers, Priests, Shavelings, and such like vermine," wrote Arthur Dent.[20]

Reading the political and social context through an eschatological lens, English Protestants could conclude that the kingdoms of the world were in their final struggle, and H. R. Trevor-Roper writes that computing when the end of the world would take place and what its final events would be was being done "in many an English manor-house, in many a vicarage or college-cell."[21] One seventeenth-century scholar, Thomas Taylor, helpfully collated all of the failed prophecies and failed timelines of his contemporaries. He did not believe that this undermined the project of anticipating Christ's coming, but he did want to point out that the searching after signs was a process full of flaws. Others did not think that Christians could overdo this particular aspect of their faith. Arthur Dent wrote, "For in this age wherein we live, the Prophesy can never be enough opened and beaten upon, that all good Protestants may be armed with it against future times."[22]

As Protestants increasingly read the Bible intimately and personally, they also began to add to the interpretation of prophetic passages for themselves. Preachers of all varieties joined in, offering their own specific interpretations, and since the age placed increasing emphasis on "the individual's response to the Spirit's illumination of the Word," men and women, lay and clergy, university-trained and not, all got into the business of prophetic interpretation.[23] Perhaps it was Augustine's worst nightmare come true. These interpreters saw themselves primarily as readers of a text meant to be taken literally, and the texts they drew on to make their own map of the future were many fewer than those of Christopher Columbus. They drew primarily on Daniel and Revelation, trying to sort out which prophecies had already been fulfilled and which remained to be fulfilled, and their work took on a finely detailed, mathematical aspect, cataloging instead of imagining. But they all agreed with William Hicks, who in 1659 spoke for many a Protestant prophecy interpreter: "Therefore ye Saints of God, lift up your heads, for the Lord is at the door, and the day of your Redemption is nigh at hand."[24]

Notes

1. Mennaseh Ben Israel, "A Declaration to the Commonwealth of England," from *To His Highness the Lord Protector* (1655), online at http://www.jewish-history.com/Occident/volume3/may1845/menasseh.html.

2. Geoffrey Rowell, *Hell and the Victorians: A Study of the Nineteenth-Century Theological Controversies concerning Eternal Punishment and the Future Life* (Oxford: Oxford University Press, 1974), 27.

3. John Calvin, *Institutes* 3.21.7. See http://www.reformed.org/books/institutes/books/book3/bk3ch21.html.

4. See John Gross, review of William J. Bouwsma's *John Calvin: A Sixteenth Century Portrait* (Oxford: Oxford University Press, 1987) in the *New York Times* (December 8, 1987), 29.

5. Calvin, *Comm. Ps. 30:6*, quoted in Bouwsma, 34.

6. Bouwsma, 42.

7. Calvin, *Comm. Luke 12:29*, quoted in Bouwsma 39.

8. Bouwsma, 80.

9. David H. Watters, *"With Bodilie Eyes": Eschatological Themes in Puritan Literature and Gravestone Art* (Ann Arbor: University of Michigan Research Press, 1981), 15.

10. Bernard McGinn, "Revelation," in *The Literary Guide to the Bible*, ed. Robert Alter and Frank Kermode (Cambridge: Belknap/Harvard University Press, 1987), 529.

11. Shalom Goldman, *God's Sacred Tongue: Hebrew and the American Imagination* (Chapel Hill: University of North Carolina Press, 2004), 132.

12. Increase Mather, *The Mystery of Israel's Salvation, Explained and Applied* (London: Allen, 1669), 8–9.

13. Ibid., 32.

14. Ibid., 34.

15. Mather, quoted in Charles Ryrie, *The Basis of the Premillennial Faith* (Neptune: Loizeaux Brothers, 1953), 31–32.

16. Bryan W. Ball, *A Great Expectation: Eschatological Thought in English Protestantism to 1660* (Leiden: Brill, 1975), 42.

17. Richard Bernard, *A Key of Knowledge for the Opening of the Secret Mysteries of St. John's Mystical Revelation* (1617), 4; quoted in Ball, 61–62.

18. Thomas Hall, *A Practical and Polemical Commentary or Exposition Upon the Third and Fourth Chapters of the Latter Epistle of Saint Paul to Timothy* (1658), 8–9; quoted in Ball, 98.

19. Hall, 8; quoted in Ball, 106.

20. Arthur Dent, *The Ruin of Rome: or, An Exposition upon the whole Revelation. Wherein is plainly showed and proved, that the Popish Religion, together with all the power and authoritie of Rome, shall ebbe and decay still more and more throughout all the churches of Europe, and come to an utter overthrow even in this life before the end of the world* (1603), 105; quoted in Ball, 133.

21. H. R. Trevor-Roper, *The Crisis of the Seventeenth Century: Religion, the Reformation and Social Change, and Other Essays* (New York: Harper and Row, 1967), 247.

22. Dent, xvi; quoted in Ball, 61.

23. Ball, 66.

24. William Hicks, *The Revelation Revealed: Being a Practical Exposition on the Revelation of St. John* (1659), 346; quoted in Ball, 88.

20

Images: Virgins of the Apocalypse

Long live religion! Long live our most Holy Mother of Guadalupe! Long live Fernando VII! Long live America and death to bad government!

—Protest banners created by
Father Miguel Hidalgo y Castilla

On a December day in 1531, an indigenous peasant and recent convert to Christianity, known to history as Juan Diego Cuauhtlatoatzin (a Náhuatl name that means "the eagle who speaks"), was walking to mass. He had been baptized by Franciscan missionaries just a few years before in the midst of intense trauma for his people. These Aztecs had been under assault from the Spanish since the arrival of commander Hernán Cortés in 1518. The Franciscan missionaries had arrived in 1523 and had quickly set about destroying every vestige of what they called "paganism." Franciscan friar Juan de Zumárraga, who had arrived in 1528, boasted of personally destroying five hundred temples and twenty thousand "idols."[1]

Juan Diego had reached the hill of Tepeyac, a hill in central Mexico in what is now Mexico City, when he heard beautiful chants coming from the hill. The hill was a traditional location for the temple of an Aztec goddess, Tonantzín, a sacred site for the indigenous people of this part of Mexico. Looking up, he saw a shiny white cloud and a rainbow. He thought that perhaps he had crossed into Paradise. "Perhaps I am there where our old ancestors, our grandparents, have said: in the land of the flowers, in the land of the corn, of our flesh, of our sustenance, perhaps in the land of Heaven?"[2]

The chanting stopped, and he heard a woman's voice calling his name from the top of the hill. He began to climb the hill toward the voice, and there he saw a beautiful woman waiting for him. "Her dress shone as the sun, as if vibrating, and the stone where She stood, as if shooting rays. Her splendor was like precious stones, like a jewel." Speaking in his native language, the woman said, "Listen, my son, the youngest, Juanito, where are you headed?" When he told her that he was going to mass, she revealed herself as "Virgin, Holy Mary, Mother of the True God." She told him to build a "little sacred house" for her on the hill where she could help "those men in this land who ... cry out to me, who look for me, who trust in me, because there I will hear their cry, their sadness, to remedy, to cure all the different sufferings, their miseries, their pains." She sent him to the palace of the Bishop of Mexico (Zumárraga) to tell him to build her temple.[3]

This was the vision of the Virgin of Guadalupe, now a deeply entrenched part of Mexican history and self-understanding. While these events are placed by tradition in the sixteenth century, in the midst of the conflict with the Spanish, actual reference to them does not occur in the historical record until the eighteenth century.[4] By this point, the legend had a clear meaning: The Virgin of Guadalupe reached out to help the people of Mexico at a time of dire need, to comfort them, and to help them find a path to healing. The Virgin of Guadalupe became a symbol of piety, a connection to Aztec roots and identity, and eventually to the national identity of Mexico.

Franciscan Missionaries

For the indigenous tribes of the Americas, the conquest of the Spanish was itself an eschatological event with world-ending portent. Many of these cultures had their own catastrophe-oriented stories about the end of time. For them, the rampant outbreak of disease and the slaughter and destruction of the people by these new invaders could only mean the end of the world.

But Christian missionaries provided an alternative interpretation of events. The Franciscan missionaries followed in the wake of the *conquistadores*, but they had their own eschatological vision for the Americas that was deeply rooted in the writing of Joachim of Fiore three centuries before. Joachim had envisioned the flourishing of the spiritual monks in the third and final age—the age of the Holy Spirit. But in the view of both the Protestant reformers and the Franciscans, the church had remained intensely materialistic. In Spain, an internal reformer named Father Juan de Guadalupe had launched a campaign to return his fellow Franciscans to the purer, poorer vision of their founder. The majority of the first missionaries to follow Cortés to the Americas were deeply influenced by the Guadalupe reform movement. They believed they were the religious of Joachim's third age, and they would bring the Gospel to the poorest of the poor—the peoples of the Americas. The missionaries who arrived in Mexico believed that they were participating in the "supernatural destiny of mankind."[5]

Just as Puritan communities came to believe that eschatological fulfillment depended on the conversion of the Jews, these missionaries believed that such fulfillment depended on the conversion of the Indians, the "last gentiles hidden until then by the impenetrable will of God."[6] This was again intricately connected with the eschatological expectation of Matthew 24: "And this good news of the kingdom will be proclaimed throughout the world, as a testimony to all the nations; and then the end will come." The Franciscans who sailed on the dangerous voyage to the New World had the urgency of this eschatological vocation in mind.

A Shift in the Eschatological Center

By the eighteenth century, preachers both indigenous to the Americas and who had come from Europe were undergoing what Alain Milhou calls the "creolization" of the eschatological and millennial teachings that had crossed the ocean with missionaries.[7] The belief that the New World was somehow especially blessed by God for eschatological purposes translated into national desires and dreams.

We can see this process at work in the spread of the veneration of the Lady of Guadalupe, Juan Diego's Virgin. Many now connected Juan Diego's description of his vision on Tepeyac as similar to the woman of Revelation 12. "A great portent appeared in heaven: a woman clothed with the sun, with the moon under her feet, and on her head a crown of twelve stars" (Rev 12:1-2). They came to believe that the birth pangs associated with this woman were the birth pangs of a new people being born in the Americas. The Virgin of Guadalupe was now depicted standing on the moon, clothed with the rays of the sun, sometimes crushing a serpent beneath her feet. The Jesuit Francisco Javier Carranza (b. 1703) published a book called *The Transmigration of the Church to Guadalupe* in which he argued that Revelation 12 was a prophecy that referred directly to Mexico. The Virgin of Guadalupe was the virgin of Revelation 12, chased out of Europe by the dragon, the antichrist. He claimed that Revelation foretold that the true church would take root in New Spain. Mexico City, where the Virgin had appeared to Juan Diego, would be the New Jerusalem.[8]

In the eighteenth century, as revolt against regional leaders grew, the creole priest Miguel Hidalgo joined with a mestizo priest Jose Morelos to organize an army largely of indigenous people. One of Hidalgo's first steps was to put an image of the Virgin of Guadalupe on their banners. The army claimed both eschatological authority and unity in this image that was at once indigenous and European. The mestizo image of Mary-Tonantzín "became the Mother of all Mexicans."[9] In 1737, Our Lady of Guadalupe was declared the Patron Virgin of Mexico, a move that was not immediately accepted by the pope.

Later, Simón Bolívar (1783–1830), in what is called his *Prophetic Letter*, continued the tradition of claiming the renewal of European civilization in the Americas and used the degeneration of Europe as a reason for Latin America to part ways with Spain. He now put this claim in secular terms, with a westward movement for all that was great in human nature: "Then the sciences and the arts, once born in the Orient and having enlightened Europe, will take their flight toward free Colombia, who will grant them asylum."[10]

This was part of broader utopian dreams that dominated European interpretation of the New World. Given Spain's ongoing struggles with Muslims, it seemed clear that the place where Christendom would be rebuilt was in the New World, where there was space and great riches. Old prophecies were read in light of this new land and reinterpreted for its era. For example, in Peru at the end of the sixteenth century, Dominican Francisco de la Cruz believed that Spain was on the brink of terrible destruction by the Turks. In Lima, he preached that the center of the church must therefore transfer to the Americas, specifically to Lima, where Solomon's Temple would be rebuilt. His personal messianic dreams went still farther. Reading Joachim in an unusual manner, he declared himself a "third David," and he believed that he would rule over a new society of mestizos. De la Cruz was, not incidentally, condemned to death and burned at the stake in 1578, but his example is instructive for its vision of a new center for Christianity.

Other New-World Virgins of the Apocalypse

The use of the Virgin Mary for eschatological identities was not confined to Mexico. In Ecuador, sculptor Bernardo de LeGarda (1700–1773) crafted the Virgin of the Apocalypse, also based on Revelation 12. While LeGarda drew on European baroque traditions, he also gave his Virgin distinctive indigenous features, drawing together the ancient text with story of the New World.[11] In Peru, the tradition of dressing up statues of Mary in indigenous costumes became a facet of private and public devotion.

The elevation of Mary as an apocalyptic figure was a distinctive characteristic of Latin American apocalypticism.

Mary had the benefit of combining both genesis and apocalypse: she could symbolize the mother of all things and the pure church escaping and defeating the antichrist at the end of time. Her cult took deep root in the Americas where ancient indigenous traditions combined with Christian eschatology.[12] As Christian eschatology went forth into these new contexts and was taken up into already existing traditions, its questions changed along with its answers.

Millennial Movements in the Americas

While there may have been utopian hopes among the many missionaries who first came to Latin America, a millennial society did not flourish. By the eighteenth century, a tremendous gap between rich and poor, between indigenous peoples and those of European descent, between slaves and free was causing foment. Just as eschatology had once participated in the questions that Europeans raised about economic, social, and religious power, now it helped to propel Latin Americans to what Robert Levine calls "insurrections with a messianic character."[13] Most of these were small, local movements undertaken by people who could not read and write and so left few written records of their protest. We can postulate that they were syncretistic—that is, they mixed together Roman Catholicism with both indigenous and African beliefs depending on their location and the particular circumstances of their people. We know of these movements mostly by their endings. For example, in 1897, a religious settlement of 25,000 people waiting for Judgment Day in Brazil was completely destroyed by government forces, frightened, perhaps falsely, of its revolutionary potential.[14]

Notes

1. Virgilio Elizondo, *Guadalupe, Mother of the New Creation* (New York: Orbis, 2002), 55.

2. Words attributed to Juan Diego in Antonio Valeriano, *Nican Mopohua*, trans. P. Mario Rojas Sánchez (Mexico City: Fundación Peregrinación, 1998), 27.

3. Valeriano, 29–33.

4. Georges Baudot, *Utopia and History in Mexico: The First Chroniclers of Mexican Civilization (1520–1569)*, trans. Bernard R. Ortiz de Montellano and Thelma Ortiz de Montellano (Niwot: University Press of Colorado, 1995), 269–70.

5. Baudot, 83.

6. Ibid.

7. Alain Milhou, "Apocalypticism in Central and South American Colonialism," in *The Encyclopedia of Apocalypticism*, ed. Stephen J. Stein (New York: Continuum, 1998), 3:21.

8. Linda B. Hall, *Mary, Mother and Warrior: The Virgin in Spain and the Americas* (Austin: University of Texas Press, 2004), 190.

9. Milhou, 26.

10. Simon Bolivar, *Prophetic Letter*, quoted in Milhou, 25.

11. https://historiadelartejuanb.wordpress.com/2012/07/18/la-virgen-de-legarda-y-sus-figuras-totemicas/.

12. Milhou, 26.

13. Robert M. Levine, "Apocalyptic Movements in Latin America in the Nineteenth and Twentieth Centuries," in *The Encyclopedia of Apocalypticism*, 3:201.

14. Ibid., 179.

21

Liberation: Eschatology and Enslaved Africans in North America

Steal away, steal away, steal away to Jesus
Steal away, steal away home
I ain't got long to stay here

My Lord, He calls me
He calls me by the thunder
The trumpet sound within-a my soul
I ain't got long to stay here

—African-American spiritual

Just before the Civil War in the United States, a slave named Thomas L. Johnson was living in Richmond, a city he called a "stronghold of the Southern States." He watched the unfolding of events carefully, and since he could read, he gathered together others to teach them what he knew. Praying for liberty, these slaves gathered together to read Daniel and search it for prophetic understanding of what was going to happen in the war.

In his memoir, he wrote, "We often met together and read this chapter (Daniel 11) in our own way." The fifth verse, "Then the king of the South will grow strong, along with one of his princes who will gain ascendancy over him and obtain dominion; his domain will be a great dominion indeed," caused consternation among those gathered. But when they put this verse in context of the whole of the chapter, they concluded that the "latter verses set forth the ultimate triumph of the North." The chapter promised that the "king of the North will again raise a far greater multitude than the former" and prevail against the South. Johnson notes that the slaves in his study group scoured the texts for "any statements which our anxiety, hope, and prayer concerning our liberty led us to search for."[1]

Exile and Enslavement

By the time Johnson wrote these words, Africans had been living on the American continents for more than three hundred years. Between 1500 and 1800, more than eleven million people crossed the Atlantic in the slave trade. Many died en route. Others died soon after. In North America, those who did survive were often separated as quickly as possible from anyone who spoke their language or shared tribal or kinship connections. Thus the central experiences of Africans in the Americas were exile and enslavement. The number of West Africans caught up in the slave trade made Africans the largest immigrant population in the Americas by the eighteenth century.[2]

Africans brought with them, of course, music, language, and

ancient cultural and religious traditions that were placed under enormous pressure in slavery. They were "torn away," Albert Raboteau writes, "from the political, social, and cultural systems that ordered their lives." Their centers of meaning were destroyed. People who spoke similar languages or had tribal connections were separated by slave traders as much as possible; kinship was likewise considered dangerous to the system of slavery. Thus connections to language, people, family, and tribe were all severed.[3]

In the economy of the southern colonies, some plantation owners thought that Christianity might be helpful in teaching slaves their proper place in God's order. They made scriptural arguments about the God-ordained nature of slavery and in particular God's intention that Africans be enslaved. But by the late eighteenth century, Africans were steadily making the argument that slavery was incompatible with Christianity, as well as incompatible with the emerging republic and its ideals. In a letter to the governor of Massachusetts in 1774, a group of slaves prefigured the Bill of Rights in a plea for the injustice of slavery. "We have in common with other men a natural right to our freedoms without being deprived of them by our fellowman. ... There is a great number of us sencear ... members of the Church of Christ. ... How can the master be said to Beare my Borden when he Beares me down with the Have (heavy) chanes of slavery and operson against my will?"[4]

Eschatology as Language of Liberation

Over the course of the development of specifically African-American forms of Christianity, eschatology became central, specifically what we have been calling prophetic eschatology. African-Americans drew on the Hebrew Bible as a source of inspiration and hope in order to transform these ancient stories into messages that spoke of their own coming freedom. Multiple aspects of these texts resonated with enslaved Africans: the story of the Hebrews and Pharaoh, the time spent in the wilderness, the hope of the Promised Land. Under the conditions of American slavery, these were no longer about the past; they were stories alive in the present, and with increasing intensity they formed the basis for how slaves told the story of the future. The movement of God—the Hebrew Bible vividly instructed—was a movement from slavery to freedom. This became the foundation for African-American Christianity, and it drew a great deal of its power from the prophetic eschatology of the ancient past.

When logical arguments to whites about the conditions of slavery failed, slaves turned to eschatology to explain and transform the situation in which they found themselves. They used the question of death and salvation, for example, to cast aspersions on the hypocritical faith of their masters. They wondered how a master could imagine him- or herself saved at the time of death when he or she had been the source of so much misery on earth. The question about the ultimate salvation of slave owners became an important part of the tradition through stories, jokes, and songs. Slaves noticed that with some frequency, their masters would call them to their death beds in order to ask forgiveness. One man recorded his experiences in a memoir, *Slave Life in Georgia*, that published in the mid-nineteenth century. He wrote, "It is a common belief amongst us that all the masters die in an awful fright, for it is usual for the slaves to be called up on such occasions to say they forgive them for what they have done. So we come to think their minds must be dreadfully uneasy about holding slaves."[5] Raboteau records this popular anecdote:

A slave named George was informed by his master that he was to be buried in a good coffin and placed beside his master's earthly remains in the same vault with the white folks. George's response to this news is mixed, "I like to have a good coffin when I die," but "I fraid massa, when de debbil come take your body, he make mistake, and get mine."[6]

While slaves used the liminal moment of death as an opportunity to reflect on the moral conditions of slavery, they also used the stories of the Hebrew Bible to talk about their expectation of God's deliverance. Over time, through private religious meetings, art and performance, storytelling and biblical study, slaves developed a culture—an "inner world"—apart from slaveholders in which an all-powerful God who did not will slavery would transform the world and the conditions of slaves and draw them toward freedom. The slaves claimed the promises of the Hebrew Bible as their own.[7] This story shaped a common identity for slaves and gave them a vision for the future. While white Christians and slave owners wanted to emphasize Christ's spiritual deliverance, black Christians drew on Moses and the possibility of a physical and earthly deliverance, a transformation of this-worldly suffering and pain.

Sometimes this hope took the form of imagined bloody vengeance. The prophetic tradition on which African Americans drew had a lot of room for both mythic hope and the violent destruction of oppressors and enemies. A New England governess who spent time in the American south recorded the words of one slave, a woman named Aggy, who reacted after her master beat her daughter. She used the familiar language of the judgment to curse her master:

Thar's a day a-comin'! Thar's a day a-comin'! ... I hear de rumblin' ob de chariots! I see de flashin' ob de guns! White folks blood is a-runnin' on de ground like a riber, an' dead's heaped up dat high! . . . Oh, Lor'! hasten de day when de blows, an de bruises, an' de aches, an' de pains, shall come to de white folks, an' de buzzards shall eat 'em as dey's dead in the streets. Oh, Lor'! gib me de pleasure ob livin' till dat day, when I shall see white folks shot down like de wolves when de come hongry out o' de woods![8]

Aggy's words are a kind of psalm resonating with the words of ancient Hebrew poets who ached for the destruction of their enemies. She used eschatological language to imagine it and gave urgency to the future in the "day" that is "a-comin'."

Eschatology as Metaphor

In 1850, Harriet Tubman, who had been a slave in the South, escaped. After her successful escape, she became the most famous "conductor" on the Underground Railroad, an informal set of networks, safe houses, and connections that could guide slaves from the south to the north. Tubman guided perhaps as many as three hundred slaves to freedom using these mechanisms, and she became known as "Moses."

Tubman was adept at using the language of eschatology to signal various aspects of both aid and help in the secret movements of the Railroad. But she also helped to give the movement from slavery to freedom an eschatological character. For example, she was famous for using African-American spirituals like "Go Down Moses" to signal to slaves that she was nearby and ready to help. She also used "map songs" to tell people where to go. All of these songs had multiple meanings. They not only gave directions or signaled help, but also created a context for religious and eschatological understanding.

The hope espoused by enslaved people and their supporters was an earthly hope. It was invested in specific earthly events, like the Civil War, in order to bring about freedom on earth for an oppressed people. The end result was not imagined to be utopia, although there were certainly utopian elements, but simply basic human dignity and freedom. Whereas much of Christianity's investment in the future had been about the impending end of the world, this prophetic strand of Christian eschatology imagined a more just future on earth.

As we've seen, Christianity never resolved well the question of the fate of an individual and the fate of the world or the question of individual judgement in relation to collective judgment. These two strands of Christian teaching had been in conflict with each other since the writings of the apostle Paul. But the contrast had perhaps never been so sharp as when it was delineated by slaves and masters in the American south in the nineteenth century.[9] Pious slaveholders preferred to focus attention on otherworldly salvation because it seemed, at least on the surface, to protect the social order. They could make the claim that disobedience and insurrection were sins that put one's immortal soul at risk. But slaves and abolitionists drew on the second strand that imagined a society transformed into something closer to the kingdom of God. They also drew on biblical language that suggested a time of blood and fire might be necessary to bring this transformation about.

The reading that enslaved Africans gave Jewish and Christian texts in their own particular historical circumstances transformed the tradition they had inherited. They passed on this tradition with new readings, heightened metaphors, and artistically rendered images that have made it impossible for any North American to hear the words "River Jordan" or "Let my people go," or Isaiah's words, "He has sent me to proclaim release to the captives and recovery of sight to the blind, to let the oppressed go free," and not hear the liberative strains of African-American Christianity.

Notes

1. Thomas L. Johnson, *Africa for Christ: Twenty-eight Years a Slave* (Chapel Hill: University of North Carolina Press, 2001), 29–30.

2. Philip Curtin, *The Atlantic Slave Trade* (Madison: University of Wisconsin Press, 1969).

3. Albert J. Raboteau, *Slave Religion: The "Invisible Institution" in the Antebellum South* (New York: Oxford University Press, 1978), 4.

4. Petition cited in St. Clair Draje, *The Redemption of Africa and Black Religion* (Chicago: Third World, 1970), 23–24.

5. John Brown, *Slave Life in Georgia*, ed. L. A. Chamerovzow (London, 1855), 203–4.

6. Raboteau, 292.

7. Ibid., 311.

8. Mary A Livermore, *My Story of the War* (Hartford: Pickle Partners, 1889), 260–61.

9. Geoffrey Rowell, *Hell and the Victorians: A Study of the Nineteenth-Century Theological Controversies concerning Eternal Punishment and the Future Life* (Oxford: Oxford University Press, 1974), 22.

22

Jeremiads: Jonathan Edwards and the American Republic

"God . . . will inflict Wrath without any Pity," American preacher Jonathan Edwards (1703–1758) told his eager audience. "When God beholds the ineffable Extremity of your Case, and sees your Torment to be so vastly disproportion'd to your Strength, and sees how your poor Soul is crushed and sinks down, as it were into an infinite Gloom, he will have no Compassion upon you, he will not forbear the Executions of his Wrath, or in the least lighten his Hand."

Thought it may be nearly impossible for us to understand it, these were words of inspiration to the eighteenth-century American-born Puritans to whom he spoke them. These are lines from Edwards's famous 1741 sermon "Sinners in the Hands of an Angry God," and they were in the form of a **jeremiad**.

A jeremiad was a form of oratory that was crucial in the emerging republic. Stephen Stein called it "the characteristic expression of New England's developing sense of mission."[1] The word "jeremiad" comes from the prophet Jeremiah, who offered long lamentations for his people and predicted their coming downfall. In a similar way, a jeremiad delivered by Puritan ministers offered people a long list of their sins and the coming wrath of God against them. But it was a paradoxical form of speech. While lambasting people with their sin, it was meant to impel them to goodness. It wasn't so much a warning as it was a way to compel people to work harder, live more righteously, and build the life of the new world.

"An Extraordinary Opportunity"

Jonathan Edwards was perhaps the most famous preacher of this period just before the Declaration of Independence, but he had inherited the form through a long line. He deployed it in a way that was slightly different from his contemporaries, actively seeking the awakening of his audiences for progress and even reason. Fascinated by Sir Isaac Newton and widely read in natural philosophy, Edwards drew these various strains together in revivals that came to be called the First Great Awakening.

The First Great Awakening was a series of revivals aimed to inspire the people of New England to turn toward God. For Edwards, awakening was intimately linked with the progress of the people. In 1737, Edwards reported a sense that the "noise amongst the dry bones waxed louder."[2] He felt that he could perceive the people's hunger for a glimpse of the kingdom of heaven, and it was his job to drive them toward it. By the time he delivered the sermon "Sinners in the Hands of an

Angry God," he believed that there was what he called an "extraordinary Opportunity" in front of the people.[3]

He directed the sermon "Sinners" toward young people. He urged "young Men and young Women" who "especially have now an extraordinary Opportunity" to turn toward Christ, but then he warned them, "If you neglect it, it will be with you as it is with those Persons that spent away the precious Days of Youth in Sin and are now come to such a dreadful pass in blindness and hardness."[4]

Edwards hinted that the American people living on this continent at this moment were a chosen people, a people for whom God had a special mission. But because of that, God demanded their total and utter repentance, their loyalty and unswerving commitment. Both risk and reward were great. Mark Noll notes that in this rhetoric there was a strong tie between personal transformation and national reform.[5] The moral standing of the people had a direct link to the moral standing of the new nation, and the jeremiad was an effective form for forging that link and convincing people of their duty.

But it was also a form that created a great deal of uncertainty about the future. The future was not guaranteed to bring either doom or prosperity. Sacvan Bercovitch, in his classic study of the jeremiad, points out that it was a twisted form of American progressivism. The point of the jeremiad was to drive the nation forward with no small amount of fear and trembling but also with concern for their neighbors and concern for the kind of society in which they lived.[6] The purpose of the jeremiad was a communal one, and it bade people to live up to their potential. Or else.

The Millennium

Evidence that the jeremiad was not all doom and gloom despite its heavy-handed rhetoric is to be found in the place that Jonathan Edwards gave the millennium in his own theology. All of his life, Edwards believed that God would accomplish "glorious things . . . for his church in the latter days."[7] He made notes on the millennium in his private notebooks throughout his life and wrote a separate commentary on Revelation, the only book of the Bible for which he did this. He believed that the Bible promised progress for the church on earth, and these promises gave him hope. The millennium would be the culmination of God's work on earth, the fulfillment of his kingdom. To speak of the millennium, Edwards frequently used the terms "advancement" and "glorious things." The promise of God's redemption within human history, not beyond it, was key to his eschatology.[8]

Edwards believed that God would accomplish his purposes on earth with outpourings of the Spirit like the kind that he had seen in his revivals.[9] He believed, based on his study of Revelation, that he was living in the time of the "sixth vial" in which false prophets went forth, but everything was in preparation for the great gathering of the Last Day. After the visit of George Whitefield, an extraordinarily talented preacher, to Edwards's Northampton, Edwards was ecstatic with the eschatological possibilities. "'Tis not unlikely," he wrote, "that this work of God's Spirit, that is so extraordinary and wonderful is the dawning, or at least a prelude, of that glorious work of God so often foretold in the Scriptures, which in the progress and issue of it, shall renew the world of mankind." And he saw that it was probable that this work would begin in America, even as it was the whole world that would be renewed.[10]

For someone who was attempting to follow the divine eschatological pulse as Edwards was, it was necessary also to watch it wane and wax. He made these enthusiastic pronouncements in the 1740s only to wonder a little later if God's work had become a "Measure withdrawn." Then he called for renewal once again and argued that all believers should draw together in a "concert of prayer" so that they could help to bring about the advent of the kingdom of God.[11] These cycles of renewal and withdrawal became an entrenched part of evangelical apocalyptic understanding, even when evangelicals lost some of Edwards's progressive mentality.

The Progressive Republic

Edwards's influence on the interpretation of the new republic was strong. By the time of the American Revolution, millennial hopes for the land combined with the progress of reason and science created a new sense of purpose for the emerging nation. In 1780 Timothy Dwight, the grandson of Edwards, published his poem *America* that spoke to this newly forged, particularly American eschatology.

> Celestial science, raptur'd we descry
> Refulgent beaming o'er the western sky;
> Bright liberty extends her blissful reign,
> With all the graces sparkling in her train:
> Religion shines with a superiour blaze,
> And heaven-born virtue beams diviner rays;
> Justice enthron'd maintains an equal sway,
> The poor dwell safely, and the proud obey.[12]

In Dwight's poem, America is a nation of celestial light, with science, liberty, and religion as partners in its progress toward a just society. We can hear hints of the Jewish prophetic tradition, the Christian ethics of eschatology, and new national hopes. Dwight believed that America represented the final stage of history, and the American nation was a universal nation that represented a universal story. He was not circumspect in this regard. He made precise calculations of the seven vials of Revelation and what each one meant for the unfolding of the divine plan. He saw American history as sacred history, and the combining of reason and scripture was only one more proof that it was so.[13]

These eschatological ideas and ambitions shaped the American republic and gave the people a sense of divinely ordained destiny and mission. Their scriptures pointed directly to them, telling them of the providential role they had to play. Inevitably, his sense of mission would splinter in the nineteenth century, revealing a "bewildering diversity" of ideas about the end of the world.[14]

Notes

1. Stephen J. Stein, "Transatlantic Extensions: Apocalyptic in Early New England," in *Apocalypse in English Renaissance Thought and Literature,* ed. C. A. Parties and Joseph Wittreich (Manchester: Manchester University Press, 1984), 273.

2. Jonathan Edwards, *A Faithful Narrative of the Surprising Work of God*, in *The Great Awakening*, in *The Works of Jonathan Edwards*, ed. C. C. Goen (New Haven: Yale University Press, 1972), 4:149–50.

3. Jonathan Edwards, "Sinners in the Hands of an Angry God," 18; online at http://digitalcommons.unl.edu/cgi/viewcontent.cgi?article=1053 &context=etas.

4. Ibid., 24.

5. Mark Noll, *America's God: From Jonathan Edwards to Abraham Lincoln* (New York: Oxford University Press, 2002), 38.

6. Sacvan Bercovitch, *The American Jeremiad* (Madison: University of Wisconsin Press, 1978), 7.

7. Jonathan Edwards, "Personal Narrative," in *Jonathan Edwards: Representative Selections*, ed. Clarence H. Faust and Thomas H. Johnson (New York: Hill and Wang, 1962), 65.

8. Gerald R. McDermott, *One Holy and Happy Society: The Public Theology of Jonathan Edwards* (University Park: The Pennsylvania State University Press, 1992), 43–45.

9. Stein, 282.

10. Goen, ed., 353.

11. Jonathan Edwards, in *The Works of President Edwards*, ed. Sereno E. Dwight (New York: Carvill, 1830), 1:213 and 240.

12. Timothy Dwight, *America: or a Poem on the Settlement of the British Colonies* (New Haven: Yale University Press, 1780), 3 and 9.

13. Richard M. Gamble, "'The Last and Brightest Empire of Time': Timothy Dwight and America as Voegelin's 'Authoritative Present,' 1771–1787," *Humanitas* 20/1–2 (2007): 13–35.

14. James Moorhead, "Apocalypticism in Mainstream Protestantism: 1800 to the Present," in *The Encyclopedia of Apocalypticism*, ed. Stephen Stein (New York: Continuum, 1998), 3:75.

23

Utopias: Postmillennial America

Thine are these orbs of light and shade;
    Thou madest Life in man and brute;
    Thou madest Death; and lo, thy foot
Is on the skull which thou hast made.

Thou wilt not leave us in the dust:
    Thou madest man, he knows not why,
    He thinks he was not made to die;
And thou hast made him: thou art just.
        —Alfred Lord Tennyson, from *In Memoriam*

The two bestselling novels of the nineteenth century both reflected one strand of Jonathan Edwards's vision of a progressive America moving toward the millennium. One was *Uncle Tom's Cabin* (1852), written by Harriet Beecher Stowe, a white abolitionist. This was a story of a fugitive slave that inspired many white Americans to take seriously the problem of slavery and to imagine a society in which everyone could be free. The other novel was called *Looking Backward* (1888), written by Edward Bellamy. It imagined the United States in the year 2000, when humans would have perfected the relationship between technology and society and thus would live with utopian ease. Both novels, one with a primarily religious vision and one with a primarily secular vision, were invested in the eschatological project that scholars have come to call **postmillennialism.**

Postmillennialism

In the nineteenth century, in the brief decades between the establishment of the American Republic and the beginning of the Civil War, American intellectuals forged a compromise with their eschatological heritage, which had imagined an impending disaster for so long. Instead of imagining the millennium as something that Christ would inaugurate in Jerusalem, these Christians imagined the kingdom of God as something they would build with their own hands. Christ would come *after* the millennium, when human progress and hard work had created a just and peaceful global society. James Moorhead calls this a compromise between apocalyptic and evolutionary understandings of time. In an apocalyptic understanding of time, history is "characterized by dramatic upheavals and supernatural events." In an evolutionary understanding, history is "governed by natural laws of organic development."[1] Rationalism combined with apocalyptic hope to create the belief that humans would *achieve* the millennium rather than be mere recipients. If the idea of human progress was to take root in a democratic republic, then people had to abandon the tyrant God who was always jumping in to undo what humans were constructing or who was threatening them with imminent disaster. Kingdom builders of the nineteenth century had little use for this God.[2]

In the United States especially, postmillennialism took root in many social projects: abolition, temperance, women's suffrage, manifest destiny, prison and education reform, and missionary societies to name a few. While postmillennialism was different from the prophetic eschatology developing among African-Americans, it did allow for white and black allies in a way that other forms of eschatology did not. The colonial and missionary version of postmillennialism was creating "civilized" and Christian citizens globally. The domestic version was transforming society into the kingdom of God. With so much work to do on earth, it no longer made sense to these Christians that God would prematurely coerce his kingdom at will. "By delaying the second coming and the last judgment to the far side of the millennium, the eschatology assured that God would not bring down the curtain of history prematurely or coerce an earthly kingdom into existence via displays of supernatural might."[3] Instead God would work in cooperation with humankind via "moral government," individual persuasion, and transformation of the human heart. The saints would cooperate with all the "accoutrements of progress"—technological, scientific and governmental—to bring about God's kingdom.[4]

Utopian Experiments

This kingdom building mentality led to a variety of utopian experiments and utopian visions of the future, and not only in the newly formed United States. In England, a woman named Jane Wardley formed the United Society of Believers in Christ's Second Appearing. This group—the Shakers—believed that they were receiving direct communication from the Holy Spirit telling them about the end of time.

In 1774, a small group of Shakers under the leadership of Ann Lee sailed to the United States and established a community at a place they called New Lebanon in New York State. Ann Lee established particular practices among her followers, including sexual equality and chastity. These practices eventually led Shakers to argue, after Mother Ann's death, that the millennium had already come, and they were living under new rules that they called "Millennial Laws."[5] But because Shakers did not believe in sexual reproduction, they eventually died out as their popularity faded.

Other social experiments spread widely in the post-millennial era. Boston Congregationalist minister George Ripley resigned his position in 1840 to found with his wife, Sophia Dana Ripley, a community outside of Boston that came to be called Brook Farm. Their goal was "to ensure a more natural union between intellectual and manual labor than now exists; to combine the thinker and the worker, as far as possible, in the same individual." They believed that this combination of thought and physical labor would "guarantee the highest mental freedom ... and thus to prepare a society of liberal, intelligent, and cultivated persons, whose relations with each other would permit a more simple and wholesome life, than can now be led amidst the pressures of our competitive institutions."[6]

They were joined in the experiment by Nathaniel Hawthorne, among others, and visited by Ralph Waldo Emerson, Bronson Alcott, Margaret Fuller, and other leading intellectuals. Nathaniel Hawthorne eventually abandoned the project, finding the balance between labor and reason not conducive to writing.

In 1821, a group of former slaves from the United States sailed to the coast of Africa and began a settlement that would become the nation of Liberia. They had a complicated understanding of their mission that included postmilliennial, utopian, and missionary goals. By 1870, 13,000 former slaves had arrived in Liberia.

There were dozens of communal experiments that began in the nineteenth century and spread from Boston to Louisiana, from Alabama to Kansas—and to the coast of Africa. Each of these was invested in some version of the perfection of human society. They imagined perfect equality among the sexes, "complex marriages," or "free love." Some offered new revelations or alternative ways to balance the demands of work and art or other kinds of alternative economies. Some were anarchist, some socialist, some apocalyptic, some missionary, some spiritualist.[7] Nearly all of them demonstrated the striving after human perfection that characterized postmillennialism, the belief that humans could find the answer to social, technological, and religious puzzles.

Judgment

Even with widespread social experimentation, an older conversation about the nature of the last judgment continued throughout the nineteenth century. In 1866, one American woman noted in a collection of essays called *The Church and the World* that "no one interested in theology could have lived through the last few years without having the awful question of future punishment forced upon his thoughts."[8] Edwards's "angry God" continued to haunt the imaginations of reformers and progressives deep into the century, and an ongoing argument about heaven, hell, judgment, personal salvation, and communal salvation dominated the religious landscape.[9]

Christianity's conflicted heritage—resurrection of the body or immortality of the soul? Judgment immediately after death or a millennium on earth? The fate of the individual soul or the fate of the entire world? An imminent end or a prolonged waiting?—weighed on this new era. The paradoxes of the inherited eschatologies felt increasingly awkward.[10]

Hell thus became, by the end of the nineteenth century, hotly debated. On the one hand was the fire and brimstone preaching inherited from the Puritans and honed by the evangelical tent preachers of the Second Great Awakening, the call of the individual soul to awaken and avoid eternal torment. On the other side were the growing questions of Christian intellectuals who were grappling with science and the very different picture of humanity and the earth that it provided.

Some theologians argued that the idea of hell was at odds with natural religion, in which God and the soul are imagined as continuous with the natural world, not radically separate from it.[11] Some thought, hearkening back to Augustine, that hell could still be useful for moral reasons, that is, by encouraging good behavior, but by the end of the century, this argument looked silly. Theologians came to argue that hell was a punishment that didn't fit the crime, that virtue induced by threat was not in fact virtue, and that no one who talked of hell actually thought he was going there.[12] Progressive Christians became increasingly comfortable with a theology that excluded hell.[13]

But then what, precisely, was the immortal soul, if it was not an entity to be judged by God on "that day"? And what was the meaning of Christ's death and resurrection? If it was not to save the soul from hell, what was it? Progressive Christians did not have an answer to these questions and instead drew heavily on the romantic tradition to suggest that the immortal soul had something to do with human yearning and was tied in to human emotion. They thus dropped questions of judgment and replaced them with questions of desire.

Science and Eschatological Doubt

When poet Alfred Lord Tennyson's (1809–1892) aunt, a devout Calvinist, looked at him, she would frequently say, "Alfred, Alfred, when I look at you, I think of the words of Holy Scripture—'Depart from me, ye cursed, into everlasting fire.'"[14] This aunt damned Tennyson because of the doubts that he articulated in his poetry, but the questions of hellfire and damnation, of the fate of the soul after death, pressed with new urgency on a Protestant society that had abandoned the compromise of purgatory and had to reckon with the new stories it was receiving from science.

Tennyson was one of the first poets who wrestled in his work to reconcile religious teachings and scientific discoveries, one of the first poets who needed a new language because of the rapid shift in how the world's basic properties were understood. *In Memoriam* was his 1849 attempt to articulate the struggle between traditional Christian teachings about the afterlife and the new understandings of the earth and its inhabitants that were being increasingly articulated by science.

The poem wrestles with human knowledge, on the one hand, and God's knowledge, on the other. Did the two need to be in conflict? Or could they find reconciliation? In each verse of the poem, Tennyson poses this question and tries to answer it, then poses the question again and seeks an answer.

We have but faith: we cannot know;
    For knowledge is of things we see
    And yet we trust it comes from thee,
A beam in darkness: let it grow.

In this verse, human knowledge has its origin in God's will, but in the next verse, Tennyson asks for something that has become more elusive.

Let knowledge grow from more to more,
    But more of reverence in us dwell;
    That mind and soul, according well,
May make one music as before.

Can mind and soul "make one music"? Or have they now parted company? Tennyson's prayer seems to be *in memoriam* of a harmony that has ceased to exist. Doubt has entered between the believer and God, and knowledge is the vehicle of doubt. At the same time, Tennyson wants to believe that human knowledge, properly understood, leads to reverence, that God has placed the natural curiosity and the ability for exploration in humankind. *In Memoriam* attempts a reconciliation, but the reader senses that its chances have become thin.

Two dramatic shifts in scientific perception cast the entire problem of Christian eschatology into new relief. One was the discovery of geologic time. While it was well into the twentieth century until Christians widely understood and perceived the problem that geologic time posed to their inheritance, discoveries of the nineteenth century heralded the change. In the eschatologies from Augustine to Luther, the world was understood to have a lifespan of roughly six thousand years. Augustine thought the world was in its decrepit old age in his own day, in rapid decline. Luther did the math and imagined the earth could not possibly have much longer to exist. But the growing field of geology began to place the age of the earth at ninety-six million years.[15] This was a radically different time frame than the ones that Christians had been using, and it threw questions of the future—which had long been an attempt to understand history comprehensively—into a strange new light. With such a vast horizon, how could a human being tell the story from beginning to end? Scripture began to lose its ability to tell a truly comprehensive, literal story of the earth—past, present, and future.

The other dramatic shift was, of course, Charles Darwin's (1809–1882) theory of evolution. For Christians willing to take on Darwin's theory, the course of history was transformed. Instead of seeing a God of sudden comings, who makes radical change, Christian thinkers engaging with Darwin began to propose theories of a God within human and natural history, a God "equated with gradual, continuous, and progressive development."[16] The integration of Darwin's theory into Christian theology resonated with postmillennialism and gave it a scientific undergirding. Others, of course, passionately rejected Darwin's theory, seeing it as tending toward atheism and any meaningful, traditional reading of scripture. This divide widened in the twentieth century.

Notes

1. James Moorhead, *World without End: Mainstream American Protestant Visions of the Last Things, 1880-1925* (Bloomington: Indiana University Press, 1999), xiii.

2. See Paul Tillich, *Perspectives on 19th and 20th century Protestant Theology* (London: SCM, 1967), 47–48.

3. James Moorhead, "Apocalypticism in Mainstream Protestantism: 1800

to the Present," *The Encyclopedia of Apocalypticism*, ed. Stephen J. Stein (New York: Continuum, 1998), 3:81.

4. Ibid.

5. Stephen Stein, "Apocalypticism Outside the Mainstream in the United States," in *The Encyclopedia of Apocalypticism*, 3:112–13.

6. George Ripley, "A Letter Addressed to the Congregational Church in Purchase Street," online at http://transcendentalism-legacy.tamu.edu/ideas/letter.html#ripley.

7. A list can be found at https://en.wikipedia.org/wiki/List_of_American_Utopian_communities.

8. Geoffrey Rowell, *Hell and the Victorians: A Study of the Nineteenth-Century Theological Controversies concerning Eternal Punishment and the Future Life* (Oxford: Oxford University Press, 1974), 1.

9. See Rowell and Moorhead, *World*, 47–76.

10. Rowell, 22.

11. Ibid., 28–29.

12. Ibid., 30.

13. Ibid., 212.

14. See *Alfred Lord Tennyson: A Memoir* (London: Macmillian, 1897), 12.

15. J. G. C. M. Fuller, "Smith's Other debt, John Strachey, William Smith and the Strata of England 1719-1801," *Geoscientist* (July 17, 2007). That age has, of course, only expanded as scientists have examined the question. Currently the age of the earth is considered to be 4.543 billion years.

16. Jon H. Roberts, *Darwinism and the Divine in America: Protestant Intellectuals and Organic Evolution, 1859-1900* (South Bend: University of Notre Dame Press, 2001), 145. See also Moorhead, *World without End*.

24

Charts: Prophecy Belief 1850-1950

All society everywhere, with its politics, its philosophy, and its religion, is in a perturbed condition. . . . The stream of earthly things is overflowing its old banks, and spreading out in every direction, in wild, disordered, ungovernable, and overwhelming volume. Old systems and modes of thought and belief, which have stood for ages, are everywhere tottering.

—Reverend Joseph Seiss, *The Last Times* (1856)

The Great Disappointment

On Tuesday, October 22, 1844, a man named Henry Emmons waited for the coming of Jesus Christ. He waited until noon on Wednesday, but soon after began to feel faint. He described his condition later in a letter as "sick with disappointment."[1] Emmons was a Millerite, and he had been awaiting the coming of Jesus Christ based on the advice of a farmer and preacher named William Miller. Miller had been studying his Bible, much like his seventeenth-century predecessors, for clues about the end of time. He concluded that the day of judgment predicted by the Bible would fall in 1843 or 1844. At first he did not name a specific date, but after some pressure from his growing number of followers, he landed on March 22, 1843.

That date passed uneventfully, but Miller continued to preach and teach all over New England in tent meetings and large venues. He revealed the biblical secrets that he had discovered through careful calculation of Daniel's seventy weeks. He argued that the first sixty-nine weeks took place from 457 BCE to 27 CE, and that since then, humans had been living in the "seventieth week," which would soon end. Thousands of people listened to him explain "his interpretative system in a low-level schoolmasterish fashion."[2] Miller and his followers used mass-produced tracts and publications to spread the word, and in early 1844, Miller's followers set a new date: October 22, 1844, a date that became known in American history as the Great Disappointment. Millerites had spread word of the world's end far and wide. Thousands believed them. Hundreds believed them so completely that they did not plant crops or prepare for winter. On the night of October 22, believers gathered on hilltops all over New England to wait for the coming of Christ. Nothing of an eschatological nature happened.

From the disarray and confusion of the Great Disappointment, however, came several new religious movements and new ways of engaging biblical eschatology. It was the root event of the Seventh-Day Adventist Church and of the Jehovah's Witnesses, who formed in the wake of the Millerite catastrophe and maintained an apocalyptic stance, even while they avoided specific dates.[3] The Millerites had demonstrated that popularizing techniques could spread apocalyptic messages quickly using frameworks that were outside traditional church institutions.

The Secret Rapture

The nineteenth century saw many itinerant preachers like Miller, who traveled around the growing expanse of the United States preaching a wide variety of eschatological theories. If some spent the nineteenth century envisioning alternative realities, others continued in the tradition of Jonathan Edwards in a different way: imagining a perilous, imminent end. Even though these Christians have often been understood as anti-modernists, they used modern techniques for calculating, elucidating, and publicizing the events of the imminent end.

One of these was a man named John Nelson Darby (1800–1882), an Anglo-Irish preacher from the Plymouth Brethren. Through an unlikely route, Darby ended up giving Christianity an enduring and widely popular understanding of biblical eschatology. Darby's apocalyptic theory had the great benefit of not linking itself to a specific date. He and other post-Miller preachers mastered "the art of keeping end-time yearning at a peak of expectation," without the pitfall of specific date-setting.[4]

Darby preached that the Bible taught that the second coming of Christ would happen not once, but twice. The first coming would be in secret, an event that Darby called "the secret rapture." The word "rapture" was indeed a biblical term, though it had never been used the way that Darby used it. It came from 1 Thessalonians 4:17: "Then we who are alive, who are left, will be caught up in the clouds together with them to meet the Lord in the air; and so we will be with the

Lord forever." In Latin, the verb for *caught up* was *rapiemur* and became in medieval Latin a noun, *raptura*, and in English, finally, rapture. The secret rapture was the moment when true believers—the invisible church—would be taken up to heaven in a sudden signal that the events of the end of time had begun.

According to this reading of scripture, which would be elaborated in a widely popular theory, the secret rapture would be followed by seven years of suffering called the tribulation. Many of the images and prophecies of Revelation—famines, plagues, the sea turned to blood, the strange locusts—would come about during this period. At the end of the tribulation would come the events of Revelation 20, the great battle between the warrior Christ and Satan that would bind Satan for a thousand years.

Scholars have called versions of end-times events like Darby's **dispensational premillennialism**. "Dispensational" refers to the division of time into specific ages, each with a specific purpose. Dispensationalists believed they were living at the last stages of the Church Age, which would be followed swiftly by the millennium and the eternal heavenly kingdom. "Premillennialism" refers to the fact that Christ would come before the millennium—the very opposite of what we have seen from other "kingdom building" Christians of this same era. In this version of events, the world actually would go into steep decline before the coming of Christ, and the secret rapture would come suddenly to save the elect from the imminent suffering. For these Christians, every war or rumor of war, every political battle lost, every moral boundary breached was a sign that the end was near.

Engineering Eschatology

To understand the appeal of dispensational premillennialism, we need to look at the broad social context. Dispensational premillennialists were part of what Brendan Pietsch calls "broad aspirational movements" in the late nineteenth century "that placed profound faith in the power of taxonomic thinking and engineering methods to produce confidence in religious knowledge."[5] Inheritors of Isaac Newton's methods, they developed these methods by making maps and charts for every aspect of eschatology. The tribulation was broken down into individual years, and each chapter of Revelation was mapped onto these charts. Daniel's seventy weeks were mapped in multiple ways; explanations for the elusive "time, times, and half a time" of Daniel and Revelation were likewise charted.

Because of the expansive growth in popular publishing in this period, dispensationalist charts combined rapidly with mass culture. These came in tracts, brochures, and pamphlets, and taught a very modern way of reading prophetic texts. One Baptist minister named Clarence Larkin (1850–1924) drew elaborate charts detailing the "resurrection and the judgments," the "millennial land," and heaven and hell that look like charts drawn to detail factory processes and work flows for the Industrial Revolution. He believed that the Bible could be charted, like the "drawings and specifications of a building."[6] His charts served as tools that believers could use to map the future.[7] It was part of a cultural logic that produced certainty through categorization and classification. This cultural logic was simultaneously and enthusiastically engaged with selling its products to as wide a public as possible.

This approach to Christian eschatology spread rapidly

among white Protestants, many of whom felt threatened by the growing number of immigrants in the United States, the rapid changes to traditional life brought by the Industrial Revolution and urbanization, and the changing intellectual landscape. At the end of the nineteenth century and the beginning of the twentieth century, conservative Protestants, a large number of whom were a part of the network of evangelist Dwight L. Moody (1837–1899), began to meet in a series of Bible conferences. Advertisements for a conference held in New York in 1878 proposed that "those who hold to the personal pre-Millennial advent of Jesus Christ and who are 'looking for the blessed hope' should meet together . . . to set forth in clear terms the grounds of their hope, to give mutual encouragement in the maintenance of what they believe to be a most vital truth for the present times."[8] In other words, conference goers sought broad agreement on questions of prophecy, beginning with belief in the secret rapture.

In conjunction with these conferences, Congregationalist minister C. I. Scofield (1843–1921) codified many of the ideas of dispensational premillennialism into his pamphlet *Rightly Dividing the Word of God* and then into the *Scofield Reference Bible*. Scofield took the King James translation of the Bible and footnoted it in such a way that revealed precisely how dispensations were part of the biblical text. Scofield's note for 1 Thessalonians 4 read, "not church saints only, but all bodies of the saved, of whatever dispensation, are included in the first resurrection." He then directed readers to other scriptures that he said referred to the "blessed hope," the secret rapture of the church. Scofield advertised his Bible as primarily methodological as opposed to theological. He wanted people to be able to read and see the truth for themselves, and to make that truth self-evident on every page. The *Scofield Reference*

Bible, with its divisions and dispensations, classification and organization, became the authoritative Bible to be studied in conservative Protestant churches and Bible colleges throughout the twentieth century. Today it is available as an app.

Parallel Stories

Despite the "scientific methods" of conservative scholars like Scofield, by the late nineteenth century the dialogue between science and religion had broken down to such a degree that conservative biblical scholars felt deeply threatened. Biblical higher criticism—that is, reading the Bible through the lens of archeology, critical literary theories, and scientific discovery—had taken deep root in institutions of higher learning that wanted biblical studies to be as scientific as any other discipline.[9] But this meant that traditionally orthodox scholars were left holding a bag of old stories that appeared to lack facts and evidence. In response to this conflict, conservative Protestants began to invest their energies in their own institutions, seminaries, colleges, publishing organizations, and missionary societies. They developed enclaves in which apocalyptic readings of biblical texts flourished. Paul Boyer notes that the "fundamentalist apocalyptic" "flourished at a grassroots level, fed by a shadowy but powerful network of itinerant evangelists, prophecy conferences, Bible schools, books, and magazines."[10]

Missionary work was central to this worldview. Whereas previous eschatological thinking had focused on "nations," these Christians believed that until every individual had had the opportunity to accept or reject Christ, the end would not come. Salvation was a question of individual choice, and they did not believe as earlier Christians had that nations or governments could ever be converted to Christ. They had become highly skeptical of institutional power overall. Instead each individual within each nation could and must have the opportunity to "be saved" before the end could come.

"As Fresh as Tomorrow's Newspaper"

Meanwhile the twentieth century seemed to be unfolding in such a way as to make dispensational premillennialism seem more relevant than ever. Beginning with the events leading to World War I, followed by the Russian Revolution, the League of Nations, the Treaty of Versailles, and finally and most significantly the founding of the state of Israel in 1948, these dispensationalist Christians believed that God was laying out the signs of the end one after another. Since the sixteenth century, the return of Jews to Palestine had been the dream of many a prophecy-driven Christian. But in the late nineteenth century, the opportunity for sudden progress was available.

When the Zionist movement was officially launched in 1897 at the World Zionist Congress in Basel, associates of Scofield and Darby, such as William Blackstone, were excited by these events. Blackstone wrote to President Benjamin Harrison in 1891 that the United States should do everything it possibly could to support the return of Jews to Palestine. In part, this was because Russian Jews were pouring into Ellis Island, and Blackstone, like many Christian fundamentalists, had a contradictory isolationist and nativist orientation. He wanted Jews to go to *Palestine*, not New York. This had been true of Christian Zionists for three hundred years. Their dream was eschatological in nature: they wanted to return Jews to their ancient homeland, at any cost, so that the events that would lead up to the end of the world could unfold.

Despite a now three-hundred-year-old campaign—the letter-writing to kings and presidents, the bid for public support, the exploratory missions—prophecy-oriented American Christians living at the turn of the twentieth century were surprised by Zionism and treated it as a God-directed sign of the times. "Of all the signs of the times," wrote Arno Gabelein, a German immigrant and prophecy teacher in 1900, Zionism is the "most startling."[11]

Dispensationalist Christians experienced Zionism as God's sudden gift. The way was being prepared. God was laying out the signs just for them, and because they had knowledge of the right way to interpret biblical texts, they could read the world that God was unfolding before their very eyes. World War I put an end to the Ottoman Empire, which had held sway over the Holy Land for four hundred years. Britain, with its ever-expanding and ever-more-fragile empire, now was in "possession" of Palestine. The long dream of many in the West to wrest control of the Holy Land from the Muslims had at last come true. When the Jewish National Council proclaimed Israel a nation on May 14, 1948, the outpouring from prophecy believers was intense. This was as sure a sign of the coming of Jesus Christ as any they could imagine. The creation of Israel was not a strategic move by western powers, not an outcome of the Holocaust, not a result of more than a thousand years of antisemitic sentiment and action by European Christians from one edge of Europe to the other, not the result of more than three hundred years of pressure on governments and kingdoms. It was clear fulfillment of biblical prophecy.

Throughout the twentieth century, the practice of reading the signs of the times through the lens of dispensational premillennialism became ever more common. A common refrain of dispensationalists was that biblical prophecy now read "as fresh as tomorrow's newspaper."[12] This message was spread through every new available technology: tracts, an expanding book publishing industry, radio, television, and, by the end of the century, the Internet. There was no end to fodder for this particular reading of biblical eschatology. The very words "Russia" or "China" or the "Middle East" could now invoke the ancient forces of Gog and Magog, Armageddon, and the final battle now unfolding before their very eyes. If anything, this form of eschatological belief became only more convincing as the twentieth century progressed. By the end of the century, there were far more dispensationalist premillennialists worldwide than there had been in 1900. They had become a political and social force to be reckoned with.

In *The Sense of an Ending*, Frank Kermode reflected on the capacity of apocalyptic endings to be ever renewed. "The world sometimes seems to collaborate with our apocalypse," he noted. At the same time, apocalyptic thought has an extraordinary capacity to "be disconfirmed without being discredited."[13] As predictions occur and even as they fail, a pattern develops, and the pattern carries forward even while individual pieces are discarded. This occurred with striking regularity in dispensationalist thought of the twentieth century. Dispensationalist eschatology became an indispensable pattern for interpreting the future.

Notes

1. Quoted in George Knight, *A Search for Identity: The Development of Seventh-Day Adventist Beliefs* (Hagerstown: Review and Herald, 2000), 53.

2. Paul Boyer, "The Growth of Fundamentalist Apocalyptic in the United States," in *The Encyclopedia of Apocalypticism*, ed. Stephen J. Stein (New York: Continuum, 1998), 3:146.

3. Ruth Alden Doan, *The Miller Heresy, Millennialism, and American Culture* (Philadelphia: Temple University Press, 1987); Boyer 145–47; Stephen O'Leary, *Arguing the Apocalypse: A Theory of Millennial Rhetoric* (New York: Oxford University Press, 1994), 93–110.

4. Boyer, 147. Stephen O'Leary unpacks the rhetorical benefits of not setting a specific date in *Arguing the Apocalypse*.

5. B. M. Pietsch, *Dispensational Modernism* (New York: Oxford University Press, 2015), 43.

6. Clarence Larkin, *Dispensational Truth; or, God's Plan and Purpose in the Ages* (Philadelphia: Clarence Larkin Est., 1920), 19.

7. Pietsch, 210.

8. Nathaniel West, ed., *Second Coming of Christ: Premillennial Essays of the Prophetic Conference* (Chicago: Revell, 1879), 11–12.

9. Pietsch tells some of this fascinating story in *Dispensational Modernism*, 73–95.

10. Paul Boyer, *When Time Shall Be No More: Prophecy Belief in Modern American Culture* (Cambridge, MA: Harvard University Press, 1992), 100.

11. Arno C. Gabelein, "The Fourth Zionistic Congress: The Most Startling Sign of Our Times," *Our Hope* 7 (September 1900): 72; quoted in Boyer, *When Time*, 186.

12. An example of this particular phrasing comes from an apocalyptic novel, Timothy LaHaye and Jerry Jenkins, *Tribulation Force* (Wheaton: Tyndale, 1996), 67.

13. Frank Kermode, *The Sense of an Ending: Studies in the Theory of Fiction* (New York: Oxford University Press, 1967), 8.

For Further Reading

Ball, Bryan. *A Great Expectation: Eschatological Thought in English Protestantism to 1660.* Leiden: Brill, 1975.

Barnes, Robin. *Prophecy and Gnosis: Apocalypticism in the Wake of the Lutheran Reformation.* Stanford: Stanford University Press, 1988.

Boyer, Paul. *When Time Shall Be No More.* Chicago: University of Chicago Press, 1992.

Brown, Peter. *The Body and Society: Men, Women, and Sexual Renunciation in Early Christianity.* New York: Columbia University Press, 1988.

Bynum, Caroline Walker. *The Resurrection of the Body in Western Christianity, 200–1336.* New York: Columbia University Press, 1995.

____, and Paul Freedman, eds. *Last Things: Death and the Apocalypse in the Middle Ages.* Philadelphia: University of Pennsylvania Press, 2000.

Chilton, Bruce. *Visions of the Apocalypse: Reception of John's Revelation in Western Imagination.* Waco: Baylor University Press, 2013.

Daley, Brian. *The Hope of the Early Church.* Cambridge, UK: Cambridge University Press, 1991.

Daly, Robert S., ed. *Apocalyptic Thought in Early Christianity.* Grand Rapids: Baker Academic, 2009.

Doan, Ruth Alden. *The Miller Heresy, Millennialism, and American Culture.* Philadelphia: Temple University Press, 1987.

Doody, John, Kari Kloos, and Kim Paffenroth, eds. *Augustine and Apocalyptic.* Lanham: Lexington, 2005.

Hill, Charles E. *Regnum Caelorum: Patterns of Millennial Thought in Early Christianity.* Grand Rapids: Eerdmans, 2001.

Kermode, Frank. *The Sense of an Ending: Studies in the Theory of Fiction.* New York: Oxford University Press, 1967.

Koester, Craig R. *Revelation and the End of All Things.* Grand Rapids: Eerdmans, 2001.

McNamara, Martin, ed. *Apocalyptic and Eschatological Heritage: The Middle East and Celtic Realms.* Portland, OR: Four Courts, 2003.

McGinn, Bernard. *Antichrist: Two Thousand Years of the Human Fascination with Evil.* San Francisco: HarperSanFrancisco, 1994.

____. *Visions of the End: Apocalyptic Traditions in the Middle Ages.* New York: Columbia University Press, 1979.

Moorhead, James. *World without End: Mainstream American Protestant Visions of the Last Things, 1880–1925.* Bloomington: Indiana University Press, 1999.

O'Leary, Stephen. *Arguing the Apocalypse: A Theory of Millennial Rhetoric.* New York: Oxford University Press, 1994.

Palmer, James. *The Apocalypse in the Early Middle Ages.* Cambridge, UK: Cambridge University Press, 2014.

Patrides, C. A., and Joseph Wittreich, eds. *Apocalypse in English Renaissance Thought and Literature.* Manchester: Manchester University Press, 1984.

Pietsch, B. M. *Dispensational Modernism.* New York: Oxford University Press, 2015.

Raboteau, Albert J. *Slave Religion: The "Invisible Institution" in the Antebellum South.* New York: Oxford University Press, 1978.

Rowell, Geoffrey. *Hell and the Victorians: A Study of the Nineteenth-Century Theological Controversies concerning Eternal Punishment and the Future Life.* Oxford: Oxford University Press, 1974.

Russell, Letty M., Margaret A. Farley, and Serene Jones, eds. *Liberating Eschatology: Essays in Honor of Letty M. Russell.* Louisville: Westminster John Knox, 1999.

Williamson, Arthur A. *Apocalypse Then: Prophecy and the Making of the Modern World.* Westport, CT: Praeger, 2008.

PART III

Contemporary Challenges

25

Theories: From Albert Schweitzer to Karl Rahner

Some say the world will end in fire,
Some say in ice.
From what I've tasted of desire
I hold with those who favor fire.
But if it had to perish twice,
I think I know enough of hate
To say that for destruction ice
Is also great
And would suffice.

—Robert Frost, "Fire and Ice"

When the nineteen-year-old Albert Schweitzer (1875–1965) headed out to do maneuvers for his year of German national service, he took with him a copy of the Gospel of Matthew in Greek. He was preparing for his university exams, and so while other young men smoked and slept, he immersed himself in the text. There, a discrepancy between what he had been taught and what was in the text struck him. In the tenth chapter of Matthew, he read that as the apostles went out into the world to heal the sick and cast out demons, they were instructed by Jesus to preach that the "kingdom of heaven" was "at hand." His professors, informed by higher biblical criticism, had taught him that Matthew was merely an extended version of Mark, and that there was nothing of significance in Matthew that was not also in a seed form in Mark. But when he looked at a similar passage in Mark in which the disciples are sent out to perform miracles, it said nothing about the "kingdom of heaven." Why and from where would Matthew import these words, especially since the kingdom of heaven had proven to be anything but "at hand?" If the text had been written generations after Jesus's death, why would his inheritors continue to repeat that the kingdom of heaven was at hand, if that was not in some way integral to the message they believed Jesus to have brought?[1]

This was the question that became Schweitzer's 1901 book, published in English in 1906 as *The Quest of the Historical Jesus*. It was a book that would change drastically how Christian eschatology was taught, understood, and fought over in the twentieth century. Combined with the tumultuous events of that century, this book helped set the stage for a new reckoning with Christianity's eschatological heritage.

Apocalyptic Experience

If the nineteenth century had brought to the Americas messianic visions, the twentieth century brought to Europe—and thus to the Americas—a great deal of what Thomas Altizer has called "apocalyptic experience."[2] Empires fell. World wars spread mass destruction. The Holocaust and other mass genocides made possible by developing human technologies challenged the notion of human progress at its most root level. The invention of the nuclear bomb meant that for the first time in human history, humans could themselves destroy the world without waiting for the hand of God.

While the intellectual ideas that accompanied these drastic events are important and worth exploring, we need first to pause to understand the level of the devastation. World War I killed more than thirty-eight million people in Europe, Asia, and Africa. In part, the war was so devastating because it was so senseless. While Europeans had been touting the height of their civilization, they were suddenly drowning in a battle mind-boggling in its barbarism. And before the skies could clear and the dead be counted, they became embroiled in a Second World War that killed more than sixty million people, the deadliest conflict in terms of total numbers in world history. Again the barbarism that new technologies made possible was especially astounding. Hitler's mass extermination of European Jews was done with modern logic and organization using modern devices. The new capacities of bombs and bombers transformed war so that civilian casualties were not avoided by any side. Mass bombings of cities were standard operating procedure for all.

The war was capped off by the decision of American President Harry Truman to drop two nuclear bombs on Japan. It was effective in ending the war, but the demonstration of nuclear technology, its ability to vaporize human beings, was like nothing that had been seen before. We will explore the effect of this particular technology on Christian eschatology in a later chapter. For now, it is enough to note that when Altizer talks about apocalyptic experience, he is describing something that touched millions upon millions of people all over the world in the most intimate way possible. Postmillennialism and belief in human progress took a deep, but perhaps not fatal, hit.

Rethinking Jesus, Rethinking Time

But before World War I, Schweitzer's *The Quest of the Historical Jesus* had entered the scholarly arena and set off a series of chain reactions. Schweitzer argued that Jesus's message in the New Testament was incomprehensible without an understanding of Jesus's eschatology. The turn away from the eschatological messages of Jesus in the Age of Reason, Schweitzer argued, had made the Gospels all but unreadable. Jesus could not be understood as a wise teacher, as biblical scholars had cast him. He had to be understood as an eschatological prophet, and this had to lead to understanding Jesus as a *failed* eschatological prophet, since he had wrongly predicted that the end was near. In the nineteenth century, Jesus's more apocalyptic statements had become all but an embarrassment for more progressive Christians, who wanted a more progressive Christ that they could use in kingdom-building projects.

Schweitzer's book was one installment in a broader reconsideration of eschatology in Christian theology. The eschatology of Jesus, writes Hans Schwarz, became one of the most important questions in Christian theology and biblical studies in the twentieth century. Scholars were on a quest for a proper understanding of the New Testament informed by archeology, historical criticism, and, beginning in 1946, the discovery of the Dead Sea Scrolls.[3] Interestingly, while scholars argued about how to understand the eschatology of Jesus, they did not embrace it. Thomas Altizer argues that "no mainstream Christian theology" of the twentieth century was truly open to the eschatological perspective of Jesus or did not have to "wholly transform it" in the search for a usable theological inheritance.[4]

Thus twentieth-century theologians had to reckon with three new understandings of time. One was the time of the Bible, which was now understood as the product of multiple ancient civilizations, each with their own unique concept of time. Another was the concept of time inherent in the nuclear age, with the clock ticking toward a human-made disaster. And the third was the mysterious endlessness of geologic and cosmic time, that made human stories about God-oriented disasters look very small indeed.

This new complexity led to a century richer in theological thinking about time than any perhaps since Augustine. Instead of what Geoffrey Rowell called the "celestial and infernal mapmaking" of the Middle Ages, and instead of the taxonomic chronologies of the early modern period, twentieth-century theologians and biblical scholars plumbed the questions of the nature of time and the eschatological questions that accompany it.[5]

Rudolph Bultmann: The Future of No Future

Some twentieth-century theologians rejected the concept of an eschatological future altogether. Rudolph Bultmann (1884–1976), a German Lutheran theologian, argued that Jesus's acts on earth were intended to turn human attention to the present, within which we can find glimpses of the kingdom of God. Jesus calls us to moments of personal decision within the context of our own lives. These moments of decision are ethical, spiritual, and intimate, but they have little to do with the future, and almost nothing to do with a collective future.

This led Bultmann to underplay references to Jesus as the Messiah. Messianic thinking is inherently future-oriented, and history itself has demonstrated, Bultmann argued, that this form of thinking is incorrect. In an article called "New Testament and Mythology," Bultmann argues, "The mythical eschatology is untenable for the simple reason that the *parousia* of Christ never took place as the New Testament expected. History did not come to an end, and as every schoolboy knows, it will continue to run its course."[6]

Instead of looking for the eschaton in the future, Bultmann argued, the individual Christian looks for it in his or her own life, the in-breaking of Christ in to the present. "In every moment," Bultmann argued, "slumbers the possibility of being the eschatological moment. You must awaken it."[7] The future is determined by the "course of history," but the kingdom of God is met and fulfilled in the present in an individual life. Bultmann redefined eschatological to mean existential: it does not tell us about the future; it tells us something critical about existence itself.

Jürgen Moltmann: Theology of Hope

Other theologians passionately disagreed that Christianity was well-served by closing off the future. One such theologian was Jürgen Moltmann (b. 1926). Moltmann extended the role of the future fully into the present. He believed that the future (God's kingdom yet to be fulfilled) ought to play a role in every aspect of the Christian life, especially politics, justice, ethics, and personal spirituality. All of Christian theology ought to be understood in light of the "end." In his first major work,

Theology of Hope, Moltmann focused on biblical stories. He noted that even when God fulfilled a promise in the Bible, there is always an "overspill that pointed to the future," a tension between promise and fulfillment that draws us ever forward.[8] In the same way, Christ is both a fulfillment and a promise. Christ was, and is, and is to come, as Revelation says. Hans Schwarz summarizes Moltmann's thought: "Cross and resurrection point toward the future in promising the righteousness of God, the new life as a result of the resurrection from the dead, and the kingdom of God 'in the new totality of being.'"[9] We can anticipate that God will continue to mold the world in the same way, by promise and fulfillment, by the overspilling of promise into the future, and by the ongoing "realization of the eschatological *hope of justice,* the *humanizing* of man, the *socializing* of humanity, *peace* for all creation."[10]

These are radical hopes when considered in the light of the Holocaust and the devastation of World War II. But Moltmann saw these events not as the failure of God's promise and fulfillment but as the failure of human progress. He believed that God's promise is always challenged by the threat of the "antichrist's destruction of the world in a storm of fire," and this should be a powerful motivator for humans to turn to God. Christians need both the promise of a tangible kingdom of God held out in front of them and an understanding of the threat of the alternative.[11] We can see here that for Moltmann the antichrist is not a person with a specific biography, as he was for Adso or Pseudo-Methodius. Moltmann was not looking for the antichrist to arise from a particular geographic location. Instead, the antichrist was a powerful and destructive force alive in human hearts. Christians should never allow the force of the antichrist to undermine their fundamental theology of hope, but they also should not be surprised that this force has destructive effects.

Some have accused Moltmann of falling too far on the side of emphasizing human action over divine action. With this intense focus on justice and his insistence that eschatology is a matter for everyday life, Moltmann believes that Christians have a great deal of work to do in the world. But he also does not think that working for personal salvation is one of them. Life after death is not as interesting as the coming future of God to be fulfilled in God's kingdom. Moltmann's is a social vision, not an individual one. Moltmann evokes the last judgment not by employing the jeremiad, as in the American tradition, but in a way that is reminiscent of Julian of Norwich. He argues that God will indeed judge all sinners. But in that judgment, "the wicked and the violent, murderers and the children of Satan, the Devil and the fallen angels will be liberated and saved from their deadly perdition through transformation into their true, created being, because God remains true to himself, and does not give up on what he has once created and affirmed, or allow it to be lost."[12]

Thus in contrast to Bultmann, Moltmann believes that Christian theology is eschatology "from first to last." Eschatology is not an epilogue in the drama of salvation but instead provides Christianity with the fuel of hope "forward looking and forward moving and therefore also revolutionary and transforming the present."[13] A Christian without a future is not a Christian at all.

Karl Rahner: Already/Not Yet

Karl Rahner (1904–1984) was a theologian absorbed in questions of time and its theological implications. Rahner synthesized the "already" of Bultmann and the "not yet" of Moltmann to produce a theology that drew on tradition but also recognized its limitations. A Jesuit, Rahner was steeped in the Christian intellectual tradition, but he argued that much of inherited Christian eschatology was of little use to a contemporary person. He saw two aspects of traditional Christian eschatology that were especially difficult to translate. One was the idea that God's will is absolutely imposed on human creatures. Through the Enlightenment, humans had come to a very different understanding of their place in creation. They could no longer accept that God's will was something imposed on them externally. They saw themselves as active participants in and shapers of the future. The danger of this worldview, Rahner said, is that humans can quickly imagine a world without God at all, with humans as the only actors on the stage of the future. Rahner called these "modern militant political world-heresies of secular utopianism."[14] Christian theology, as we've inherited it, is ill-equipped to address this challenge, because it has emphasized God's will imposed on humankind.

The other problem that Rahner perceived was a problem inherent in the Enlightenment itself. Christian thinkers had become too focused on the fate of the individual as the only interesting eschatological question. Personal and individual salvation was the sole preoccupation of the modern believer, and modern theologians had followed suit. "A cosmic eschatology involving the whole of history has become very colourless and insignificant as compared with a doctrine of the individual immortality of spiritual souls and of their individual destiny," he wrote.[15] Biblical eschatology was all but impossible to reconcile with this perspective and thus could only be read superficially. Christians were going to need to return to the older sources with fresh eyes *and* develop a new vocabulary to meet these challenges. Throughout his own life, Rahner moved from a personal understanding of eschatology to an interpersonal one, to a social and moral vision that was ever more comprehensive.[16]

But developing this new vocabulary was extremely difficult because, Rahner argued in vivid contrast to the many prophecy investigators before and since him, the future of the world in God is radically hidden from us. "The future is announced and promised in Christ, but it is announced and promised precisely as a hidden mystery." Eschatology cannot be demythologized, à la Bultmann, because mystery is an essential element.[17]

Even as the future is unknown, paradoxically, it is also an "inner moment of the present." The future is a fulfillment of, not a radical departure from, the present. The seed of our redemption is already present, and material reality will not be discarded but further transformed.[18] Thus the orientation of the Christian to the future is one of openness. The future is God's promise, not God's threat. Our attitude should be one of "abiding openness to the question of the absolute future which seeks to bestow itself, which has definitively promised itself as coming in Jesus Christ, and which is called God," Rahner wrote in his *Theological Investigations*.[19]

Rahner distinguishes the eschatological from the apocalyptic in an interesting way. The eschatological, he argues, is a future projection from the present. It is a forward-looking gesture rooted in the present moment. The apocalyptic is when we inject the future into the present. We attempt to look at the present from the point of view of the future.[20] Rahner called this a "false apocalyptic," because the future is genuinely open. The apocalyptic can really only unveil a deeper reality of the present. It cannot, as has so many times been attempted in the

Christian tradition, tell us the future. Thus Rahner argued that the future projection of eschatology is based on the present salvation in Jesus Christ. He spoke of eschatology as a "reaching out" both to God and to the future, and he called both God and the future a "distant presence."[21]

Humans live now with the mystery of divine communication. God does reach out to us in our human condition. But the consummation of the individual will be in the beatific vision. We currently experience God's relationship with us through grace. Then we will experience it through vision. "What grace and vision of God mean are two phases of one and the same event . . . two phases of God's single self-communication to man."[22]

But God's individual communication—although intimate and essential—is not enough. God also has the work of transforming all of humankind and redeeming the earth. Humans themselves cannot be fully redeemed except in relation to the world. ("Through bodiliness the whole world belongs to me from the start in everything that happens."[23]) Resurrection thus plays a key role. While Rahner could not fully account for the bodily nature of resurrection, he did insist on it.[24] Resurrection and *parousia* are collective experiences of perfection—the world and the individual both completed in Christ's coming.[25]

Rahner made a bold attempt to bring traditional eschatology into the contemporary moment. He was heavily criticized and even censured by the establishment for insisting on innovative theology. But his work gives us an important record of attempts to reconcile ancient images and sacred mysteries with contemporary understandings of the nature of the person and the earth.

Notes

1. Adapted from James Brabazon, *Albert Schweitzer: A Biography* (Syracuse: Syracuse University Press, 2000), 50–54.

2. Thomas J. Altizer, "Modern Thought and Apocalypticism," in *The Encyclopedia of Apocalypticism*, ed. Stephen J. Stein (New York: Continuum, 1998), 3:346.

3. Hans Schwarz, *Eschatology* (Grand Rapids: Eerdmans, 2000), 105–6.

4. Altizer, 346.

5. Geoffrey Rowell, *Hell and the Victorians: A Study of the Nineteenth-Century Theological Controversies concerning Eternal Punishment and the Future Life* (Oxford: Oxford University Press, 1974), 311.

6. Rudolph Bultmann, "New Testament and Mythology," in *Kerygma and Myth: A Theological Debate,* trans. R. H. Fuller, ed. Hans Werner Bartsch (London: SPCK, 1953), 1:5.

7. Bultmann, *History and Eschatology* (Edinburgh: Edinburgh University Press, 1957), 155.

8. Schwarz, 147.

9. Ibid., 148, quoting Jürgen Moltmann, *Theology of Hope: On the Ground and Implications of a Christian Eschatology,* trans. James W. Leitch (Minneapolis: Fortress, 1993), 203.

10. Moltmann, *Theology of Hope*, 329.

11. Moltmann, *The Coming of God: Christian Eschatology,* trans. Margaret Kohl (Minneapolis: Fortress, 1996), 201.

12. Ibid., 255.

13. Moltmann, *Theology of Hope*, 16.

14. Rahner, "Eschatology," in *Sacramentum Mundi: An Encyclopedia of Theology,* trans. W. J. O'Hara et al., ed. Karl Rahner, Cornelius Ernst, and Kevin Smyth (New York: Herder & Herder, 1968), 2:244.

15. Ibid., 242.

16. Peter C. Phan, "Eschatology," *The Cambridge Companion to Karl Rahner,* ed. Declan Marmion and Mary E. Hines (Cambridge: Cambridge University Press, 2005), 177.

17. Morwenna Ludlow, *Universal Salvation: Eschatology in the Thought of*

Gregory of Nyssa and Karl Rahner (Oxford: Oxford University Press, 2000), 134.

18. Denis Edwards, "The Resurrection of the Body and Transformation of the Universe in the Theology of Karl Rahner," *Philosophy and Theology* 18/2 (2006): 7.

19. Karl Rahner, *Theological Investigations*, trans. Cornelius Ernst (Baltimore: Helicon, 1961), 12:190.

20. Phan, 178.

21. Rahner, *Foundations of Christian Faith: An Introduction to the Idea of Christianity*, trans. William V. Dych (New York: Crossroad, 1982), 119. See Ludlow, 125–26.

22. Rahner, *Foundations of Christian Faith*, 118.

23. Karl Rahner, "The Body in the Order of Salvation," in *Theological Investigations, Vol. 17: Jesus, Man and the Church*, trans. Margaret Kohl (London: Darton, Longman & Todd, 1981), 87–88.

24. See Peter C. Phan, *Eternity in Time: A Study of Karl Rahner's Eschatology* (Cranbury: Associated University Presses, 1988), 179.

25. Ludlow details some of the theological problems with this attempted synthesis on pp. 234–35.

26

Protests: From Martin Luther King Jr. to Leymah Gbowee

Now is the time to rise from the dark and desolate valley of segregation to the sunlit path of racial justice. Now is the time to lift our nation from the quicksands of racial injustice to the solid rock of brotherhood. Now is the time to make justice a reality for all of God's children.

—Martin Luther King Jr.

In January 1963, Alabama governor George Wallace stood on the steps of the state capitol and declared "segregation now, segregation tomorrow . . . segregation forever." For almost a decade previous, demonstrators had been working to break down the wall known in the southern states as Jim Crow—a collection of laws and practices that separated blacks from whites. But the pace of change was intensifying.

In 1960, four young black men sat at a lunch counter at Woolworths in Greensboro, North Carolina, knowing that they were risking their lives. In the three years from that moment to Wallace's declaration, a national movement, and indeed an international movement, had been growing. Between 1960 and 1963, Togo, Mali, Senegal, Zaire, Somalia, Benin, Niger, Burkina Faso, Ivory Coast, Chad, Central African Republic, Congo, Gabon, Nigeria, Mauritania, Sierra Leone, Tanganyika, and Jamaica all became independent from the colonial powers that had previously controlled their governments. "The new sense of dignity and self-respect on the part of the Negro (in America)," Martin Luther King Jr. (1929–1968) wrote in 1960, was due in part to "the awareness that his struggle is a part of a worldwide struggle."[1] By August 1963, King and others had organized a national march on Washington, DC, and from the steps of the Lincoln Memorial, King would deliver one of the most important eschatological speeches ever given by an American leader.

Christ Comes Now

In the wake of the Civil War and the abolition of slavery, governments and municipalities in the American South created an elaborate system of laws and social customs to prevent African-Americans from attaining true equality. Collectively known as "Jim Crow" laws, these were the target of the Civil Rights Movement. The Civil Rights Movement was an eschatological movement in that it both posited a future of peace, freedom, and equality and argued for dramatic social change in the present. A prophetic eschatological movement, its vision was one of earthly transformation as opposed to an otherworldly "end." The language of the biblical prophets was central.

While still in seminary, King wrote that modern Christians

needed to reject the notion of a physical second coming of Christ that lay in the future at some unknown time. Christ comes, he argued, in our words and deeds, in our actions toward our fellow human beings.[2] This was the relevant coming, not an abstract future one. Likewise, judgment was not a later event but something that was happening at this moment. This perhaps explains King's frequent impatience with white theology, which was always delaying the moment of justice until some later time, just as whites were always telling African-Americans to be patient in their struggle for justice, that now was not the right time. In "Letter from a Birmingham Jail," King wrote with no small amount of exasperation, "For years now I have heard the word 'Wait!' It rings in the ear of every Negro with piercing familiarity. This 'Wait' has almost always meant 'Never.' We must come to see, with one of our distinguished jurists, that 'justice too long delayed is justice denied.'"[3]

At the same time that King displayed this righteous impatience, he was a master of the millennia-old Christian tension between the now and the not yet. He simultaneously created an urgency around the present moment and projected the future toward which he and others were struggling. He used this tension to inspire the movement.

"I Have a Dream"

King had given versions of his famous "I have a dream" speech before. But on the steps of the Lincoln Memorial in the late summer of 1963, his goal was to take many small political actions and transform them into a national movement. He had to give people involved in an intense political struggle fuel to keep going in the face of both violent opposition and the tedium of minute political action.

"We have come to this hallowed spot to remind America of the fierce urgency of Now," he began. "This is no time to engage in the luxury of cooling off or to take the tranquilizing drug of gradualism. Now is the time to make real the promises of democracy. Now is the time to rise from the dark and desolate valley of segregation to the sunlit path of racial justice. Now is the time to lift our nation from the quicksands of racial injustice to the solid rock of brotherhood. Now is the time to make justice a reality for all of God's children."

This was a powerful call for action in the present. But just as he was about to send his audience back to the trenches of their work, gospel singer Mahalia Jackson called out from behind him on the podium, "Tell them about the dream, Martin!" Almost imperceptibly, King slid over his prepared notes. He began to speak extemporaneously. His speech writer, Clarence Jones, remembers turning to the person next to him and saying, "These people don't know it yet, but they are about to go to church."[4]

Drawing on the African-American Christian tradition, biblical prophecy, and patriotic language about the meaning and destiny of America, King began to improvise using both the polemic and poetic modes of eschatology. "And so even though we face the difficulties of today and tomorrow, I still have a dream. It is a dream deeply rooted in the American dream," he began as though for a second time.[5] He stumbled a little as he found his way into the theme, but finally launched into a prophetic vision that became the turning point of the movement.

I have a dream that one day every valley shall be exalted and every hill and mountain shall be made low, the rough places will be made plain, and the crooked places will be made straight, "and the glory of the Lord shall be revealed and all flesh shall see it together." This is our hope and this is the faith I go back to the South with. With this faith, we will be able to hew out of the mountain of despair a stone of hope. With this faith, we will be able to transform the jangling discord of our nation into a beautiful symphony of brotherhood. With this faith, we will be able to work together, to pray together, to struggle together, to go to jail together, to stand up for freedom together knowing that we will be free one day.

At every turn, as he used the refrain "I have a dream today," King broadened the "we" to whom he referred. By the end of the speech, that "we" included "little black boys and black girls" who "will be able to join hands with little white boys and white girls as sisters and brothers." All of these were the people who shared in the faith and would claim the future that King described. His dream, he said, was "deeply rooted in the American dream." But he drew on a yet more ancient language, from the psalms and prophets of ancient Israel, to give his vision of the future its most passionate articulation.

King's speech marked the year when the Civil Rights Movement came into its own. The writer James Baldwin described the moment later: "That day for a moment it almost seemed that we stood on a height and could see our inheritance; perhaps we could make the kingdom real, perhaps the beloved community would not for ever remain that dream one dreamed in agony."[6]

The Fish Market Women

Almost forty years later, a woman was sleeping in the cramped offices of the Women In Peacebuilding Network, an NGO in Monrovia, Liberia, when she had a dream. In the dream a voice told her to "Gather the women and pray for peace." War had been raging in Liberia for more than two decades with factions of rebels and a corrupt government engaged in a never-ending cycle of violence. Leymah Gbowee, who won the Nobel Prize for Peace in 2011, was baffled by the dream's instruction. She did not see herself as a religious leader but as a single mother with an education disrupted by war and a part-time job from which she barely managed to pay a few bills. "It was like hearing the voice of God, yes, but . . . that wasn't possible," she writes in her memoir. "I drank too much. I fornicated! I was sleeping with a man who wasn't my husband, who in fact was still legally married to someone else. If God was going to speak to someone in Liberia, it wouldn't be me."[7]

Later that day she tentatively shared her dream with a co-worker at the church compound where she worked. A few others overheard the conversation and said, "We need to pray." Twenty women started to pray once a week. These women gathered more women. They started visiting churches on Sunday to spread their message, then market stalls on Saturday, and mosques on Friday. From the first group of twenty, thousands of women, who became known as the "fish market women" and later as the Women of Liberia Mass Action for Peace, began to organize, mobilize, and recruit. The women began to stand on the edges of roads, dressed all in white, holding signs demanding peace. At first no one noticed or cared about them. When filmmaker Abigail Disney was searching for footage of these early protests for her film *Pray the Devil Back to Hell*, there was nothing. Gbowee writes that the response from local photographers to the request was, "Why would we [have filmed them]? They just looked pathetic."[8]

The women drew on theories of nonviolence and liberation that they had gleaned from King and from Mahatma Gandhi's revolution in India. As the movement grew, leaders sat down every night to consider their actions from that day and what they could do to build peace the next day. They kept the message simple: "We want peace. No more war." When they gathered early in the morning, they began with Christian and Muslim prayers. They developed a repertoire of songs and listened to one another's stories. Meanwhile, the civil war raged on, displacing thousands of Liberians from their homes.

"We Want Peace, No More War"

Gradually, with some coverage from the BBC's *Focus on Africa*, the women's movement was able to put pressure on President Charles Taylor and rebel groups to enter into peace talks. Taylor agreed to meet rebels in Accra, the capital of neighboring Ghana. Gbowee and other women decided to camp outside the hotel where the talks were taking place. The talks went on for weeks, while war in Monrovia and across Liberia continued to rage. From his place next to the pool in the hotel, Taylor declared that his people "will fight street to street, house to house." The women felt helpless and foolish camped outside waiting for a peace agreement that would never come, while so-called negotiators made battle plans inside the hotel.

One day, after the negotiators went into a conference room, the women moved inside to block the door. They sent a note in through the glass doors. No one would come out, the women said, until a ceasefire agreement was signed. In a moment that was caught on tape, hotel security officers moved in to arrest Gbowee and other women. Gbowee responded, "I will make it very easy for you to arrest me," and then she began to take off her clothes. Other women rose to do the same. She was responding intuitively, without forethought, she says. Her thoughts were "a jumble." The point was to say: "Okay, if you think you'll humiliate me with an arrest, watch me humiliate myself more than you could have dreamed."

Later she recognized that her actions had "summoned a traditional power" that conjures up a curse for a man who sees a married woman naked.[9] The president of Nigeria, General Abdulsalami Abubakar, intervened and urged the men back to the negotiating table.

From this confrontation a fragile peace was born, a ceasefire was signed, and within a month, Charles Taylor resigned and went into exile in Nigeria. The next president, Ellen Johnson Sirleaf, was the first female president of an African nation.

We can look at Gbowee's work from the perspective of political action, and it will no doubt be studied by peace builders for decades to come. But we can also look at it from the perspective of Christian eschatological protest, a form of prophetic eschatology. Like other dreamers in this tradition, Gbowee heard a voice directing her to take action. Like many others before her, she drew on Christian tradition to find language and meaning for her work. She also extended the tradition by finding a way to speak across religious traditions in order to bring together women with a common vision for the future.

Christian eschatological protest in the twenty-first century must be context-specific. It must draw on a particular situation in a particular place. But it must also connect to universal values of peace and justice, and speak across boundaries. It also does not hurt to connect to global media, and tell one's story to as broad an audience as possible. Movements like King's and Gbowee's now have a deep reservoir of techniques and strategies for nonviolent action built through the anti-colonial, anti-apartheid, and Civil Rights movements of the twentieth century, and the rich language of Christian eschatology—and not Christian alone—to create lasting social change. They have demonstrated the power of protest to transform societies and their futures.

Notes

1. Martin Luther King Jr., "The Rising Tide of Racial Consciousness," quoted in Gary Younge, *The Speech: The Story Behind Dr. Martin Luther King Jr.'s Dream* (Chicago: Haymarket, 2013), 18.

2. Martin Luther King Jr., "The Christian Pertinence of Eschatological Hope," online at https://kinginstitute.stanford.edu/king-papers/documents/christian-pertinence-eschatological-hope.

3. King, "Letter from a Birmingham Jail," online at http://www.uscrossier.org/pullias/wp-content/uploads/2012/06/king.pdf.

4. Some have questioned Jones's interpretation of events. For Jones's version, see https://www.youtube.com/watch?v=KxlOlynG6FY. For other versions, see Gary Younge, *The Speech: The Story Behind Dr. Martin Luther King Jr.'s Dream* (Chicago: Haymarket, 2013), 95.

5. According to Jennifer Scanlon, biographer of Civil Rights activist Anna Arnold Hedgeman, Hedgeman was also in the audience, and when King said, "I have a dream," she scribbled angrily on her program, "*We* have a dream." See http://www.nytimes.com/2016/02/28/books/review/until-there-is-justice-by-jennifer-scanlon.html?_r=0.

6. James Baldwin, *No Name in the Street* (New York: Dell, 1973).

7. Leymah Gbowee with Carol Mithers, *Mighty Be Our Powers* (New York: Beast, 2011), 122.

8. Ibid., 211.

9. Ibid., 162.

27

Clocks: The Atomic Age

Gee, I wish we had one of them doomsday machines.
—General Buck Turgidson
in *Dr. Strangelove*

In the final scene of the 1964 film *Dr. Strangelove: Or How I Learned to Stop Worrying and Love the Bomb*, Major "King" Kong (played by the comic actor Slim Pickens) rides a nuclear missile like a cowboy on a horse on his way to activate the "doomsday machine" that will destroy the entire planet. An American general has "gone rogue" and ordered the attack without fully understanding the consequences. The Pentagon's leaders gather in a "war room" to try to figure out what to do, but as the film ends, we see mushroom clouds exploding and hear the haunting, ironic tune, "We'll Meet Again."

"The Like of Which Has Never Been Seen"

In August 1945, in the final stages of World War II, the United

States dropped two atomic bombs on two cities in Japan, Hiroshima and Nagasaki. Hundreds of thousands of people were killed and thousands more affected by radioactive fallout. The U.S. had been experimenting with nuclear fission for almost a decade, but had successfully detonated a nuclear bomb in New Mexico only a month before this attack. They knew they had a new and deadly weapon that in the words of Harry Truman contained "a rain of ruin from the air, the like of which has never been seen on this earth."[1]

While this remains the one and only use of nuclear weapons in an act of war, the post-bombing generation was the first to imagine, vividly, the end of the world caused by human means. The film footage of Nagasaki and Hiroshima allowed people to see first-hand other human beings instantly vaporized. It showed the aftermath of devastating burns, cancer, and disease. While the nuclear age paralleled ancient Christian teaching about the "end" being "at hand," it also was a radically secular version of that teaching, and it became the most vivid example of a catastrophic ending that the modern world could imagine.

The Doomsday Clock

In 1947, the *Bulletin of Atomic Scientists* introduced the world to the Doomsday Clock—a symbol of how close the world was to its own destruction. Stephen O'Leary called this the "most enduring and universally recognized" symbol of the atomic age.[2]

The atomic scientists set the Clock at seven minutes to midnight. Midnight was the representation of disaster, the coming of global nuclear war. The seven minutes was, of course, symbolic time. Twice a year since 1947, the *Bulletin's*

Science and Security committee has met to decide how close to midnight to set the Clock. In 1953, they set the Clock at two minutes to midnight to symbolize the danger of the escalating arms race between the United States and the Soviet Union. It was moved back in 1960 when the U.S. and the Soviet Union seemed more interested in preventing global disaster than provoking it. Scientists have since added global climate change and the disposal of nuclear waste to the factors that influence the Clock's proximity to midnight.

In 2015 the committee set the Clock to three minutes to midnight as a signal of the committee's sentiments about the U.S.'s failure to act on global climate change. After the Paris accord, in which 188 countries agreed to limit their carbon emissions aggressively, some thought that the Clock hands might move back. Instead, the *Bulletin* issued a statement saying that they saw no reason to adjust the assessment of risk. Rachel Bronson, executive director and publisher of the *Bulletin*, said, "Last year, the *Bulletin*'s Science and Security Board moved the Doomsday Clock forward to three minutes to midnight, noting: 'The probability of global catastrophe is very high, and the actions needed to reduce the risks of disaster must be taken very soon.' That probability has not been reduced. The Clock ticks. Global danger looms. Wise leaders should act—immediately."[3]

These factors that the *Bulletin* uses for its determination all have the paradoxical combination of being both under human control and outside it. The Clock is a polemical symbol intended to influence the choices and actions of world leaders. But it is effective as a rhetorical device because of the way that it combines the ancient Jewish apocalyptic language of the day of the Lord with the ticking symbol of modernity, channeled through Christian sensibilities about the nearness of the "end."

What could represent modernity more perfectly than a clock, which had catapulted humans into a new experience of time? But the Doomsday Clock also reminds us of the ticking of a bomb waiting to go off.

The Doomsday Clock creates both a sense of "urgency and inevitability, of the necessity to act while there is still time, and the irreversibility of time's passage toward the end that awaits us all."[4] But as symbolic time, it moves both forward and backward—and its movement reflects collective action. It paradoxically communicates that the future is in our hands even while we have little control over it. Like medieval Christians, O'Leary argues, people who live under the Doomsday Clock have to reckon simultaneously with the "psychological weight of imminent judgment on every moment of passing time, and come to terms with the perpetual postponement of judgment and the heavenly kingdom" that follows it.[5]

Post-apocalyptic?

In the terms as we've been exploring them, the phrase **post-apocalyptic** makes little sense. Apocalyptic eschatology is the revelation of the true nature of reality that points toward a particular kind of God-ordained future. An apocalypse is a literary genre that vivifies this reality, which has a kind of timelessness. What comes after the true nature of reality? But in the twentieth century, apocalyptic changed meaning. It came to mean a final catastrophe that marked the end of human history. The post-apocalyptic became that which followed "the end," the aftermath of catastrophe.

The collective psychological pressure of living in the atomic age resulted in a creative outpouring on the subject of nuclear disaster in the late twentieth century. Popular and elite books, movies, comic books, music albums, and art explored these themes. Movies provided a visual mechanism to explore mass destruction, rooted in news footage of the Hiroshima and Nagasaki bombings.

By the 1980s, filmmakers and novelists were beginning to explore a different imaginative territory—the territory beyond disaster. The post-apocalyptic offered a new form of speculation about the future. Russell Hoban's 1980 novel *Riddley Walker* is set 2000 years after the nuclear disaster, when human civilization in "Inland" (England) is in a primitive stage. Only fragments of the old world remain. At the very end of the novel, humans have begun to develop the weapons that, the novel hints, will lead them back on the path to their own destruction.

Riddley Walker suggests that human history is on an endless loop that produces the means for its own destruction, destroys itself, and begins again. This is a kind of inverted millennium. If, for thousands of years, Christians imagined that history would somehow result in the thousand-year reign of Christ on earth, that the final battle would result in the binding of Satan, the post-apocalyptic has humans living with the one-thousand-year consequences of their actions. There is no final victory for the forces of God. In the atomic age, we live with original sin without redemption.

Notes

1. http://news.bbc.co.uk/onthisday/hi/witness/august/6/newsid _4715000/4715303.stm.
2. Stephen O'Leary, "Apocalypticism in American Popular Culture: From

323

the Dawn of the Nuclear Age to the End of the American Century," in *The Encyclopedia of Apocalypticism*, ed. Stephen J. Stein (New York: Continuum, 1998), 3:400.

3. http://thebulletin.org/press-release/doomsday-clock-hands-remain-unchanged-despite-iran-deal-and-paris-talks9122.

4. O'Leary, 400.

5. Ibid., 401.

28

Failures: The Limits of Christian Futures

In our rooms filled with laughter
We make hope from every small disaster.

—The Weepies

One day in the early spring of 2011, I was driving from Boston to Amherst, Massachusetts, when I saw a billboard that said, "Judgment Day, May 21, 2011. The Bible guarantees it." Despite having studied Christian apocalypticism for more than a decade, I had never heard of this billboard's sponsors: Harold Camping and Family Radio. Harold Camping was indeed a modern day William Miller who, from the desk of his radio program in California, had studied the scriptures, calculated a date, and with the help of his followers, put together a slick marketing campaign to reach people in the one location in the United States where they perhaps felt most vulnerable to apocalyptic eschatology: their cars.

Failed Predictions

Camping's version of the end of the world, with his old-fashioned calculations and his worldwide radio broadcasts, captured popular imagination in the spring of 2011. He was featured in the *New York Times*, the *Wall Street Journal*, and the *Times of London*. A caravan of his followers traveled across the United States hoping to convince as many people as possible to save themselves before the final date. His broadcasts detailing his belief were heard in forty-eight countries. "God has given us soooo much information in the Bible about this," Camping said in an interview with *New York Magazine*. "And so many proofs, and so many signs, that we know it is absolutely going to happen without any question at all. . . . When the clock says 6 PM, there's going to be this tremendous earthquake. . . . And the whole world will be alerted that Judgment Day has begun."[1]

What Camping did so effectively, what still surprisingly works to inspire the imagination in American culture, was to connect ancient beliefs and texts with the ordinariness of contemporary life—cars, billboards, radio, advertising. He was able to tap into the sense among twenty-first-century people that our life is unsustainable. He gave that uneasiness supernatural meaning and connected it to his own expertise. To some extent, he was successful. Imaginations were ignited. Camping gained a shockingly large following. And even while he will hardly be remembered, a blip on the radar screen of Christian apocalypticism, for a few moments he had a hold on something that is alive in our culture. A fear. A hope. An energy.

I remember exactly where I was when 6:00 p.m. PST came and went without a worldwide earthquake. I was at my nephew's graduation party, standing near the cheese plate and the guacamole. I looked at the clock—I couldn't help myself. The hour struck while conversation buzzed around the kitchen and out onto the patio. And then it passed without cosmic disruption.

Camping is not alone in making predictions, and despite the Great Disappointment and repeated admonitions that no one will know the hour or the day, many dispensational premillennialists from the nineteenth century to the present have made their livelihoods on predictions. Hal Lindsey, who wrote what has frequently been called the bestselling book of the 1970s, *The Late Great Planet Earth*, has continued to make failed predictions for forty years without apology. The Internet spreads predictions like wildfire, and while we may face all kinds of disasters—personal, social, environmental—none of them add up to Judgment Day.

DIY Eschatology

Some cultural critics scan global popular culture and see an obsession with apocalyptic eschatology that seems to have no end. Lorenzo DiTomasso notes that in the 1990s, Hollywood released twenty-four films with apocalyptic themes. This was considered a period of enormous apocalyptic fervor with the Y2K preoccupation, the rise of the *Left Behind* series, and articles in every magazine and newspaper about the anticipation of our apocalyptic demise. (In popular culture, apocalypticism has become now entirely collapsed with the notion of disaster. It no longer has notes of unveiling a truer reality.)

But instead of this apocalyptic outpouring slackening in the period after the year 2000, the pace continues to grow unabated. Twice as many apocalyptically themed films were produced in the first half of the 2010s. Television shows like *The Leftovers* explore apocalyptic themes reminiscent of dispensational premillennialism but without the pious overlay. Add in video games, comic books, and other fare of popular culture, and DiTomasso sees a global "apocalyptic turn."[2]

Popular culture's version of apocalypticism cannot be precisely described as Christian. While Harold Camping's version was Christian, Michael Barkun notes a do-it-yourself bricolage of most of popular culture's apocalyptic overtones: Christianity mixes with beliefs about UFOs, Maya calendars, and prophesiers of many stripes. Richard Werbner describes this as "the formation of fresh cultural forms from the ready-to-hand debris of old ones."[3] Contemporary popular culture's many versions of the "end" have a debris-like quality. Like Camping, they make up a dynamic part of the landscape and yet are unlikely to be remembered in ten or twenty or fifty years. They remind me of plastic action figures in Happy Meal boxes: fun for a few minutes, and off to the landfill.

DiTomasso argues that the Internet has "fundamentally changed how apocalyptic speculation is conceived, manufactured, and disseminated."[4] Endless content is produced, and people have instant access to any apocalyptic prediction. But what DiTomasso calls the "vertical dimension"—something with depth or nuance—is almost nonexistent. "Intellectual depth and critical nuance" have been "sacrificed to unlimited content."[5] Apocalypticism appears to be a strategy that brings coherence, however briefly, to the vast amount of information available to us. A "sense of an ending" quickly shapes meaning, and yet somehow, just as quickly, it dissolves into the vast river of information.

Apocalypticism as a form of knowledge has devolved over the course of the Enlightenment from a comprehensive expertise to a conspiracy theory. Much apocalypticism in contemporary popular culture is a form of "special knowledge" that "they" have and are hiding from us. As opposed to a total theory of knowledge that draws from every available field, contemporary apocalypticism is predicated on a secret piece of information that we don't have access to. At the same time, Frank Kermode points out that "the paradigm of apocalypse continues to lie under our ways of making sense of the world." But it does this by offering us one crisis after another, an endless sense of transition. We always feel that we are living at a turning point in history.[6]

This may be in part why other scholars have argued that the twenty-first century is the *least* apocalyptic century in Christian history. Caroline Walker Bynum and Paul Freedman argue that apocalypticism has become difficult for most people to take seriously. "The underlying assumptions, certainly of most Americans, [is] that things will go on pretty much as they are now except with some new and slicker technology." This, they argue, "contrasts dramatically with the real apprehensiveness of the mid-twentieth century or the most sweeping confidence . . . at the turn of the last century."[7] Both apocalypticism of the cataclysmic variety and the progressive eschatology of the nineteenth century seem of little note in the early decades of the twenty-first.

Personal Eschatology

In this book, we've been tracing two strands of eschatology that we've called the apocalyptic and the prophetic. But the twenty-first century may require us to add a third strand: the personal. Twenty-first century Christians are by no means the first to worry about what happens after death. We've seen this as an important question since before Augustine. But the level of individualism that this question entails in the twenty-first century perhaps transforms it. No longer held in tension with apocalyptic eschatology—which is now just another form of death—personal eschatology can take on new importance.

In contemporary imagination, life after death is a mildly happy journey: a white light, a sense of love, a fuzzy, happy ending. Bynum and Freedman call this "confused and blandly optimistic" in comparison with medieval versions of life after death. "At the end of the twentieth century," they write, "we are neither very apocalyptic, nor very eschatological, nor even very scared. Not, perhaps, as much as we ought to be."[8]

But we do proliferate stories about life after death, attempting to peer behind the veil. *Proof of Heaven, The Day I Died, My Descent into Death, Encountering Heaven and the After Life, Embraced by the Light*: all of these titles and dozens more recount personal, individual experiences of death or near-death. For us, such stories are authentic only if they are personal. We are less likely to accept "truth" about the afterlife if it comes from a religious authority. But if an ordinary person with no particular spirituality stops breathing, sees a light, and comes back to tell us about it, we are prepared to accept these stories as true. The beatific vision is no longer confined to those who labor for holiness or have gone through a painful purgation. It is freely available to all.

Such a vision, however, lacks the rich complexities of the past, where social and moral visions were held in tension with personal hopes. And for Christians, these reports have a thinness that disconnect them from their tradition. They are fine for momentary consolation about the uncertainties of death, but they do little to speak to the meaning of life, either in the present or in the future.

All over the world, Christians recite the words of the Nicene Creed: "We believe in the resurrection of the dead and the life of the world to come." But resurrection of the dead itself has become an ever more difficult thing to conceptualize. The idea of physical immortality retains some of its ancient draw. Some have attempted to imagine physical immortality through cryogenics or cyborgs. Many of us merely try to prevent the physical decay of our bodies through diet and exercise, fascinated by the possibility of ever-longer lives. Modern medicine likewise seeks to preserve individual lives for as long as possible. But physical transformation into Paul's sheaf of wheat or Dante's butterfly is a strain on the contemporary imagination. It is difficult to know what the future of such a doctrine will be. If the resurrection of the dead will continue as a story by which Christians live, then it somehow has to take on new meanings.

Taking Note of the Past

There are as many failed Christian versions of the future as there are Christian pasts. Each Christian past has its attendant future, and each has risen and fallen with its own time. Christians believed that human kingdoms and divine kingdoms could be identified with one another. Kings and emperors and popes claimed the status of God's most important actor on earth—the one through whom God's kingdom comes. Each of these semidivine actors claimed their own moment as an eschatological one, and each became another footnote in what Walter Benjamin saw as the great wreckage of history.[9]

In the modern period, the same impulse has been at work,

but the "great actors" have not always been kings. We saw this impulse in Christopher Columbus and in the Shakers' Mother Ann Lee, and perhaps we see it today in cult leaders like Jim Jones and David Koresh. Even Harold Camping started his calculations of the end of the world based on his own decision to leave the Church of Christ in 1988. He called this very personal end the end of the entire "Church Age." This kind of eschatology contains a striking narcissism.

Another failure of Christian eschatology is the too-frequent choice to read the Bible as a kind of code. This is an ancient impulse that was honed during the Enlightenment and continues unabated to this day. This mysterious collection of texts, with all its numbers and symbols, has been read, reread, and picked apart, autopsied, with the numbers run again and again, and each one of this kind of reading has produced nothing. These chronological calculations are "made to bear the weight of our anxieties and hopes."[10] We use the numbers of the Bible to create what art historian Henri Focillon called a "perpetual calendar of human anxiety."[11]

After Harold Camping's calculations failed, he first did what many others have done. He recalculated. He decided that perhaps God meant that the first "earthquake" that he had predicted would be a spiritual one, felt only in the heavenly realms. The second, earthly quake would take place on October 21, 2011. By then, fewer were paying attention. Popular culture and media had moved on. The twenty-first of October came and went, with only the usual earthquakes: fifty per day, geologists tell us. After that, Camping, who was a very old man and not the first apocalypticist to predict the end of the world in close timing with his own death, did something remarkable: he apologized. "I do not think," he said, "that God intends for us to read the Bible this way at all. I will go back to studying the scriptures, but not for them to tell me the time and date of the end."[12] Camping died just a few months later, but the next Bible code breaker could learn from him. This idea of gleaning secret eschatological knowledge from biblical texts is a strategy that has failed countless times in the history of Christianity.

Time, Times, and Half a Time

For most of Christian history, eschatology has been too small, the span of time too short. Humans have had the tendency to imagine God's Great, Divine Clean Up as something that they could put inside their limited imaginations. Salvation belonged to these people and not those. Cosmic grace would hit this place and time and not that one. We have a strong tendency, demonstrated by failed Christian eschatologies, to over-estimate ourselves and to underestimate the work of God. Whatever redemption looks like, the history of Christian eschatology teaches us that it is almost always imagined as too small, and meanwhile both the universe and our ideas about the universe outgrow it over and over again. Whatever Christian eschatology can mean for the future, it cannot be parochial or ethnic or even merely earthly. Contemporary theologian John Polkinghorne reminds us that no matter what happens to humans, that will be just a small episode in cosmic history. Our eschatologies have been relentlessly and, he says, "unduly" anthropocentric.[13]

We might also learn something from the tendency in Christian eschatology to imagine disaster over and over again. In the contemporary world, this tendency is perhaps stronger than ever. The next great catastrophe—meteorite, flood, earthquake, famine, war, nuclear disaster, tsunami—will be a part of our world and, at least to some degree, outside of our control. We do live with catastrophes, both earthly and personal. We try to give them cosmic meaning. But, as Julian of Norwich tells us, our lived reality is always a mix of "well and woe"; our work is to seek God through these experiences. If we invest in an imagination of catastrophe, we more often than not participate in calamity but fail to do the good work that is right in front of us. To whatever degree Christian eschatology leads us to neglect our neighbors and our communities and the care of our fragile planet, it is a failed eschatology.

Notes

1. http://nymag.com/daily/intelligencer/2011/05/a_conversation _with_harold_cam.html.

2. Lorenzo DiTomasso, "Apocalypticism and Popular Culture," in *The Oxford Handbook of Apocalyptic Literature*, ed. John J. Collins (New York: Oxford University Press, 2014), 473.

3. Quoted in Michael Barkun, "Politics and Apocalypticism," in *The Encyclopedia of Apocalypticism*, ed. Stephen J. Stein (New York: Continuum, 1998), 3:449.

4. DiTomasso, 477.

5. Ibid., 501.

6. Frank Kermode, *The Sense of an Ending: Studies in the Theory of Fiction* (New York: Oxford University Press, 1967), 28 and 14.

7. Caroline Walker Bynum and Paul Freedman, introduction to *Last Things: Death and the Apocalypse in the Middle Ages* (Philadelphia: University of Pennsylvania Press, 2000), 17.

8. Ibid., 16–17.

9. Walter Benjamin, "Theses on the Philosophy of History," in *Illuminations*, trans. Harry Zohn (New York: Schocken, 1968), 253–64.

10. Kermode, 11.

11. See Henri Focillon, *The Year 1000*, trans. Fred D. Wieck (New York: Harper & Row, 1971). Quoted in Kermode, 11.

12. http://www.christianpost.com/news/harold-camping-admits-hes-wrong-about-doomsday-predictions-full-statement-71008/.

13. John Polkinghorne, *The God of Hope and the End of the World* (New Haven: Yale University Press, 2002), 11 and 17.

29

Questions: Science and Christian Eschatology

People like us, who believe in physics, know that the distinction between past, present, and future is only a stubbornly persistent illusion.

—Albert Einstein

In the news recently came the story of a gravitational wave—the news media called it a chirp—that registered on detectors in the states of Washington and Louisiana that had been especially built for the purpose of receiving it, but never had. The gravitational wave—a bending of space and time—came, scientists believe, from a time a billion years ago in a faraway galaxy when two black holes merged. Their union was so powerful it sent waves through the universe, growing fainter across space and time until it reached the Laser Interferometer Gravitational-Wave Observatory on September 14, 2015, at about 4:00 in the morning, making a small blip "a fraction of the width of a proton," the *New York Times* said. From this event so small it hardly registers as an event, scientists were able to demonstrate, after many years of waiting, Einstein's theory that gravity is a wave.

The story of our earth is as old as these black holes. It goes back approximately 4.543 billion years, and if the predictions of astrophysicists are right—and they might be or they might not be—the earth is likely to die as our sun brightens and our atmosphere thins. This will burn up the water on the planet. Life will end on earth anywhere from 500 million years to 1.5 billion years from now. Or in about five billion years, our sun will dim to the degree that it can no longer support life. The earth will grow cold and become just another floating rock. Neither of these stories about the end of life on earth are easy to reconcile with Christian eschatology as we've inherited it.

Time as Mystery

In this book, we've been looking at Christian eschatology as a comprehensive form of knowledge, one that, for centuries, drew on every field of knowledge available to its given society—from astronomy to textual studies—in order to discern the divine will for the future. But it did this with a story of earth that was a far more manageable to the human mind: six thousand years. It had an ancient—but not that ancient—creation story and apocalyptic texts that spoke of a particular kind of end. The climax would come through God's own saving action. With a beginning, climax, and end, the narrative demands of a good story had been met, and Christians have been telling this story for thousands of years.

But recent scientific discoveries have made new demands on Christian theology. Without question, Christian eschatology needs to shift to a larger plane of knowledge. We must grapple with the "extraordinary length" of the "developmental chain of being," as philosopher of religion Anthony Aveni puts it.[1] Time is not what we thought it was. This is true in terms of both ancient and modern concepts of time. Time is neither a set of events predetermined by God nor is it the neutral ticking of a clock without end and without meaning. Instead time is an inherently bendable reality tied up with space. The flow of time is a mystery that quantum physics cannot yet fully explain. That gravitational wave is a new piece of evidence that underscores the complexity.

If Christian eschatology is to meet the challenge of these new questions about the nature of time, the immense age of the universe, and these accounts of the universe's and the earth's beginnings and ends, it has a great deal of work to do. Heretofore, theology has been too terrestrial and too anthropocentric. It has not been big enough to take into account the vastness and strangeness of the space and time of the universe.

What Is to Come

Science alone, however, cannot meet the demands of theology. Theoretical physicist and Nobel prize winner Steven Weinberg has said that with science alone, we would have to conclude that the universe is pointless. "There is no point in the universe that can be discovered by the methods of science. I believe that what we have found so far, an impersonal universe, which is not particularly directed toward human beings, is what we are going to continue to find. And that when we find the ultimate laws of nature they will have a chilling, cold, impersonal quality about them."[2] Given this "chilling, cold, impersonal quality," Weinberg is suspicious of any account of the universe that makes us feel better about the state of things, any account that might be, at the end of the day, wishful thinking. Theology, he argues, is perhaps just a developed form of wishful thinking.

In her book *The Givenness of Things*, Marilynne Robinson takes the discourse of contemporary science to task for just this kind of assertion. Given the partial nature of the scientific enterprise, one cannot extrapolate, she argues, from the findings of theoretical physics to statements about the nature of the universe. Even less so about the future. We stand on what Robinson calls the frontier where *"what is* fronts on *what is to come."*

> It is an error of much scientific thinking to extrapolate ... from our radically partial model of reality, a model curtailed, unaccountably and arbitrarily, by the exclusion of much that we *do* know about the vast fabric, and the fine grain of the cosmos in which we live and move and have our being. Cosmic and microcosmic being are so glorious and strange that nothing marvelous can be excluded on the grounds of improbability.[3]

Our understanding of reality—of the ultimate nature of space and time—is too partial to extrapolate certainties about the future or the ultimate nature of reality. Except maybe that we will be surprised. "Where were you," Robinson might ask Weinberg, "when God laid the foundation of the earth?"[4]

The business of science is predicated on a model of repetition. The experimental method is one in which scientists attempt to replicate the past in order to predict the future. Thus continuity is central to the scientific enterprise. But theology asserts what John Polkinghorne calls "God's free action" that "may be expected to bring about the kind of discontinuity essential for the ultimate fulfillment of the divine purpose."[5] Because theology has an emphasis on the particular, the strange, and the unexpected, it can introduce a concept like Isaiah's "new heavens and a new earth" (Isa 65:17). This, Polkinghorne says, "is what distinguishes theological eschatology from a secular futurology."[6] Both Polkinghorne and Robinson agree that theology may have a new vocation: to disturb the certainties of science and scientists, as it was once and continues to be so thoroughly disturbed by science.

But discontinuity does not mean a wiping clean of the slate, that there is no connection between our current reality and our future reality. For theologians who take seriously a dialogue with science, an emerging understanding of God is one in which God is "patient and subtle, content to achieve divine purposes in an open and developing way, in which creatures themselves collaborate."[7] Quantum theory has noted the way in which any two subatomic entities that have interacted with one another remain "entangled" no matter how far apart they may get. This is called the EPR (Einstein, Podolsky, Rosen) paradox. It means that all matter is related to all other matter—affecting and interaffecting—in ways that, for the most part, we don't yet understand.

The impact of this question has yet to be felt fully in Christian eschatology, but it opens up new forms of dialogue and new ways to interpret ancient texts. For example, what does quantum entanglement mean for a doctrine like the resurrection of the dead? How do space, time, and matter become a part of the new creation? What is the nature of time in which it even makes sense to talk about the future? If the universe is always expanding, what is it expanding into?

Eschatology remains an essential, if more humble, part of theology because it engages us in questions of the meaningfulness of creation, in both its connection to the past and its unfolding in the future. Maybe the eschatology of the twenty-first century is best understood not as a comprehensive form of knowledge but as a comprehensive form of questioning.

Notes

1. Anthony Aveni, "Time," in *Critical Terms in Religious Studies,* ed. Mark C. Taylor (Chicago: University of Chicago Press, 1998), 317.

2. Interview with Steven Weinberg, PBS, "Faith and Reason," at http://www.pbs.org/faithandreason/transcript/wein-frame.html.

3. Marilynne Robinson, "Reformation," in *The Givenness of Things* (New York: Farrar, Straus & Giroux, 2015).

4. Ibid. Drawn from Job 38:4.

5. John Polkinghorne, *The God of Hope and the End of the World* (New Haven: Yale University Press, 2002), xxiv.

6. Ibid.

7. Ibid., 15.

30

Towardness

To crave and to have are as like as a thing and its shadow. For when does a berry break upon the tongue as sweetly as when one longs to taste it, and when is the taste refracted into so many hues and savors of ripeness and earth, and when do our senses know any thing so utterly as when we lack it? And here again is a foreshadowing—the world will be made whole. For to wish for a hand on one's hair is all but to feel it. So whatever we may lose, very craving gives it back to us again. Though we dream and hardly know it, longing, like an angel, fosters us, smooths our hair, and brings us wild strawberries.
—Marilynne Robinson, *Housekeeping*

All I need to know is there is no end to love.
—U2

In Marilynne Robinson's novel *Lila*, Lila is the wife of John Ames, a minister who has lived in Gilead, Iowa all his life. She, however, is a newcomer to the town, and she has lived a wandering life as the "stolen" child of a migrant worker. When she arrives in Gilead, she has no particular purpose beyond survival. One day, camped outside of Gilead in an abandoned shack, she stops into Ames's church while he is in the midst of a baptism.

The idea of baptism begins to haunt Lila and follows her through both memory and ordinary life until she decides that she wants Ames to baptize her. In a sensual, even erotic, scene, Ames does baptize Lila on the bank of a river.

Lila eventually marries Ames, and they have a child together. But in the midst of this new life, Lila harbors deep anxieties about her choice; we might call it an eschatological pain. She understands that baptism has in some sense "saved" her, but she is troubled by the idea that she is saved where others are not, because of a random act of Ames's kindness. She decides that she has no interest in the kingdom of God if it means a form of unearned inclusion and exclusion. She would turn away from heaven, if that is what it means to be redeemed. But as she continues to follow this line of thought, she begins to grasp the tension between the now and the not yet that has always driven Christian eschatology forward.

> For now there were geraniums in the windows, and an old man at the kitchen table telling his baby some rhyme he'd known forever, probably still wondering if he had managed to bring her along into that next life, if he could ever be certain of it. Almost letting himself imagine grieving for her in heaven, because not to grieve for her would mean he was dead, after all.

It was, Lila realizes, the "light of eternity" that allowed her to see the potential for redemption in all things, even in herself. Robinson weaves together personal and cosmic eschatology in the imagination of one simple woman grappling with her own existence. She expresses Christian eschatology as an act of the imagination, behind which is the forward motion of love. Love for Ames, love for her child, belief in her own deserving of love allowed Lila to accept not the certainty of a good ending but the risk of loving into eternity.

In an interview, Robinson says, "I expect to be very much surprised by the Second Coming. I would never have imagined the Incarnation or the Resurrection. To be astonishing seems to be a mark of God's great acts—who could have imagined Creation? On these grounds it seems like presumption to me to treat what can only be speculation as if it were even tentative knowledge. I expect the goodness of God and the preciousness of Creation to be realized fully and eternally. I expect us all to receive a great instruction in the absolute nature of grace."[1]

Towardness

What Robinson calls a "foreshadowing," Daniel Hardy calls an element of "towardness" that is in all of creation. Towardnesss, he argues, is even more essential to God's nature than creation and redemption. Even if there had never been sin, God still would have wanted to do more. Creation would still have been an ongoing process.[2] Towardness is paradoxical because it exists both with and without a "sense of an ending." It implies the future but without a certainty of outcome.

Towardness is also an expression of the now and the not yet that we have been tracing. It suggests that we concern ourselves with the present moment: the geraniums on the windowsill, the old man teaching the baby rhymes. We invest this world with love. But the present contains a longing that also needs our attention. This longing draws us forward into the future. Ben Quash calls this the Holy Spirit's work of "unfolding-in-connection." Creation is not separate from this process; we are not merely the process's victims, but we also are not its controllers. "Unfolding-in-connection" is always bigger than our own lives and always draws us beyond the present.[3]

Quash uses the eschatological image in Romans 8 as an ancient source for understanding what it might mean to unfold in connection. In this passage, Paul writes that "the whole creation groans and suffers the pain of childbirth together until now." A woman in childbirth is neither a passive recipient of new life nor is she fully in control of what is happening in and through her. This, Quash says, is a "powerful image in which the chain of events in which the human being is wholly invested (in body, mind, and emotion) at the same time unfolds with its own 'independent' and certainly unstoppable momentum."[4] The life unfolding through the woman's labor does not belong to her, and if the inevitable event stops, both she and the child will die.

The New Day Breaks

Christian eschatology, as we noted from the beginning, has been over the course of two millennia both spectacularly wrong and eerily right. It has contributed to the end of some worlds and helped create new ones. It has given us a sense of forward motion, and it has implanted itself within the DNA of our culture. The task for the twenty-first century is to claim the richest, deepest, and most powerful eschatological tendencies of Christian theology as an essential part of meaning making. Meaning making is an essential human activity. Even if we were to try to leave it behind, we would reinvent it.

Meanwhile, amidst these thousands of years of eschatological yearning, the poet Philip Levine writes, the new day breaks "to find us in the valleys of our living." Whatever

Christian eschatology will be going forward, its most powerful forms are those that involve human creativity. Throughout the history of Christian eschatology, we've seen how belief in the overwhelming power of God, the possibility of God's imminent and awesome coming, has inspired both paralyzing fear and social transformation—sometimes at the same time. Belief in God as the sole eschatological actor and belief in humans as the only actors both have had disastrous consequences. Those who urge us to see the connection between the world we make and the creative work of God are the most meaningful voices for this new day. Taken together, these voices draw on that tantalizing aspect of Christian eschatology: its ancient tension between the now and the not yet, between what was, what is, and what is to come. This is the edge on which Christians have always lived as they have attempted to understand, interpret, live into, accept, transform, and hope in the future.

Notes

1. Wyatt Mason, "The Revelations of Marilynne Robinson," *The New York Times Magazine* (October 1, 2014), n.p.

2. Daniel Hardy, quoted in Ben Quash, *Found Theology: History, Imagination, and the Holy Spirit* (London: Bloomsbury, 2014), 252–53.

3. Ibid., 219.

4. Ibid., 227.

For Further Reading

Bultmann, Rudolph. *History and Eschatology*. Edinburgh: Edinburgh University Press, 1957.

Gbowee, Leymah, with Carol Mithers. *Mighty Be Our Powers*. New York: Beast, 2011.

King, Martin Luther, Jr. *A Testament of Hope: The Essential Writings and Speeches of Martin Luther King, Jr.* Edited by James M. Washington. Reprint. New York: HarperOne, 2003.

Moltmann, Jürgen. *Theology of Hope: On the Ground and Implications of a Christian Eschatology*. Translated by James W. Leitch. Minneapolis: Fortress, 1993.

Polkinghorne, John. *The God of Hope and the End of the World*. New Haven: Yale University Press, 2002.

Quash, Ben. *Found Theology: History, Imagination, and the Holy Spirit*. London: Bloomsbury, 2014.

Rahner, Karl. "Eschatology." Pages 2:242–46 in *Sacramentum Mundi: An Encyclopedia of Theology*. Translated by W. J. O'Hara et al. Edited by Karl Rahner, Cornelius Ernst, and Kevin Smyth. New York: Herder & Herder, 1968.

Robinson, Marilynne. *The Givenness of Things*. New York: Farrar, Straus & Giroux, 2015.

Schwarz, Hans. *Eschatology*. Grand Rapids: Eerdmans, 2000.

Glossary of Terms

Apocalypse—a literary genre that describes an otherworldly agent revealing to a human one the nature of divine reality and, often, important information about the future.

Apocalyptic eschatology—refers to beliefs about events at the end of time that will occur almost entirely outside human control.

Beatific vision—a direct and personal seeing of God, either in heaven or through another mystical mechanism.

Chiliasm—belief in an earthly reign of Christ. See **Millennium**.

Dispensational premillennialism—belief that divides human history into eras and then prophesies that Jesus's defeat of Satan will usher in the millennium.

Eschatology—the study of ultimate things, using biblical texts as a primary source.

Jeremiad—a form of speech that invokes lamentation and urges people to take moral action.

Kingdom of God, kingdom of heaven—in the New Testament, a term that is repeatedly used to refer to the presence and/or coming of God's reign. It is placed in opposition to earthly or worldly power.

Messiah—the deliverer of the Jewish people promised by the Hebrew Bible.

Messianic age—the age after the Messiah has come, typically imagined as an age of unparalleled peace and prosperity.

Millennarianism—belief in the transformation of society with the aid of supernatural action.

Millennium—the one-thousand-year reign of Christ on earth. A reference to Revelation 20.

Parousia—a Greek term for the second coming of Christ.

Premillennialism—belief that Christ's return will usher in the millennium.

Post-apocalyptic—a contemporary term that refers to life following a cataclysmic event like a nuclear war.

Postmillennialism—belief that Christ will return to earth after the millennium, a time of peace and prosperity that will be ushered in by human action in the perfection of society.

Prophetic eschatology—refers to the work that humans and God do together to create the kingdom of heaven.

Pseudepigraphic—relating to works that are falsely attributed to biblical or other famous actors of a previous era.

Son of Man—a mysterious term first used in Daniel to refer to an eschatological figure who will "appear" in the clouds. Used in the New Testament to refer to Jesus.

Zoroastrianism—an ancient Persian religion based on the teachings of Zoroaster. Strongly influential on exilic Judaism.

Index